MONTERREY IS OURS!

I0652525

MONTERREY IS OURS!

The Mexican War Letters of
Lieutenant Dana
1845-1847

Edited By
ROBERT H. FERRELL

THE UNIVERSITY PRESS OF KENTUCKY

Copyright © 1990 by The University Press of Kentucky
Scholarly publisher for the commonwealth,
serving Bellarmine College, Berea College, Centre
College of Kentucky, Eastern Kentucky University,
The Filson Club, Georgetown College, Kentucky
Historical Society, Kentucky State University,
Morehead State University, Murray State University,
Northern Kentucky University, Transylvania University,
University of Kentucky, University of Louisville,
and Western Kentucky University.
Editorial and Sales Offices: Lexington, Kentucky 40506-0336

Library of Congress Cataloging-in-Publication Data

Dana. Napoleon Jackson Tecumseh, 1822-1905.
  Monterrey is ours! : the Mexican war letters of Lieutenant Dana,
1845-1847 / edited by Robert H. Ferrell.
    p. cm.
  ISBN: 978-0-8131-5242-4
  1. Dana, Napoleon Jackson Tecumseh, 1822-1905—Correspondence,
2. United States—History—War with Mexico, 1845-1848—Personal
narratives. 3. Monterey, Battle of, 1846. 4. Soldiers—United
States—Correspondence. I. Ferrell, Robert H. II. Title.
E411.D25   1990
973.6'28—dc20   8-29351
                                                         CIP

                                  ∞

Contents

Maps

Introduction

Napoleon Jackson Tecumseh Dana—what a name, so fully reminiscent of his time!—was born in Eastport, Maine, on April 15, 1822, and died in this present century, July 15, 1905, in Portsmouth, New Hampshire. His life thus bridged most of the nineteenth century, if one defines it historically, from the final defeat of Napoleon Bonaparte at Waterloo in 1815 until the First Battle of the Marne in 1914. Dana came from an illustrious family, the descendants of Richard Dana who settled in Cambridge, Massachusetts, in 1640. The Danas were lawyers, clergymen, poets, essayists, and novelists. Napoleon Dana was the nephew of the famous chemists James F. and Samuel L. Dana. His father, Nathaniel Giddings Dana, was a graduate of West Point and a professional army officer. The son was born at a U.S. Army fort.

Young Dana entered the U.S. Military Academy in 1838 at the age of sixteen and graduated four years later with the class of 1842. He was commissioned in the Seventh Infantry and was still a second lieutenant when the Mexican War opened in 1846. Promoted to first lieutenant the next year, he was brevetted after the Battle of Cerro Gordo, which he barely survived. He had been among the men storming Telegraph Hill, was severely wounded, and was left on the field for dead but was picked up by a burial party after thirty-six hours.

After the war with Mexico he was eventually stationed at Fort Snelling, Minnesota, where he observed the opportunities in what was then the American West. He left the army in 1855 to open a banking business in St. Paul.

The Civil War proved as notable a chapter in Dana's life as had been the Mexican War a decade and a half earlier. He had continued his interest in military affairs, serving as brigadier general of the Minnesota militia, and in 1861 he became colonel of the First Minnesota Infantry. A unit composed of lumbermen, fully able to withstand the first shocks of battle, the regiment participated in the Battle of Ball's Bluff, in the main a Union disaster, and afterward helped evacuate the defeated troops to the Maryland shore of the

Potomac. A brigadier general in 1862, Dana commanded a brigade of the Second Corps in the peninsular campaign and at Antietam, where again he was badly wounded. After a long convalescence, during which he was promoted to major general, he organized the defenses of Philadelphia at the time of the movement into Pennsylvania of General Robert E. Lee's Army of Northern Virginia. General Dana later took a command in Texas and drove the Confederate forces from territory around the coast where he had fought the Mexicans in 1846-47. Toward the end of the war he held commands in inactive areas along the Mississippi.

Resigning from the army in 1865, Dana resumed his business career and until 1871 was general agent of the American-Russia Commercial Company of Alaska, during the era of the purchase of Alaska by the United States and its organization as a federal territory. He then became an executive of railroad companies, holding among other offices the presidency of the Chicago, Burlington, and Quincy. In the latter 1890s he was deputy commissioner of pensions in Washington. Under a special Act of Congress in 1894 he received back his regular army rank of captain and retired with a pension.

Dana's letters are a remarkable testimony to his many qualities and demonstrate that he was a man of his time. They show a youth in the full vigor of life, looking to advancement of his career, to be sure, but also to the increasing greatness, he believed, of his country. Like so many young men during the 1840s he envisioned the United States as Young America, a country not yet afflicted, perhaps never to be afflicted, by the ineptitudes of the countries of Europe. As in that wonderful, lively decade there was a Young Italy and a Young Hungary, so the United States in its youthfulness was ready to take the lands of weak Mexico.

Racism formed a part of Dana's outlook. As the war turned into hard fighting, more than the Americans expected, he revised his views of Mexican abilities. By the time of Cerro Gordo, he was willing to believe that Mexican soldiers were worthy enemies of the U.S. Army. Still, he continued to feel that Mexicans were hardly the equals of Americans.

In his letters Dana appears as an imaginative soldier, never just a commentator remarking movements of the foe. He possessed an eye for strategy and discerned the purposes of colonels and generals, not merely listening for army gossip but attempting to determine how the army's leaders were solving their problems in Mexico. He watched for tactical leadership, measuring it against principles he had learned at the little academy along the Hudson where a few dozen cadets had sought to absorb the wisdom of aging veterans of the War of 1812.

Dana also had a remarkable relationship with his wife, the former Susan Sandford, whom he married in 1844 just before his regiment went down to the Texas border to join the forces of General Zachary Taylor. The "Dear Sue" of the letters, known also as "Dearest Sue" and "My own darling wife," etc., was a bundle of contradictions, and Dana had all he could do to handle her. She was a prim, correct girl when Dana happened upon her. She was also emotional and young. She was receiving the attentions of a suitor, whom her future husband promptly sent packing, but she seems to have sent him away too. At that moment her father resolved matters. He bade Dana take his daughter as quickly as possible—which, after all, was the way Major Sandford was himself about to acquire a new wife. Dana pressed his case, and Sue acquiesced.

As the reader will discern, the marriage began with Sue in love yet subject to bouts of melancholia that sometimes drove her absent husband wild. In November 1845, when he was on the Texas border and the Mexican War was only a few months away, he was so moved by Sue's inability to cope that he took leave of his regiment and hastened back to her. After she had settled down, he returned to his post.

Sue seems to have been careless with money. After her husband left for Texas she paid little attention to the cost of her lodgings or to arrangements for boarding. Sometimes she let bills go for months. Admittedly Dana was equally improvident. He had gotten several hundred dollars into debt before he married Sue, borrowing from fellow officers a few dollars for some emergency or convenience, another few when a paymaster was not around. He also borrowed from his men. In the army of Dana's time soldiers possessing small amounts of cash placed them in the hands of officers. At the beginning of the war, Dana found himself trustee for the estate of a sergeant killed during the siege of Fort Brown, and when a paymaster decided to settle the sergeant's affairs it was up to Dana to produce the money—which he had spent. But Sue gave little attention to such problems. To them she simply added her own.

Sue displayed other awkwardnesses. She wandered at will up and down the Mississippi, aboard steamboats, taking passage from New Orleans Barracks to Jefferson Barracks in St. Louis, traveling as far as Covington, Kentucky. Each time she moved she informed her husband belatedly, perhaps failing to write while she enjoyed a period of melancholia. Such behavior aroused her husband's consternation. It also took time for him to write four-page letters in small script, full of descriptions of his life on the border or in Mexico. He envisioned the letters filed away in postoffice pigeonholes in New Orleans or St. Louis or Covington. Sometimes Sue carelessly gave her own letters to officers who claimed to be en route to the Rio Grande.

As one would suspect, the "Dear Sue" letters eventually show a remarkable change in the relationship between husband and wife. Well into the campaigning of 1846-47, Dana's attitude toward Sue was one of the dominant partner in a business enterprise in which she was the minority stockholder. Then, suddenly, after he had boasted for months how other officers and men were killed or badly wounded and he was not, he was struck down on Telegraph Hill. Rescued, taken to a house near the battlefield, removed to a nearby town, he could think only of Sue. The roles now were reversed. His letters home are poignant about what had happened; as he told her, he was in her hands.

After Dana returned from the Mexican War it was, of course, possible for the couple to lead a normal life. Their daughter Mary Langdon Dana had been born in June, 1845, and Charles Peaslee and Alfred Sandford Dana followed. During the Civil War, when Napoleon Dana again was away in the army, the Dear Sue letters resumed, and it is clear that the by-then middle-aged husband and wife were as much in love as during their first long separation.

Nearly a century and a half after Dana wrote these extraordinary letters, the U.S. Military Academy at West Point acquired them. Post archivists have always sought papers of graduates, and in 1986 word came that a manuscript dealer in Massachusetts possessed Dana material. There were 120 letters. The largest collection of Mexican War letters in the New-York Historical Society, a major manuscript depository, contains about twenty letters. The U.S. Army's archive at Carlisle Barracks has a similarly small collection. Mostly in two numbered groups, the Dana letters make a pile three inches high. The paper is almost as usable as when Dana put his pen to it. Edges have frayed, but otherwise the letters are in fine shape. Final pages contain fragments of purple wax, remnants of the seals Sue broke when opening her mail. The size of pages varies, but most approximate present-day typing paper, perhaps eight by ten inches. The letters are usually four pages long, written on folded double sheets. Dana wrote with a small hand because paper was expensive and he had much to say. Sometimes he supplemented the usual four pages with loose pages or took another double sheet and wrote a total of eight. One letter describing the relief of Fort Brown by the battles of Palo Alto and Resaca de la Palma required ten pages.

The rarity of such letters is easy to understand. Generally speaking, few from the Mexican War have survived. Fewer men by far were involved than fought the Civil War—General Taylor's force ranged between four thousand and six thousand, and Winfield Scott's was about ten thousand. And sending letters home was difficult. Roads were hardly highways and were subject to vagaries of the seasons. Part of the passage from Texas and Mexico was by sea. Within the United States it often was by river, notably the Mississippi. Steamboats were unreliable teakettles, having a tendency to blow up. Dana's brother-in-law, Captain Daniel P. Whiting, a considerable artist, lost a precious packet of drawings when a steamboat sank en route to the engraver. It was a wonder that Dana's letters got through and to the peripatetic Sue at that.

Let it be said that not all of Dana's letters are of historical value. Many contain commentaries on Sue's day-to-day activities, or about relatives, and page after page, almost beyond belief, describes his love for Sue. Dana wrote 300,000 words, and less than a third are worth attention.

When Dana was writing, however, of what lay at hand in camp or along the line of march or on the battlefield, he had much to say, and he expressed it with the crispness and address that readers of later years have come to admire in writers. Dana at his best is very good indeed. Through these letters Americans of the present time can look back to an era that now lies far into their country's past.

A Note
on the Editing

To make the letters easier for present-day readers, I have taken
some minor liberties. Abbreviations have disappeared, and cap-
italization now accords with modern usage, as does punctuation.
Misspellings stand corrected. Dana infrequently used italics, and
what few he used are gone, together with an occasional Victorian
"Oh!" I divided material into paragraphs; Dana ran everything
together. As is customary, ellipsis points indicate an omission;
when there are four, the first is a period. I used no points at the
beginning or end of an entry, even if the quoted material did not
represent all that Dana wrote on that date.

Perhaps a special explanation is necessary for "Monterrey,"
rather than "Monterey." The latter was the American spelling of the
time. It seemed better to use present-day spelling even though
Dana on September 26, 1846, wrote Sue, "Monterey is ours."

MONTERREY IS OURS!

1
On the Nueces
August-October 1845

Arrival in the Grand Camp. Appointment as Quartermaster. In Bed with Rattlesnakes. Intimate Advice to Sue. Terrible Accident to the *Dayton*. Funeral. Lipan Indians. Mrs. Hawkins. Flies, Cockroaches. Toothache. Alf. Cool Weather. A Horseback Ride.

The antecedents of the Mexican War of 1846-48 need no recital. Suffice it to say that during the presidential election of 1844, between the supposed dark horse candidate of the Democrats, James K. Polk of Tennessee, who had actually been a prominent member of the House of Representatives, having occupied the post of Speaker, and the Whig candidate Henry Clay of Kentucky, the issue became the annexation of Texas—which was likely to produce war with Mexico. The Texas issue was nothing if not complicated. The Mexican government claimed Texas as its rightful northern territory. Texas, however, had made itself independent in the revolution of 1835-36. Upon the success of that revolution, the people of Texas sought to bring Texas into the Union. Such an arrangement had not happened immediately less because of Mexican displeasure—the government in Mexico seemed too weak to intervene—than because of the uneasy sectional balance within the United States. Addition of what was then called Texas, which comprised not merely present-day Texas but the upper Rio Grande valley, might have required a division into several states, which would have destroyed the balance in the U.S. Senate between slave states and free. But annexation was a popular issue in the American South and in the West, and the Democrats under Polk decided it was a winner. In part because Clay could not make up his mind about expansion, Polk won. John Tyler, then president, signed a joint resolution of Congress annexing Texas. Upon taking office, Polk sent General Taylor into Texas with a few thousand troops as an army of occupation. The Mexicans said the border between their province of Texas and Mexico's other provinces was the Nueces River. The Americans said it was the Rio Grande. Taylor's troops were soon in the disputed area. The situation was, to put things mildly, uneasy. Polk trusted that a show of force would suffice to confirm the annexation of Texas, but if the Mexicans were foolish enough to challenge Taylor,

*the president was willing to go to war—in which case the soldiers of
the United States would seize New Mexico and California.*

August 29 ✦ Here we are on the banks of the Nueces in the
grand camp of the army of occupation. I am seated in . . . a chair
upon my chest, and writing in the chair, myself sitting in the
rocking chair (what luxury for the camp), with a piece of candle
lighted by me flaring, so that I find difficulty in writing. There is
always a very strong sea breeze blowing here, which renders the
land very pleasant and Corpus Christi Bay the roughest piece of
water for its size I have ever seen.

Well, how did we get here? My dearest wife, I will go 'way
back to St. Joseph's Island, thirty-five miles, and tell you. Yesterday
morning at seven o'clock we loaded, with two companies and their
baggage, a schooner to which the one we went to Pensacola in was a
splendid palace. No exaggeration. She was the ugliest and nastiest
craft I ever saw. Well, we crowded ourselves on board of the cranky,
tarry, filthy concern and started, with the hope of getting to General
Taylor's headquarters by twelve o'clock.[1] But oh, the fallacy of
human expectations! We little knew what a fix we had got into. We
had not gone more than two miles before we had been aground
twice and the men had to jump overboard and shove the vessel off.
After a good deal of fuss and no fun, we made out to reach the head
of a bayou, five miles, where the wind was dead ahead. Here the
men had to get out into the water waist-deep and with a line
cordelle us for three hours.[2]

Not liking the accommodations on board, I took my gun and
jumped overboard too. After stubbing my boots entirely out I came
on board again with two whole birds.

Well, to make a long story short, we did not arrive at Corpus
Christi till after sunset, and there we had to anchor four hundred
yards from the shore and land in small boats with a tremendous sea
running. I tell you the waves were bigger than ever you saw. Where
we were it was out of the question to land any of the baggage in the
night. So we had to take the [illegible] and jump overboard to our
hips to do that and there we were again on the sand beach with no
tents and I no blanket. Captain Lee went up to the dragoon camp to
sleep with Sibley, his brother-in-law, the adjutant, who was kind
enough to send me a buffalo robe as I had to pass the night with the
company on the beach.[3] So without any supper, and only hard
biscuit for dinner, we laid ourselves down with nothing over us but
(as Crittenden says) the starry canister of heaven. But would you

Camp of the army of occupation. Lithograph after Daniel P. Whiting.

believe it, in spite of this real soldier fare I slept so soundly that I could not even dream of my sweet wife and babe, far, far away. . . .

We have been hard at work all day clearing ground for our camp, pitching tents, digging wells, etc. We have a great deal yet to do, in fact we will continue to have hard work till we go home again, which will be God knows when. I don't think there is to be anything done in the way of fighting. If there is, it will be a long time first. If Mexico declares war, I believe General Taylor means to march us right on Matamoros. If he does, it is to be hoped that we will not get a whipping. . . .

I believe, my dear Sue, that I have not changed my shirt for five days, but as soon as I stop writing I am going to undress to my shirttail and slippers and go to the beach some thirty yards behind my tent and take a fine bath. Then I will go to bed and think of you and wake up in the morning and think of my loved one again. You are always my first and my last thought, my alpha and my omega, and so you ever shall be. I have not shaved for a week and do not intend to till I see you. You never saw such a hairy looking set of fellows in your life as we have here. Nobody shaves, some have hair all over their faces, and some you can see nothing but their eyes.

1. For Gen. Zachary Taylor, see Holman Hamilton, *Zachary Taylor*, 2 vols. (New York, 1941-51); Brainerd Dyer, *Zachary Taylor* (Baton Rouge, 1946); Silas B. McKinley and Silas Bent, *Old Rough and Ready* (New York, 1946); and K. Jack Bauer, *Zachary Taylor: Soldier, Planter, Statesman of the Old Southwest* (Baton Rouge, 1985). Also see John S.D. Eisenhower, "Polk and His Generals," in Douglas W. Richmond, ed., *Essays on the Mexican War* (College Station, Tex., 1986), 34-65.   2. A cordelle is a towline or towrope.   3. Francis Lee graduated from West Point in 1822, was a captain at the outset of the Mexican War, was promoted to major in 1847, and was brevetted to lieutenant colonel that same year. He died in St. Louis in 1859. George W. Cullum, *Biographical Register of the Officers and Graduates of the U.S. Military Academy . . .*, 2 vols. (New York, 1868), I, 234-35. Caleb C. Sibley graduated from the Academy in 1829 and was a captain in the Fifth Infantry in 1845. He served as a lieutenant colonel and colonel in the Civil War (Cullum, I, 353). The brevet rank of Francis Lee, mentioned above, requires explanation. Intended to reward officers for combat, it became a way to promote men unable to receive promotion because of lack of retirements. Normally brevet rank carried no increase in authority or pay, but General Taylor received a larger command while enjoying brevet rank—he was a brevet brigadier general in 1845 (K. Jack Bauer, *The Mexican War, 1846-1848* [New York, 1974], 33-34).

September 1   ✦   How I wish I could know how my sweet little Sue is coming in all that she does and all that she feels in the absence of her husband. If I could only get one look at you, I do not say that I would be satisfied, but it would repay me for many of these sad and lonesome moments. You must have been home now some five or six days, and with your father and sisters, and you must be comparatively happy.[1] I have no doubt that you have a good many cries, and a good many hours of low spirits, but you must welcome them and patiently await the distant day of our meeting. We can, none of us, give any guess when that day will come. Probably it will be long first, quite long. . . .

The skin, dear wife, [is] off of two places on me, it is burned off of my face by the hot sun and rubbed off of my tail by a hard-trotting horse. You did not know that I am a mounted officer, though, and I belong to the regimental staff. Yesterday I was appointed quartermaster to the regiment by Major Brown, under an order from General Taylor. It has nothing to do with the company, but quartermaster alone.[2] So that I have charge and conduction of all the transportation, mules, horses, oxen wagons, baggage train, etc. of the regiment. It is a high compliment paid me by the major when there are so many officers senior to me. The task is very arduous and responsible and will keep me riding about pretty near all the time. I have a good horse and saddle and have used him a good deal already. This will give me back the sixteen dollars a month which I lost by leaving Fort Pike. How long I shall keep the appointment I cannot tell, because there are three quartermasters ordered out here from Washington, and one of them may be required to perform the duties for this regiment. Should I retain it and we commence our marches, all my energies will be called out, every one of them in full play. The office, if faithfully fulfilled, is no sinecure.

Besides being a mounted officer, I have also mounted my bed. Until last night I have slept on the ground, but the reptiles were so abundant I could stand it no longer, so I made Evans cut me four crooked forks and plant them at the four corners of my bed. Across these I laid two crooked poles and again across these I laid some flour-barrel staves. This is my bedstead. It broke down this afternoon and I rolled out of the tent, to the great amusement of Britton and all hands.[3] When I rolled out, the horse kicked and Bascomb barked and everybody laughed.

But the snakes are really bad here and are the only bedfellows we have. Yesterday morning Whiting found a huge rattlesnake coiled up at the foot of his bed. He woke all around him with his nine rattles. They killed him and Whiting has his skin.[4] A Lieutenant Smith had one crawl over his bare legs one night and he laid still until His Snakeship crawled off. We all get used to the varmints here and you must not be surprised if I bring home a few pets of the kind.

1. Major Sandford was then living in Gold Springs, Missouri, a locality not on present-day maps.   2. Jacob Brown served in the War of 1812 and was promoted to captain in 1825 and major in 1843 (Francis B. Heitman, *Historical Register and Dictionary of the United States Army,* 2 vols. [Washington, D.C., 1903], I, 252). Years later, Dana recalled some of the officers of the Mexican War and wrote about Major Brown: "The Seventh Infantry was the first regiment which received the fire of the enemy in Mexico. Having lost its lieutenant colonel, Hoffman, who died at Corpus Christi the preceding winter, it marched to Matamoros under the command of Major Brown, who was a veteran of the War of 1812, having been a sergeant in that war and promoted for gallantry from the ranks. When General Taylor found it necessary to take his whole force with him to his base of supplies for rations, knowing that a strong Mexican army was on our side of the river, as he mounted his horse (Old Whitey) the officers of the regiment gathered about him to bid him farewell. He had selected this regiment from his army to garrison the fieldwork which the army had thrown up right in front of Matamoros on the riverbank, at point-blank range of the batteries of the Mexicans on the opposite side, and with Bragg's battery of light artillery of four guns (in which George H. Thomas, 'the Rock of Chickamauga,' was a second lieutenant) and Captain Lowd's company of artillery with four eighteen-pounders, making us about five hundred all told for a garrison. He said to us as he mounted his horse, 'Gentlemen, this fort has no name. It will be named for the first officer that falls here.' He knew full well that we would be attacked as soon as he left, and the first officer who fell was the commanding officer, Major Brown, from whence comes the name of Brownsville, opposite Matamoros today" (Undated typescript in Dana MSS.)   3. Forbes Britton, an 1834 Academy graduate, was a first lieutenant with the Seventh Infantry in 1845. He attained a captaincy in 1847, resigned in 1850, and died in

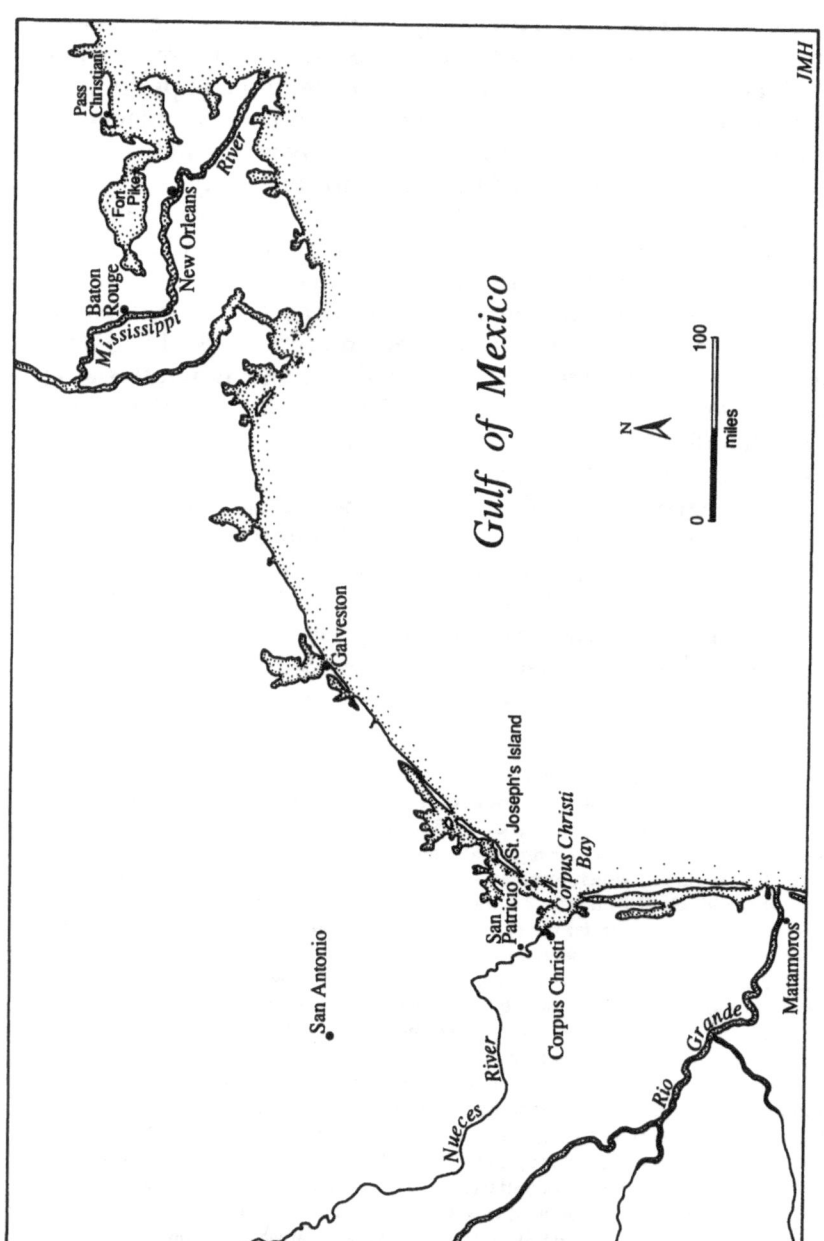

The Texas Border

1861 (Cullum, I, 460-61). 4. Capt. Daniel P. Whiting was Dana's brother-in-law. A short biography appears in Cullum, I, 410. See also Mary B. Saunders, *In Memoriam: Daniel Powers Whiting* (n.p., n.d.), a copy of which is in the archives of the U.S. Military Academy. Born in New York State in 1808, Whiting graduated from West Point in 1832, served in the Indian War in Florida, was promoted to captain in 1845, and was brevetted major after the Battle of Cerro Gordo. After further garrison and frontier duty, during which he took part in the Utah expedition in 1858-60, he entered the Civil War as a lieutenant colonel but retired in 1863 because of ill health. After spending years as an invalid, he died in Washington in 1892. From the time he left West Point until near his death, he kept a detailed diary and after the Mexican War wrote an autobiography. He placed these documents in the charge of his youngest daughter, Mary Saunders. Alas, diary and autobiography seem to have disappeared. Whiting did arrange for publication of five lithographs. The first, of the army of occupation at Corpus Christi, was initially done in Baltimore in two hundred copies; the lithographer was Charles Fenderich, the publisher Edward Weber. It was not to the captain's taste, and he arranged for republication in New York, together with four scenes of Monterrey and vicinity, under title of *Army Portfolio;* Fenderich did one of the Monterrey scenes, Charles Parsons the others, and the portfolio was published by G. and W. Endicott in 1847. According to a tradition of the Whiting family, only twenty-four sets were made. As related in the introduction, drawings to continue the series were en route to Baltimore when they were lost in the sinking of a Mississippi steamboat.

September 4 ✦ Crittenden is lying on my bed, and I was going to allow him to take a snooze whilst I say a few more words to my darling wife. We are in the same place, my dearest, and are likely to remain as we are for an indefinite period, three or four weeks longer at any rate, after which we may move some thirty miles up the Nueces to San Patricio.

This is the dirtiest place, I believe, I was ever in. It is almost impossible to keep clean, although the bay is just behind our tents where we can bathe whenever we wish. If I sit down to read or to write, I get my face, hands, eyes, papers all full of sand, sticks, etc. There is a constant wind blowing from the sea, so hard that we can hardly wear straw hats. As for clothes, I do not pretend to keep them clean. That checked coat I have worn ever since I have been here and shall wear it a week longer. I have got on a dark woolen purple shirt, which will stand two or three weeks' wear without beginning to show dirt. It may smell a little after the second week, but the strong breeze carries off the odor. I have just been begging Crittenden to remove himself at a little distance from me, wash himself, and to paint his red beard, but he appears like all the rest to have no regard whatever to the nasal or optical organs of his fellow wallowers. I never shall be a white man again in the world, and some of us I am sure will not be permitted into the front doors whenever we get home, even if we go through a scraping process first. . . .

We have given Brewer up. I at last made the captain believe that it was a bad arrangement and more expensive and less comfortable than we might have. I persuaded him to get Mrs. Lindsay to cook and wash both for us. Now, we were obliged to pay Uncle Sam for Brewer, merely for a waiter, eight dollars apiece, and about three dollars a month to someone else for washing, making eleven dollars a month. Now we agreed to give Mrs. L. each six dollars for doing both. Moreover, Crittenden was ordered to join our regiment today, and we invited him to our mess and give Mrs. L. three dollars more for him. So that makes only $5 a month each. So that by that operation we save $6 a month. Worth saving, isn't it, dear wife? . . .[1]

I think, though, dearest, that we never will go back to our little Fort Pike again. I tell you it looked sad to see the *Monmouth* and the *Creole* out here and to think of the happy home we had left behind us.

1. In a letter of August 26, Dana had testified that Brewer was doing poorly: "Let me tell you, my darling one, how sumptuously Captain L. and myself fare at our mess. Brewer feeds us in the morning on coffee, boiled ham, pickles, and hard biscuit. At dinner boiled ham, hard biscuit, and pickles. At supper hard biscuit and coffee. We have no lobscouse, and we have no potatoes, and no gloves to wipe out our plates with. We sit on two boxes and eat off of a chest." "Lobscouse" was a nautical word for a combination of meat with vegetables, ship biscuit, etc., sometimes stewed, often baked. Brewer's essential problem was drunkenness. See also Darwin Payne, "Camp Life in the Army of Occupation: Corpus Christi, July 1845 to March 1846," *Southwestern Historical Quarterly* 73 (1969), 326-42.

September 7 ✦ Why, my own dearest wife, did I forget to give you a caution in my last letter, a caution I had so often thought of and so much dreaded lest you would not take care of it yourself? I had laid it up in my mind to give you warning and then, anxious though I was and will always be about that very thing, still I closed my letter without telling you of it. It is this. If your courses return upon you, that you take the greatest care that you do not expose yourself to take cold at or before that time. Be heedful and thoughtful about it and when it is time for your courses to come upon you, which is now, do not sit out in the evening air, even though others do, and do not allow the slightest chance to take cold or expose yourself in any way about that period.

I will be delighted if you are not pregnant. You must not forget to tell me all about it, and if you are so, bear it as well as you can and tell your husband all your feelings. If he cannot be with you to nurse you in your troubles, he can feel for you and sympathize with you. Should you be in that way, you and your new mother will be within a month of each other. Then there is your sister too. Her belly was getting quite large at Fort Pickens.[1] She can outdo any woman I ever saw. If ever there was a woman liked it, it is her.

But do you mind, dearest wife, and be careful of yourself whether you are in that way or not. If you are not, be exceedingly careful about your courses. If you are so, be very careful to prevent a miscarriage.

Also endeavor to keep up cheerful spirits and when I return be able to show me, for I will look, a nice plump pair of legs, and good round soft titties, rosy cheeks, and long hair. Cut off the ends of the latter often and be sparing of your oil.

1. Fort Pickens was on Santa Rosa Island in Pensacola harbor.

September 12 ✦ It is late at night, but I make haste to finish this letter and dispatch it to you in order that you may have a correct account of a terrible accident which has occurred here this afternoon, for should newspaper rumors reach you before you hear from me, they will be so much exaggerated that you might feel uneasy about some of your friends. Providence has seen fit to order us today with a very severe calamity, which carries tears and mourning into some poor broken hearts. A little old high-pressure steamer called the *Dayton*, from Galveston, a miserable apology for an old boat, worse than the one which used to bring our wood at Fort Pike, which had been hired by the quartermaster's department, blew up today just out here on her way to St. Joseph's Island. The explosion was tremendous and the boat a complete wreck. There were some eight or ten officers on board of her at the time, two of whom, poor fellows, Lieutenants Higgins and Berry of the Fourth, were killed. Lieutenant Graham of the Fourth was badly scalded. There were seven killed in all and seventeen wounded. Among the killed was Corporal Chambers. He had been discharged and was going back home. He was mashed to a mummy. Poor Mrs. Higgins. They had been married but ten days when they were separated. Hers is a hard case. A poor widow and so young. His father-in-law, Captain Morrison, is here. Berry was a single man. Crittenden was standing talking with Higgins at the time and was not hurt. A narrow escape. The other officers on board were not hurt at all. They were Captain Crosman, Lieutenants Gordon and Woods.[1] The old craft never ought to have been hired, as she was about fifty years old in the first place, and the next place the officers ought not to have gone on board of her. They don't catch me in any such place, for if I must go I prefer a safer transport. The affair was the more unfortunate as they had discharged the boat this very day. They have two fine boats here now from Orleans, the *Neva* and the *White Wing*, both good and safe boats. Make yourself entirely easy about me, dearest wife. These officers were not obliged to go in the first place to St. Joseph's Island, and in the next there are plenty of sail vessels to go in. For myself I shall always stay at home unless I am ordered to go, which is scarcely a possibility, and if I were ordered I would go in a schooner. I suppose in reporting this affair the papers will have hundreds killed instead of tens.

1. Thaddeus Higgins, who graduated in 1840, was a second lieutenant when he was killed in 1845 (Cullum, I, 607-8). Benjamin A. Berry, a graduate in 1841, was a second lieutenant (ibid., II, 34). William M. Graham graduated in 1817 and was a captain in 1845; he was promoted to lieutenant colonel in 1847 and was killed that year at the Battle of Molino del Rey (ibid., I, 161-62). Pitcairn Morrison was commissioned a second lieutenant in 1820, a first lieutenant in 1826, and a captain in 1836. A colonel by 1861, he retired two years later and was brevetted brigadier general in 1865. He died in 1887 (Heitman, I, 729). George H. Crosman, an 1823 graduate of the Academy, was brevetted major general in the Civil War (Cullum, I, 253-54). William Hamilton Gordon, a first lieutenant at the time, became captain next year, major in 1861, and died in 1865 (Heitman, I, 465). James S. Woods, an 1844 graduate, was a second lieutenant the next year and was killed at the Battle of Monterrey (Cullum, II, 107).

September 15 ✦ Day before yesterday was a sad day here, the bodies of Lieutenants Higgins and Berry of the Fourth Regiment were brought on shore, together with a sergeant, Corporal Chambers, two privates, and two citizens, and the afternoon was set aside for their interment with the honors of war. A beautiful site was chosen for a burial ground, a charming place for a cemetery, just on the brow of a gently sloping hill surrounded and there by tufts of low brush. At the foot of the hill stretching out more than half a mile is the plain on which we are encamped, a plain about five miles long. This spot fronts on the beautiful piece of water called Corpus Christi Bay, and on the left is seen the Nueces, gently winding its way through the plain below. It is a romantic spot, and tears almost came to my eyes as I wished that you could be here to witness the scene on that sacred evening.

The time was twilight. The sun had just finished his course and sunk to rest behind the hills around us. The moon, silvery bright, was well nigh full and looked down from heaven to light us on our way to lay the corpses of our brothers in the dust. On the brigade parade ground of the First Brigade a long line of sad and mournful-looking soldiers might be seen waiting the moment to pay the last honors to departed soldiers. All wait in mournful silence. All seem impressed with the deep solemnity, the unusual sadness of the occasion.

Now from silence, scarcely to be heard, attentive ears may catch the sound, a low and mournful sound, of covered, muffled drums, and low and plaintive notes upon the fife. It swells and swells into a wild and touching wail, an escort of forty men present their arms, and slowly down their front is borne a deep black pall, borne by eight officers in uniform with white scarfs about their shoulders. Slowly it passes with the funeral dirge to the left of the escort and is there placed in a wagon with four horses. Upon the pall is laid a stand of colors and a sword. The pallbearers take their places on each side of the funeral car. Beneath this pall there lies the mingled corpse of poor Higgins, all that remains of him on this earth, and that soon to disappear. Alas, what burning tears await the tidings of his sad end. What heartbreaking sobs shall greet dread news of his untimely death. After the pall follows an old soldier in deep mourning, the father of her who is left so young a widow. The corpse has taken up its place in line and waits to obey the last military command upon its last field.

A silence again prevails, when softly commences again that slow and dirgelike strain and rises to a wild and heartfelt wail, and from a tent close by a pageant precisely similar to the former is seen to issue, passing around the right of a second escort and receiving its salute; the corpse of poor Berry is borne to its place in line similar too in ceremonies with the ranking corpse. Thrice again the same is repeated and the remains of a sergeant and two privates are placed on the left of their respective escorts. Thrice females in closest black seek the nearest place to the deceased sergeant and appear both to leave the mourning pall.

All now wait the word of command, which is given, and the separate escorts followed by their respective corpses wheel into column and move off to the mournful "Dead march in Saul" from the band. After the escorts and corpses follow the soldiers of the Fourth Regiment to which all the deceased belonged. Next came the officers of the same regiment, and after them about sixty officers of the other corps. In this order the procession moved for half a mile to the graves of those whom we were to lay to rest. Here we formed in line, and with the silvery light of the moon we let the coffins into the grave. Then all uncovered and by a lantern's glimmer the service for the dead was read from the church prayer book in solemn voice by an appropriate officer, and then three pieces of arms gave to the dead their last salute, and there we left them.

The beating of the waves of Corpus Christi Bay and the murmur of the river shall make a long, long requiem, which will sing its strains long after the tears of those who love shall cease to flow. There, Mexico, lie the first who have fallen. In your foolhardiness will more be sacrificed? If so, a terrible vengeance follows. The [illegible] will be appeased.

All who were lost by the explosion of the *Dayton* have been found. Nine killed, seventeen wounded, which were about all she had on board.

September 16 ✦ One thing let me again charge you, that is, to believe none of those idle, foolish rumors which are continually going the rounds of the newspapers. Some of them are the excess of absurdity and many of them without any foundation. For instance, there was a report at Orleans and Baton Rouge that the *Alabama* with all of us on board had perished, when we had a quick, pleasant, smooth passage, without anything to render it disagreeable.

Then there are many ridiculous reports, and will be many more, of our being cut to pieces by the Mexicans. We will have no fight. That is almost a certainty. And even if Mexico were to declare war, we are too strong for her and are growing stronger and stronger every day. She cannot fight us, that is out of the question. She cannot raise the means. So fear not that any action will take place. Our troops will not molest each other. She has not a force equal to us within two hundred miles of us, and that would dwindle to one half before she could reach us. Then the moral effect is great for us. We have a contempt for them, and their soldiers have a terror for our name. We have sixteen companies of artillery expected here daily with more field cannon than all Mexico can raise. That renders us vastly superior to them. The Fifth Regiment, or five companies of them, arrived here yesterday. It appears that they did not reach Jefferson Barracks, but orders met them on the way to keep on for Texas.[1] I presume six companies of the First are at the barracks by this time. I saw Lieutenant Whipple yesterday.[2] He saw your uncle on the way, and he told him of Cass's death. We expect the Eighth Regiment every day. We have now here five regiments—twenty-five hundred men. When all arrive who are on the way, we shall have four thousand of our army here. Then in addition we have one thousand Texan volunteers at their homes who can be called out at a moment's notice. If need be we could at twenty days' notice have thirty thousand men here, which would bear all Mexico before us.

1. Jefferson Barracks was on the right bank of the Mississippi nine miles below St. Louis.   2. Joseph H. Whipple of the Fifth graduated in 1835 and was a first lieutenant. He died in Mexico two years later (Cullum, I, 489).

September 21 ✦ Yesterday we had a visit from some Lipan Indians, regular wild, fierce warriors, fine-looking Indians, mounted on horseback, painted red and brown, and dressed off with buckskins, buffalo tails, and other ornaments.[1] One fellow had a pair of leggings I would much liked to have got, but I was afraid to ask him for fear he would want to eat a piece of me. Their dresses were very funny. One fellow had his navel painted vermilion, with black around it. They are a bold set of fellows, but their tribe is small. The Comanches are the sovereigns of the prairies of Texas.

1. The Lipans were of the eastern or buffalo-hunting group of Apache tribes, which formerly ranged especially in central and western Texas.

September 22 ✦ The chief of the Lipan tribe of Indians was shot by some rascal last night in a very cowardly manner. I should think the old fellow had nine lives, for he will not die from this, and he was shot enough to kill a half a dozen men. Some rascal got him out in the dark to take a drink, and then drew a six-barreled pistol and shot the chief in the forehead. He fell, but the ball did not penetrate. It traveled round the skull. He was again shot in the breast, when miraculously again the ball struck a rib and instead of penetrating it traversed around and came out at the back. He then got up and ran, when the ruffian took him in the neck and shoulder with a load of buckshot. A Colonel Cook here, a leading man at this place, but an outlaw from the States, with ten-thousand dollars reward on his head, was suspected, but he stoutly denies it to General Taylor and says he had gone to bed. A long time ago this colonel had his eye put out in a fight by an Indian arrow, and he says this is the man who did it. For which he swears to kill him if he finds him on the altar. All the people around here are rascals. There is not a man of them who is not a renegade from justice from our country, some for crime, some for debt.

We had a visit from the Texan secretary of war and some officers the other day, ordinary looking men enough. The best of them looked as if they could steal sheep. This is secret, you know. The best-looking man among them was Captain Hays, the commander of a company of Texan rangers, a very remarkable man, and one of the most daring men of the day.[1] He often fights against five times his numbers of Comanches, and it is said of him that having surrounded a party of them in a piece of brush, that in his excitement he said to his men, "Boys, you stand here whilst I go in and rouse them out." He did rouse them out, and was not hurt. He too is an outlaw for killing a man in the United States. He is certainly a remarkable young man, and every Indian on the prairies knows him and fears him.[2]

The Indians are at present at peace with Texas, but Mexico is too weak to bring them to terms. The United States will have to pacify them for her by and by. That may be the condition on which she may let us have as far as the Rio Grande.

1. The secretary of war—and of the navy (it was a joint office)—was William G. Cooke.   2. John Coffee Hays was born in Tennessee in 1817 and died in California in 1883. One of the volunteers during the Texas Revolution, arriving just after the Battle of San Jacinto, he thereafter fought four years against hostile Mexicans and Indians and in 1840 became captain of a ranger company. He served throughout the Mexican War as colonel of a regiment of Texas volunteer cavalry and won distinction at Monterrey. In 1849 he went to California, where he acquired large interests in real estate, banking, and industry. *Dictionary of American Biography*, 20 vols. (New York, 1928-36; reprinted in 10 vols.), vol. 4, pt. 2, p. 463 (hereinafter cited as *DAB*). During the Mexican War, Hays and his men were an awesome sight, "a wild and motley looking crew with an inveterate hatred for all Mexicans, who in turn looked on them, with considerable cause, as the legions of the very devil himself. Bearded to the eyes, dressed in rough homespun and slouch hats, carrying no tents and little baggage, with a small sack of parched corn supplemented by wild game for rations, and with no forage for their wiry mustangs except the grass underfoot, they were individually armed to the teeth with an assortment of rifles, bowie knives, and, most important of all, the Colt repeating revolver which had made a name for itself on the great plains of Texas. They had no discipline, no scientific tactics, and it was the practice of Jack Hays to point his finger at the enemy and shout, 'Give 'em hell, boys!' " (Edward S. Wallace, *General William Jenkins Worth: Monterey's Forgotten Hero* [Dallas, 1953], 87).

September 23 ✦ Whiting and myself went out in a boat for a couple of hours to fish in the bay this morning. The swell was a little high and Whiting was seasick. After fishing for a long time we both of us lost patience, got two or three glorious nibbles, and came home without any of the scaly monsters, as Hawkins calls them.[1]

We are settling down here, dear Sue, into a real everyday life, nothing to excite us, not a great deal to do, and us poor married fellows allowed too much time to pine after our wives. We resort to all sorts of jokes and amusements to while away unhappy hours, and have our ears wide open to catch all rumors of change, and strain our eyes across the bay for the steamboat smoke which might possibly be the first tidings of news from home. Our mails come very seldom, and when a chance vessel does bring one, those who do not receive documents are much disappointed. They say that the mails are loaded down with letters for the officers' ladies. Bliss, the adjutant general, says that the married officers for writing beat the Jews. . . .[2]

Our Lieutenant Colonel Hoffman has not as yet made his appearance. He is not much wished for, and Major B. still commands the regiment.[3] He does very well indeed. The grumblers will not listen to anything in his favor, but he does well and is the best major on the field. We are decidedly the best regiment here and have the finest and most military-looking camp. As for the crack regiments, self-styled, the Third and Fourth, I do not think they can compare with us with much credit to themselves. . . .

It is long since we have heard from Orleans. The most recent papers we have received are twelve days old, and we live under the fear continually that some of our mail get lost and our valued letters never reach us, therefore number your letters, Sue, that I may know if I receive them all. I have until now received but two from you, one from Memphis, one from home, but the next mail may bring me two. If I could but know if you are well, if you get through your distresses without sickness or a nervous attack, God grant that you meet with no more sorrows.

---

1. Edgar S. Hawkins, who graduated from West Point in 1820, was a captain in 1845. He retired as a major in 1861 and died four years later (Cullum, I, 208-9).   2. Capt. William W.S. Bliss was Taylor's assistant adjutant general and later his son-in-law. An 1833 graduate of West Point and a member of the Fourth Infantry, he was brevetted major for Palo Alto and Resaca de la Palma and lieutenant colonel for Buena Vista. He died in 1853 (Cullum, I, 427-28). He was a bright young officer with a flair for writing and was suspected of being the virtual author of Taylor's dispatches, which were often cleverly and nicely written. The judgment seemed corroborated with publication of Taylor's private correspondence, which showed choler and grammatical infelicities; see *Letters of Zachary Taylor* (Rochester, N.Y., 1908). Within the general's family the intelligent son-in-law was known as "Perfect" Bliss.   3. William Hoffman, mentioned above, a first lieutenant in 1813, a captain in 1819, a major in 1838, and promoted to lieutenant colonel on July 15, 1845, died on November 26 of that year (Heitman, I, 535).

September 26 ✦   Months may pass before our government can ripen negotiations sufficiently to withdraw and canton her troops, and with those of us too who remain behind it will be a matter of great uncertainty how soon we can provide for our wives. I believe there is really a lady arrived at Joseph's Island, who I do not know. Poor thing, she will really be in a very bad fix indeed. I expect she will pretty soon find her way back to Orleans. I presume she came over from one of the Florida posts. She will find this a worse place than Florida to come to, that is, for a lady. Here we are in the field, in the true meaning of the word, living real soldiers' lives, and a lady can find nothing comfortable here. Your constitution, my dearest wife, my delicate little flower, would be undermined in this life in two weeks. Major Seawell wrote to Captain Hawkins to know if he could bring his wife, and she added in a postscript that she intended to come at all events.[1] Hawkins answered him not to think of it, not for a moment. The major will probably leave her at Baton Rouge.

1. Washington Seawell, an 1825 Academy graduate, served through the Civil War and was brevetted brigadier general (Cullum, I, 281).

September 30 ✦   Think, dearest, what a time Mrs. Hawkins is having of it here in camp. This wet weather, it must be exceedingly disagreeable to her, if not dangerous. I have heard many officers wish that it would rain ten times harder and ten days at a time, to induce her to go to Orleans. None of them encourage her to stay. It is certainly very annoying to officers in the field to have a lady in camp near them and then it is so very public for her. No privacy whatever. Old General Taylor said to her, "Well, madam, we did not expect any ladies, but since you are here we will make you as comfortable as we can, but if I had come with the command you would not have started, I can tell you." I cannot but think she will have to return to Orleans, especially when we commence a movement towards the Rio Grande.

October 1 ✦   There are millions of flies about here, thicker ever than the mosquitoes at Fort Pike. They won't let us sleep in the daytime, cover the walls of the tents at night, fly into our noses and mouths, get into our eatables on their passage from the plate to the mouth. Now don't you see what a great advantage I have in not being at all disgusted with such things? The captain and Strong make a good deal of fuss about it, but I let it pass without saying anything.[1] There is at least one fly in every cup of coffee we drink. Now you could not stand that at all, I know. Our boiled ham today was covered with dead ones, which had drowned in the fat after it was put on the table. Whilst I am writing they dirty all over the paper. We are all flyblown, our pillows and white clothing always spotted and our tempers put to the test by their annoyances.

Then this is a mighty thriving country for cockroaches too. I do not know whether there are any notices of that kind here, but those we brought from around Orleans and their eggs have bred most plentiful. Our clothes, papers, coats, trunks, and everything is full.

I think what with the mildew from the incessant wet weather, the flies, the ants, and the roaches, we will have to get entirely new clothes to make a decent appearance after the campaign is over. One of my black frock coats looks as if it had received a charge of birdshot through the tail. Bean came in here a few minutes since, asked if I were writing to you, and desired me to send his best respects. He is now lying asleep on my bed, with his face in his hat to keep the flies off.[2]

1. Erastus B. Strong, who graduated in 1844 and was a second lieutenant, was killed at Molino del Rey (Cullum, II, 106).   2. Bean was clerk to a sutler of artillery.

October 3   ✦   I was kept awake the greater part of last night with the toothache, the first regular toothache I have had for five years and upwards. I got up twice in the night and went to Dr. Crittenden to have it out, but he was afraid it would crumble and thought it unsafe to try it except by daylight. He gave me creosote but it did it no good whatever. So I had to stand it as best I could, but I thought that reveille never would come. At the first peep of dawn I dressed myself and got Crittenden up and we had it out in a few minutes. It was next the last tooth, and I thought my head was coming off. It left a big hole. So much towards my looking older when I come back again to you, my dear wife. A husband with mouth and cheeks fallen in and narrow-jawed at that. . . .

What has Alf done with himself?[1] Still nothing for him to come out here for. There can be no opening for him at this place and should there be one suitable on the Rio Grande when we get there I will make haste to let him know. When Alf does get started on the right track he will get ahead, no doubt. If he had money to start with, a little time to throw away, and was disposed to be a little venturesome, I would say come here and take a look, and if he could do nothing better he might make calculations on a mule speculation. Mules which would bring thirty-five, forty, fifty dollars and sometimes more at Orleans can be purchased here from the Mexicans from ten to fifteen. About the costs and risks of transportation I can't tell him. He would have to calculate those himself. I myself would not enter into the scheme unless I had money to place at a venture. Perhaps his uncle or someone else would advance money and stand half the losses or half the profits. Cargoes of mules frequently go from here to Orleans. Should we go on the Rio Grande, mules will be more abundant and cheaper, and a schooner would carry them from Brazos Santiago. At the present time I know of nothing else Alf could do here, and as I said before I would advise him not to come. He can do much better in a safer way somewhere else.

1. Alfred Sandford, Sue's brother.

October 5 ✦ We had quite a cool touch this morning, quite an October day. Everybody buttoned up to the neck. Blankets are very comfortable such nights as last night. How cold it must be getting with you. If you could only take wings and fly down here to warm in my bosom.

And then this is delightful weather for riding. Yesterday I had to ride five miles back in the country back of us and as I rode back all alone I was every moment vainly wishing that I could have you with me. You would be so delighted: all is so wild and romantic. Your buoyant spirit would be unchained, and you would feel so free and happy.

I saw some pretty wildflowers, and it occurred to me that I would gather them and press them for the darling I so much loved and so constantly thought of, so I gathered a large bunch and I almost cried with joy as I thought of the value you would set upon them. I walked nearly a mile, leading my horse and plucking all the prettiest I saw. I felt a great happiness in gathering flowers, which I knew were for you, and I almost dreamed as I walked along and buried myself in thought that I could hand them to you when I returned. How I cherished each flower, and how carefully I selected the prettiest and most perfect, but alas, when I returned home all my endeavors were fruitless. The poor little offsprings of nature had wilted and died, and I was sadly disappointed.

October 6 ✦ I saw Mrs. Hawkins ride through camp today in a two-horse buggy wagon with an officer. I hear nothing of her, but I know that she cannot be made comfortable in such a place as this. Were we where we could get trees, logs, boards, or anything of that kind, it would be a different matter, but here nothing of the kind is to be had for love or money. It is said that there is not a pine tree in this part of the country and none near the Rio Grande. We are waiting to see if Major Seawell will bring his wife out here. I expect he will think better of it and conclude to leave her at Baton Rouge.

I do very little reading here, scarcely any. You see I write nearly every day, if not quite, to you, darling. That occupies a good deal of my time, my duties a good deal more, and I spend a good deal in loafing around and talking and chatting with the officers of the various camps. You see, being in camp is like everybody being in one large house, occupying different rooms in the same hall. We only step out of our tents, and we are in the grand common saloon, the parade ground. Colonel Twiggs says that this business of sleeping on straw and sleeping on the ground was never intended for gentlemen but for blackguards.[1]

The blots on this paper, Sue, are a specimen of what the cockroaches will do for us here. They crawl in the inkstand and crawl over the paper, leaving their tracks behind. They are not so large as they were on board of our little old schooner. . . .

I hope our little Mary's teeth are not putting you to a heap of trouble. You must not get frightened about her, darling wife. Try and be composed, whatever trials you meet with, and know and recollect how dearly your husband loves you and let that be a consolation to you. Have you commenced feeding her yet? When you wean her, I think if you are not in a "delicate fix" you will be mighty well. God grant it. You will then get fat and rosy again and be once more as wild as a young deer, and as sprightly as a kitten, for your husband when he gets home. I will try to limber my long legs to romp about with you in the woods.

1. David E. Twiggs, son of Brig. Gen. John Twiggs, who was called the Savior of Georgia in the American Revolution, was born in Georgia in 1790 and after service in the war of 1812 joined the regular army in 1825. He had risen to the rank of colonel by the time of the Mexican War. After the battles of Palo Alto and Resaca de la Palma, in which he distinguished himself, he was promoted to brigadier general. He was brevetted major general after Monterrey, even though he had been ill and had taken no part. Years later, in February 1861, in command of the military department of Texas, he surrendered his forces and stores to the Confederacy, an act for which he was dismissed from the U.S. Army. Commissioned a major general in the Confederate army, he proved too old to take the field and died the next year (*DAB*, vol. 10, pt. 1, p. 83). "Twiggs is a man somewhat advanced in years; of a large body; full, round, red face; heavy whiskers and moustachios; but these are all white, or nearly so. Of course he had, when first seen, a singular appearance. Yesterday, he was coming along the road, through our encampment, going down to General Taylor's. Two of the men of our company, by name Dyer

and Dresser, who had never seen the general, started towards their horses, tied a hundred yards or more down the road. Dyer had a large bag of corn on his shoulder, to feed them; while Dresser had two heavy bundles of fodder. They saw General Twiggs coming up towards them: they caught a view of his red face, and white whiskers and moustachios, long and bushy. As if frightened, they suddenly stopped; looked quickly at one another, and at him again; he was coming nearer. With a look of the greatest alarm, Dyer dropped his bag of corn in the road, and ran with all speed back; while Dresser hesitated a moment, looked again, then dropped his fodder, and cleared after him. Both ran up the road, looking back over their shoulders, with the same apppearance of alarm. General Twiggs, seeing this, was much annoyed; and his countenance was of higher color. He came in view of them again, as they had stopped at the lower tent in the company line. As soon as he appeared, they ran up to the head of the line; and all eyes were upon them and the general. As he still came nearer, with the appearance of the utmost fear, they dashed head foremost into the thorny chapparal, and hid themselves in its thickets. The general's face, as he saw all this, was more red than ever; while he passed by, with a bow to those who were standing spectators of the curious scene" (George C. Furber, *The Twelve Months Volunteer* [Cincinnati, 1848], 331-32).

October 7 ✦ Good morning again, my own beloved, sweet little Sue. I will write you a few lines, in beginning this letter, although I finished No. 9 yesterday afternoon. I know that even if I repeat the same words over and over again, my darling wife will always be glad to get them or even to see the handwriting of her own fond husband, when he is so cruelly separated from her. . . .

It is another rainy day, all is damp and wet and everything feels nasty. The guard mounted in a driving rain, a guard of two hundred men. The fatigue and forage have gone out to get wet jackets at their works of cutting wood and hay. This is the kind of weather which makes the bane of a soldier's life. The sentinel, wet to the skin, has still to tread his miry post and even when relieved has but to sit still for his clothes to dry on him. The ground on which the soldier sleeps is wet, his tent is wet, his blanket is wet, his clothes are wet. The rain extinguishes the fires, and he is obliged to wait until the sun comes out to dry his disagreeable, uncomfortable property. In addition to this his meals are irregular and only half-prepared. If it rains right hard he gets no coffee, so that he is obliged to take cold comfort, and if he can get a little whiskey he is apt to raise spirits by artificial means.

October 8 ✦ You can't imagine what a crowd of officers and men we have here, quite an army for the United States to get together on a common occasion. You can ride a mile and a half along a long line of camp, the whole space white with tents.

Mrs. Hawkins has taken to riding out. She rode along the camp yesterday and today on horseback. I suppose she will march in that manner.

I was sent out this morning by Major Brown to beat the country for several miles in search of a lost man. The man was one of my woodchoppers. He wandered off from his party yesterday and has not been heard of since. I took a bugle, mounted my horse, and with a couple of men set out but found no man. I reckon he wandered away voluntarily, and such wandering as that we generally call desertion.

The country back of us is really beautiful to ride through, if you could only come along on horseback over that rolling prairie land you would be absolutely delighted. You could sing and cry out as loudly as you would want to, and say, "Oh, look yonder!" when a deer took to his flight or a pretty bed of wildflowers came into view. Every time I go over the hills I wish and wish again that you were riding by my side. Independently of your being with me, you would be so delightd with the country and the scenery. The rolling expanse of green dotted with shade in thick knots, called "spots," and occasionally through a thick growth of chaparral you get a view of a beautiful bend of the Nueces.

2
Tedium
October-November 1845

October 10 ✦ When I come home . . ., I shall want to kiss you all over, and won't you let me do it? I know you will, for you told me on the steamboat you would do everything I want. May I kiss you over and over again on your lips, titties, belly, legs, and between them too? Yes, I must. Tell me, dear one, if I may.

You don't know how anxious I am lest you are in a delicate situation. Tell me all about it, Sue. It is possible that nursing may make your courses irregular, and they may come yet, but it was after the time when you last wrote me? I really hope you are not so. It appears too much to lose. You will have all the pain and trouble, without our having all the enjoyment. If you are so, we are losing a deal of fun in bed.

Say, darling, don't you like for me to talk to you in this way? Do you ever think of me in that way? So you have not put my miniature in my place yet? Are you not going to do it? I am just as big a rascal as ever, am I not? It is my love for you which prompts it all, dearest one. I never think of anyone else in that way and when I used to talk to you of others it was only to laugh at you. A brute beast will lick the dirt from its own young but will only bite those of another. So with me, darling wife. Your parts inspire me with love and excite my desires. Other women would disgust me. Conversations which, before I was married, I would sit and listen to and join in now fill me with the deepest disgust. Will you really send me the measure of your leg right high up?[1]

Well, no paymaster came by the *Alabama* and I am sure you will want money. Captain Sanders of the engineers very kindly volunteered to lend me a check, which he has, and I will get that and send it to you.[2] It is not a large one but it will do for you until I can send you more. You shall have just as much as you want, and I want you to tell me always how much you stand in need of. I would send you a pay account of seventy-five dollars but I owe these men so much that I am anxious to keep by me all you have not use for.

1. These remarks were in response to a letter from Sue dated September 9: "As for your precious miniature, very well, old fellow. You need not think I have forgotten where you told me to put it. No, I did not put it there and am even afraid to take it to bed with me for fear of getting it injured. But I kiss it and kiss it and press it to my bosom over and over again." The Dana MSS in the archives of West Point contain about twenty miscellaneous letters, including a dozen or so from Sue to her husband. Sue's letters are not especially informative and usually offer laments over her husband's absence. The other letters, to Sue from friends or relatives, include several chatty missives from the wife of Captain Lee. The miniature, likely a daguerreotype, is not in the small group of family photographs in the West Point archives. 2. John Sanders graduated in 1834, was brevetted major in 1846, and died in 1858 (Cullum, I, 445).

October 11 ✦ There is no paymaster here, and I did not know at first how I should get a check, but Captain Sanders of the engineers happened to have a check of this amount which he kindly volunteered to lend me, so I took it to the quartermaster of the army and got him to exchange it for one in my name. I make it payable to your order on the back of it. You must write your name, "Susan Dana," under mine and get Major Mackay or someone to get you the money.[1]

My expenses this month, darling, will not exceed eighteen dollars. When I can give those men all their money, I shall feel happy indeed. They do not want it now, have not asked for it, but they might. You want me to tell you about the sums, don't you? You, my wife, shall know all I ever do and shall always know the exact state of my purse. Well, I owe Sergeant Weigart $255, Wise $69, Armstrong $20, and Burke $65. In all $409. Now at the end of this month towards paying this I shall have only $60, which will leave a balance due by me of $349. That is a pretty big sum, is it not? But if we are prudent and economical, we can pay it. It worries me a great deal all the time that debts contracted before I was married should incommode you, loved one, who never had anything to do with them. Now, if we save $30 each month, it will take a year to pay off this debt. This is the time to save, whilst I have a little extra pay. If we can manage between us to live right economically, we can save nearly $40 a month, which, when taken into account with a probable reduction of my pay by and by, it will leave an average of $30 a month. Now can we between us make out to live separately for $40 a month? If each of us can get along on $18 a month, the $4 we pay Lucinda will make the $40.[2]

1. Aeneas Mackay served in the War of 1812, became a captain in 1822, a major in 1838, and a lieutenant colonel in 1846. He died in 1850 (Heitman, I, 670).   2. Lucinda was a youthful helper sent by a family friend, Dr. Wedderburn.

October 13   ✦   Jenkins arrived last night with his goods and has been all day landing them and is employing this bright moonlight night in putting up the same house he had at Pass Christian. I believe he has brought a very fine and extensive assortment of goods and will ask very extensive prices for everything. I ordered some potatoes and onions of him today for our mess, but when I heard that the potatoes were five dollars and the onions were six dollars a barrel I very soon countermanded the order. We go on the economical plan, and all those things are luxuries here. Eggs sell here at fifty cents a dozen and butter at fifty cents a pound. People all come here to make money, and the sutlers stick fast to the troops like so many bloodsuckers.

October 14   ✦   Well, my dear little wife, I have just returned from my morning's ride back in the country, and now I am going to sit down and talk to you again for a short time, but the flies bother me so much that I have to stop between about every two letters to brush them off my face. You have no idea what pests they are here. They annoy us almost as much as the mosquitoes did. . . .

So you are anxious to commence my shirts. I expect you will have a long time to make them, but when I do get home I expect to need a complete wardrobe very badly. I doubt if I shall have anything decent to wear. I have now only three decent white shirts. The rest are either lost or torn entirely to pieces. They destroy clothes here by wholesale. My best shirts are all torn up. I think there must be something in the water to rot them. I bought a couple of flannel shirts, and three colored shirts, and one of the flannel ones has been spoiled by washing. My drawers too are fast disappearing. In fact everything. I am obliged to have those pants which Elwyn gave me made up now, and they will not be worth much then, for they have been badly attacked by the moths and cockroaches.[1] We have to spend our money in spite of all we can do, don't we? Should I return to the States in the spring, I will require an entire new outfit. I shall be very little able to afford it, too. However, we will try hard, won't we, and hope for the best? . . .

By the way, dearest, should you be pregnant, be careful about your diet, won't you? Do you recollect how much we used to talk about that last year, and how sick you got once or twice? That night when you were so sick, when we sent over for Dr. Crittenden next morning, was occasioned by eating improper food for some time. I know my Sue will be careful of all those things for my sake. I hope and pray that you are not in that condition because I always want to be with you at such times, and this would be such a fine chance for a resting spell and for you to grow fat. When you get old, Sue, you are going to be a regular little fat dumpy, as broad as you are long. Then won't you have big legs? Are you going to have all your linen chemises nicely made up when I get home, and such nice pretty drawers? I like for you to wear panties, especially when you are where you see anybody. In fact always except when I am playing rascal.

I believe the mail is about to close to go by the *Monmouth*, and I must make haste to finish this or it will not be mailed. I would not wonder if I were now too late, for the steamboat is raising her steam, and I expect the mail is closed before the time they have appointed.

1. Charles H. Langdon Elwyn was godfather to the Danas' daughter, Mary.

October 15 ✦ I left Captain Lee just before I commenced writing this to you, dear Sue. He went to bed as I left him. He is getting stronger gradually. His attack pulled him down a good deal and he will be convalescent some days longer. All the rest of us enjoy perfect health. For myself I don't know when I have been so entirely healthy for so long a time. This place agrees with me admirably. Something here keeps up a constant very gentle action on my bowels which keeps me in good order and carries off bile. I hope you will be as healthy as I have been. I would rest satisfied then, love.

Mrs. Hawkins rides by here on horseback with her husband every day. I have only seen her at a distance as yet and doubt if I have any nearer view during our stay. She has no children, I believe, in fact if she had, she would not be here, I expect, for camp is not a place to bring young children to. Still less is it a place for women to have them in.

October 17 ✦ I finished dinner about a half an hour since, my dearest little wife, and since then have been sitting and talking with the captain. He is right smart now and will soon attend to all his duties.

And let me tell you what we had today to grace our table: venison, baked potatoes, and fritters. Tomorrow we will probably vary it by changing roast beef for venison. Our fare has the very slightest variety here, and it is fortunate that neither Captain Lee, Crittenden, or myself care much about our diet. Strong grumbles a good deal, but as he is only one of four we let him take it out in grumbling. Would you believe it that I have not drunk milk in coffee since we left the *Alabama* and that I look upon butter as one of the luxuries of life? We have not had that either since we left the steamer.

Our sutler, Jenkins, has his store full of everything which can tempt. Nothing can be called for there which he has not, from the nicest fancy articles which can be bought at Madame Theodore's to herrings. But he does not get my name on his books. It will take me a long time to forget the old bill. I have only spent thirty cents with him as yet for a pair of gloves. He sells quite reasonably for Texas, and for some things he asks less than Bosworth did. You know my old determination never to run up another sutler's bill, and you also know my new one not to spend a cent which I can save. I mean to hold fast to them both, and at the first of the month I will tell you of all my expenses this month. . . .

The army here has been doing nothing but undergo reviews and inspections for the past week. An inspector general has been appointed and on Wednesday he inspected and reviewed the twelve companies of artillery in the morning and the Eighth Infantry in the afternoon. That was the First Brigade. Yesterday he reviewed and inspected the Second Brigade, the Seventh in the morning and the Fifth afterwards. Today he reviewed the light artillery and the Third Brigade, the Third Infantry in the morning and the Fourth afterwards. He has got still to take a look at the dragoons and the volunteers.

You have no idea, Sue, what a military show we have here and how much of the pomp of war with none of the glory. That is not the worst of it, too. There will be none. I wish I had all my glory and was on my way home again, but let us hold on and see what Mr. Polk is going to do.[1]

1. For President Polk, see Charles A. McCoy, *Polk and the Presidency* (Austin, 1960), and Charles G. Sellers, *James K. Polk: Continentalist, 1843-1846* (Princeton, 1966), the second volume of a projected three-volume biography. The diary of the president appears in its entirety in Milo M. Quaife, ed., *The Diary of James K. Polk during His Presidency, 1845 to 1849*, 4 vols. (Chicago, 1910), and in abridgment in Allan Nevins, ed., *The Diary of a President* (New York, 1929). For diplomacy of the time, see the definitive account by David M. Pletcher, *The Diplomacy of Annexation: Texas, Oregon, and the Mexican*

War (Columbia, Mo., 1973). A very interesting book stressing the importance of the Pacific ports for Polk's diplomacy is Norman A. Graebner, *Empire on the Pacific* (New York, 1955).

October 19 ✦ We are all but decided that we are to await here the action of Congress, which we will not hear for three months yet. However, we must have patience as there is no help, and it may be that Mr. Polk may get us out of this fix earlier than we think, for if he were in it, he would be fully as anxious to do something or other as we are, and I wish we had him here.

If our bright quartermaster in Orleans, Colonel Hunt, would send us our letters, we would be much better satisfied, but he allows schooner after schooner to arrive here without letters and waits a fortnight or more for a steamboat. That was just the way we had to wait and wait for the mail which came by the *Alabama*. There is considerable dissatisfaction here about Colonel Hunt's arrangements. . . .[1]

Last night we had a great rain again, a severe thunderstorm. Camp is not very agreeable at such times. When the storm drives hard at the back of my tent, I roll up half of my bed and sleep on the other half, and when the storm comes on at the front, vice versa, I roll it up then foot first. I told you long ago what a primitive bedstead I have. Well, the same holds fast yet. I hope very soon to have a tent to myself again, as the rest of our tents are expected from Orleans. It is very disagreeable to be living with another so long in a small tent. It would do very well on a march or in more active service where, being pretty much all the time on the move, all we would have to do would be to roll in and sleep on the ground at night. . . .

Don't you recollect, dear one, that Mrs. Lindsay had a miscarriage at Fort Pike? Well, she had to call in the doctor here yesterday. She was flooding, but she has not entirely slipped this time. Our other woman, Mrs. Dorrance, is sick, too, with an ulcer in the throat. They are both of them worthless hags, not fit for anything, and had no business to have come along with us. Don't you wish you were a camp woman, Sue, and I a soldier? Then we might always go together. How would you like deck passage? And sleeping on the ground in a common soldier's tent? Doing Mrs. Lindsay's washing for her when she is sick and washing for the men at a half dollar a month?[2]

1. Lt. Col. Thomas F. Hunt served in the War of 1812. He was brevetted colonel in 1848 and died in 1856 (Heitman, I, 557).   2. The regular army allowed four female laundresses to

attend each company. They drew rations like the men. Officers fixed their prices, and deducted their pay, which they received on payday, from that of the soldiers (George C. Furber, *The Twelve Months Volunteer*, 57). Volunteer regiments had no laundresses.

October 21 ✦ How is our little one, dearest Sue? Tomorrow is the day which makes her seven months old, and two of those months I have been away. She must have grown a great deal in that time, and when I get home she won't know anything about me. Will she let me take her with my mustaches and beard on? They have grown quite long now, and if they make me shave before I come home I mean to enclose them to you. They have been growing now about seven weeks. I have been on the point of shaving them off once or twice, but several tell me that they improve my appearance. So I will have the vanity to keep them on to show them to you. I have been raising them for you altogether.

October 24 ✦ Our government cannot in honor hold out the olive branch to Mexico when she is making so many brags and trying to borrow money to enable her to fight us. Our president has done all he has the power to do at present. He has collected all the force at his disposal here upon this disputed land, and if Mexico, in her ignorance, is not overawed by this show of strength, we must wait until Congress, that supreme power which holds all the military reserves of the country, shall convene and decide what is to be done. They can declare war and back their declaration with troops enough to overrun all the plains of Mexico. If Mexico will not come forward frankly and offer us the friendly hand, Congress will, when it convenes in December, instruct Mr. Polk to demand the intentions of Mexico, and if her answer is not satisfactory, she will be very soon driven into terms. Then, and not until then, will we meet. Then and not until then will we be happy. All depends upon treacherous Mexico. If she can quiet her internal disturbances and form a permanent government, we may meet in the spring. But I fear not till then.

October 26 ✦ It will be three months probably before we commence any operations here, for it will take that time for Congress to act and to send instructions. But after that time I really hope that affairs will approach a crisis much more rapidly.

Now it is exceedingly annoying. Here we are at a dead standstill, doing nothing, which we could now as well do anywhere else. That is perfecting ourselves as soldiers. All the army which were off duty were carried yesterday out to some tableland about a mile from here with axes and spades to clear ground for army drills. Heretofore we have been drilling by regiments and brigades, but soon General Worth is to drill the whole army together: 3,000 infantry, 250 artillery, and 400 dragoons, besides the volunteers. It will be the largest scale our army has performed on for very many years.[1] The last day of this month is muster day and the whole force is to be mustered and reviewed by General Taylor. An army like this ought to have a man of more rank than he to command it.[2]

1. William Jenkins Worth was born in 1794 in New York state, of Quaker parents, and was a veteran of the War of 1812. Wounded at the Battle of Lundy's Lane, he was lamed for life but remained in the army. For a while he was commandant of cadets at West Point, even though he was not a graduate. He participated in the Seminole War in 1838, and some years later President Polk brevetted him brigadier general. Polk sent him to Texas as second in command to General Taylor. He served Taylor well ("a grade or a grave," he boasted just before Monterrey) and then transferred to the army of Gen. Winfield Scott, where he again excelled. He was a fine commander in the field but was not much of a tent soldier. Quarrelsome and politically ambitious, he became so obnoxious that at one juncture Scott placed him under arrest. He was assigned after the war to the department of Texas and died of cholera in 1849. See Edward S. Wallace, *General William Jenkins Worth*. Fort Worth, Texas, was named for him.   2. Taylor received the brevet rank of major general after Palo Alto and Resaca de la Palma.

November 1 ✦ Here we are, another month has come in, and still we are in the same place. Little did we expect when we first landed here that this late day would still find us here. Many of us hoped to be interior or on the Rio Grande, and some tried hard to hope that this date would find them at home again. But we are still here and most likely will remain here for some time to come. Doubtless cold December will come in and find us just where November has already caught us. . . .

Everything still remains the same, dull routine of a life of military instruction. Yesterday was muster day and all hands were out. General Taylor reviewed the First Brigade. That brigade can turn out one thousand men with Worth at their head. We are pretty sure, or rather entirely sure now, that we will remain here until we receive instructions after the action of Congress. The quartermaster department, I believe, are making arrangements to get sufficient lumber out here to put us in huts for winter quarters.

The weather still continues warm here. Today was a very warm one, so that our tents are not too cool for a while yet. For the last week I have been wearing a pair of those blue checked pants which your dear little hands made and that checkered loose coat, which, by the way, I shall now have to give up, as it is worn out. The stuff turned out to be very rotten. I don't care how long the moderate weather continues, for I want to save my winter clothes as much as possible. But after a while I reckon we will all be glad to get into winter quarters. Just think of a gentleman living in a hut.

November 2 ✦ You must not think, darling little wife, that I do not like the idea of your living at the barracks with your sister. Anything which may tend to make you happy and comfortable, be assured, will meet with my warm approval. . . . The only thing which I am grieved about is the messing establishment which your sister has got up after having received so many disagreeable lessons on that score. By all means, dearest wife, I would have you in no way connected with it. I know you will think just as I do on that subject. You know my views and in your letter you tell me how nobly you will follow them out. Tell me how you manage to see these gentlemen but "once in a month." That perhaps is a little too distant, but I could never bear that you should sit down at table with them three time a day as if they were acquaintances of a life's standing or very near relations. And dearest, believe me it is your duty to urge that Kate and Sci should not be thus brought in such familiar contact with gentlemen. I am sure your father would not approve of that. . . .[1]

By the way, whilst I remember it, can't you manage to pay your mess bill every month and not let several months run in together? I hate these big bills. . . .

This, you see, is my sixteenth letter, which makes more than one every five days since we parted. And they are longer letters than I ever wrote before. Your last to me, dearest, was a nice long one, but you did not tell me half. As you say, you will have to write on two sheets in future. How much do you have to pay for my letters? Are any of them charged twenty cents?

1. Kate and Sci were Sue's sisters. Another of the sisters, known within the family as "Indiana" (Sue was called "Catawba"), had of course married Captain Whiting. The fourth sister was Orphana. Indiana for a while objected to the engagement of Dana and Sue; her father was then staying with her, and her objection was doubly awkward as a result; Dana disliked her for this reason. Then, too, Mrs. Whiting was often pregnant, and when Sue moved in with her, it was necessary to tolerate her not always well behaved children. Mrs. Whiting died in 1849 at the age of thirty-five, perhaps as a result of a difficult pregnancy. Many years later, the Whitings' youngest daughter,

Mary—there were two sons and four daughters—wrote that Gen. William T. Sherman had once described her mother as "the pride of the army" and a Dr. Dougall had spoken of her as "the grandest woman in America" (Mary B. Saunders, *In Memoriam: Daniel Powers Whiting*).

November 3 ✦ The Orleans volunteers are going home tomorrow. Their time of service expires shortly after they reach the city. I wish I were going with them indeed. I expect most of them feel very glad to have got through with their campaign. They have had but a smile of the soldier's life. The people of Orleans will doubtless make a great fuss over them and think them perfect lions. I would be glad to witness their landing in the city. . . .

John Smith, the tailor, is here dunning officers. I recognized him and shook hands with him. He is staying at Jenkins' store. I owe him $100, so I thought it best to play the most frank, open part. I went over to Jenkins' the evening after he arrived and invited him over to my tent for the discussion of business matters. I reminded him of the debt and told him how much chagrined I had been because I could not pay it, explained to him that it was utterly impossible to pay it until I had paid about $350 which I owed, and promised to pay him as soon as it was possible to do so. He appeared satisfied, was very polite, said that he had not come out here to press me, and dropped the subject and spoke of other matters as soon as I would let him. I had no idea a tailor had so much delicacy.

I shall be very sorry if Earle comes out. It is not so easy to satisfy him. If I did not owe these men here, how easily I could get out of debt. When I can once pay them, I will not keep anybody's money but my own.

November 6 ✦ Our officers here are many of them hard-pushed for amusement. About every week now an expedition of some kind or other is fitted out, and many of them volunteer and get permission to go along. Day before yesterday one left for San Antonio de Bexar, that paradise of Texas. The expedition was Lieutenants Root and Hanson from this brigade with twenty-five men to convoy a train of loaded wagons up to those companies of dragoons stationed there.[1] Many officers went along for pleasure. Among other inducements for the young officers to go is that San Antonio is said to have many pretty girls.

For me, dearest little Sue, I keep along the same as ever, taking my accustomed rides, attending to my fatigue duties and other quartermaster duties, and sitting and thinking of my dear little wife. For the last three or four days I have been a little more busy than usual, and two or three times just as I was about to write to you I have been called off. And now I have to go and get a coffin made for a dead discharged soldier.

1. William Root, a second lieutenant in 1837, resigned in May 1846 (Heitman, I, 845). Charles Hanson, a first lieutenant at this time, was killed in the Battle of Contreras in 1847 (ibid., I, 498).

November 7 ✦ Dr. Crittenden has just come in and is lying down on my bed. He is grumbling and swearing about the sick children. He has his hands full of them. They call him up at all times of night, won't let him sleep in the afternoon, and make a great fuss all the time. He says they always come to him in the eleventh hour. He has had two die on his hands in the last month, and now he has another about doing the same. Besides he has had three women to deliver here. One was that girl who lived at Mrs. Henshaw's and went to Mt. Vernon Arsenal with one of Major Rains' sergeants.[1] Girls will do it, all of them, when you give them a chance, won't they? . . .

Bosworth has got back. The captain got two or three papers from him. I don't know whether his wife died or not. Major Mackay arrived here today. He is just from St. Louis. I suppose you heard of his losing two of his children up there. I expect he does not fancy coming out here much. I don't blame him.

News reached us today that a young officer of dragoons named Cook, from Kentucky, I think, who left here about a week since for home on sick leave, cut his throat on the way to Galveston.[2] The report is believed here, as he was desponding when he left here and his mind was evidently diseased. It appears to be fated that the loss of the army should fall on the younger part of it. . . .

We had a right cold night last night. It took two blankets to keep one at all comfortable, and then I had to haul up my feet to keep them out of the cold. If it was not for the name of [illegible] thing, we might as well live out of doors in windy weather, for when the wind comes from the front of the tents it fills the tent inside like a sail. In a day or two now I expect I shall be able to get a tent to myself. Then I will be fixed much more comfortably and be private.

1. Gabriel J. Rains graduated from West Point in 1827. A lieutenant colonel in 1861, he resigned to enter the Confederate army as a brigadier general (*DAB*, vol. 8, pt. 1, pp.

328-29).   2. Augustus Cook, appointed to the Academy from Kentucky, had graduated in 1844 (Cullum, II, 104).

November 10   ✦   A large expedition started this morning for the
Rio Grande composed of two companies of dragoons, about a
hundred men with thirteen wagons and a good many officers who
volunteered to go. Dr. Crittenden was sent with them. They carried
a good deal of interest along, for if they had met a body of Mexicans
and had been attacked, they would have been obliged to fight, and
that would have been the beginning of a war. But when they had got
about a mile, General Taylor sent a messenger and recalled them.
None of us can conjecture the reason for his doing so. Several
expeditions have already been about eighty miles in that direction
for reconnaissance and have returned. But this one was to reconnoiter the country almost as far as Matamoros, where there is a
garrison of three hundred Mexicans. I suppose we will learn why
the general ordered the detachment back after it started. Although
the weather was so exceedingly uncomfortable, they were all disappointed at not starting after they had prepared themselves. I tried to
get Crittenden to make his will before he started, for we persuaded
him that he would be chained in a Mexican prison before he returned. He took along a rope to tie General Arista and a cowhide to
whip him.[1]

1. Gen. Mariano Arista, a tall, redheaded officer, commanded in northeast Mexico. He
had once lived in Cincinnati.

November 12   ✦   Mexico as she is will do well enough. Should
she revolutionize again and place Almonte at the head, it may be
quite a different question.[1] But let us hope, fondly hope. All our
intelligence goes to confirm the belief that a part of this army will go
home by springtime, and should we here remain, I hope that you
will be able to join me before late in spring. . . .

That young officer of dragoons, Cook, whom I told you about,
did actually cut his throat at Galveston but did not succeed in killing
himself. On his way from there to New Orleans, however, he
jumped overboard. So that is the last of him. He was an excellent
fellow, but if he was determined to kill himself, it is well enough that
he went.

That same reconnoitering party with which Crittenden started
the other day is to leave again at sunrise tomorrow morning. They

will go very near to the Rio Grande. C. wants to know if there isn't some danger of their catching a fellow out there and putting a chain on his leg. They will be gone about twenty days.

1. Juan N. Almonte was Mexican minister in Washington.

November 13   ✦   The party with whom Dr. Crittenden went started in a rain this morning, about a hundred dragoons, the Star-Spangled Banner floating over their heads. If the Mexicans fire at that there will be a war to a certainty. I would not wonder, though, if they went to Matamoros and were feasted and feted there. It would be rather unwelcome tidings to hear that they were all chained at Perote or that the Comanches had driven off all their horses and then attacked them.

November 14   ✦   Another mail arrived last night, my own dear Sue, and still not one word from you. But this time neither Captain Lee nor Whiting received letters, so that I did not feel a proportionate uneasiness. King arrived with the mail, and of course I seized hold of him and made him tell me everything about you that he knew. He could not tell me half plainly enough because he says that he has seen you but very seldom as you have been confined to your room upstairs a great part of the time.

My darling one, when will you get right well again? What a long period of silence for you, eighteen days. You must have been pretty sick all that time, or you would have written to me. But why do you not make one of the girls write? King could not say much about your sickness, but he told me today that your sister told him that half of it was occasioned by your fretting and worrying about me. Now, my dearest, you must cheer up and get well for me. You will not get well until you get in better spirits. Now try, loved one, won't you, and see if you cannot get right smart and come downstairs often and enjoy yourself, and run about and romp with the girls and go up to the city. You must force yourself to do these things sometimes, dear, for your own welfare. And when I come home I will romp and play with you and go everywhere with you.

We none of us know what is going on at Washington so that we can make no sure calculations. From appearances we judge that there will not be a necessity to keep this army together more than a couple of months longer. It is possible, though, that we may be kept here until the whole question with Mexico, in reference to boundaries, is indisputably settled.

All last night it rained and stormed very hard, so that we all got more or less wet, and it has continued wet all day and rainy. We are not yet dried. There are things which soldiers must become accustomed to, and as the old saying goes, they are nothing once you get used to them. Those fellows who are on their way to the Rio Grande must have had an awfully uncomfortable time of it marching in the rain all day and then lying down to sleep in it at night.

3

The Rio Grande

April 1846

The Voyage Back. Advice to Sue. No Word from the Army of Occupation. Arrival at St. Joseph's Island. General Taylor on the Rio Grande. Disappearance of Colonel Cross. At Work on the Fortifications opposite Matamoros. On Guard. Colonel Whistler. Ships Blockading the River. Exciting News about Lieutenant Porter. Finding of Colonel Cross's Skeleton. Parley with the Mexicans. Near Capture of Two Dragoons. Funeral of Colonel Cross. Rumored Arrival of General Arista. Capture of Captain Thornton and His Party.

Sue's melancholia became so great that Dana took a leave of absence and went back to Jefferson Barracks to see her. The cause of her troubles was perhaps nothing serious, quite possibly the result of her confinement and the birth of Mary, together with the miserable living conditions at the barracks, where she was unable to keep house and took meals with officers. For a young girl recently married, with her husband in Texas, it was too much. In a military sense the leave fortunately caused no difficulties. During the time Dana was away, nothing happened along the Texas border.

Belize, April 1 ✦ We have cast anchor here for a little while in order to stow away the freight a little more closely and also to allow the weather to clear up a little before we put to sea. And as the captain promises to send a boat ashore this afternoon, I will employ the few minutes in writing you a page or so in order to cheer you up a little by letting you know that I am still thinking of you and that we are likely to have as pleasant and agreeable a passage as we could wish. All the passengers are sitting around the table, talking and laughing and every now and then addressing me, so that I doubt if I can write you anything which would be worth your reading. Dobbins is sitting just opposite to me and looking as if he were surprised at my writing so soon. I suppose he does not intend to write to his wife.[1]

I really hope, dearest Sue, that you calmed off a little after I left. I thought of you all last night whilst I was awake and feared much lest you had made yourself sick with fretting.

1. Stephen Decatur Dobbins, a first lieutenant at the time, was twice dismissed from the army, the second occasion being in 1847 (Heitman, I, 375).

St. Joseph's Island, April 6 ✦ We are detained so long on our route that I fear you will be getting right anxious about me because you do not hear from me as I told you would in ten days after I left. I am fearful now that it will be three weeks before this boat returns to New Orleans.[1] We left the Belize the same day on which I wrote to you, and we were out at sea nearly three days, experiencing for the two last pretty rough weather. At noon on the third day we arrived here. That was the fourth of the month, and here we have been, lying at the wharf, ever since.

No sooner had we got well inside the bar than a tremendous storm came up which has lasted with greater or less violence until now. It has been blowing terribly, hailing, thundering, lightning, and raining. The sea outside the bar is running mountains high, and we would have fared very badly had we have been in it. We were to have left this afternoon for the Brazos de Santiago, but the weather is so violent that we will not be able to get out until it calms. Our captain will not put to sea until we have good weather, even if we have to wait a day or two longer in harbor.

I sat down yesterday to commence my letter to you, my own little Sue, but it was so very dark in the cabin owing to the storming weather that I could not even see where to commence. I tried it again this morning, but again could not get enough light, so I asked the mate to allow me to write in his room. And here I am in his small kennel with a little hole of a window and the rain beating overhead like hailstones. I cannot but think that you will be anxious lest I am out in this bad weather, and I almost wish I had wings that I might give you word of my safety and comfort in this snug harbor.

My dearest one, you must not forget now that you have promised to be cheerful and lively and not to give way to sad feelings. If Kitty has the dumps at any time, mind that you do not catch it, but leave her to herself and go to seek someone more cheerfully disposed. You must recollect, my dear Sue, that we have had a much better time than most of the married people belonging to the army of occupation and that we ought not to complain but rather feel well satisfied and thankful and invigorated for this separation. You have only to look at your neighbor to see a more unhappy case than your own. Her husband has been home nearly as long as I have, and still he has been but a very short time with her. Neither did he write to her from the Belize. And now that I am preparing this letter only on the hope of finding an opportunity to send it to you when we reach the Brazos, he is talking about nothing at all and probably wishing in his heart that I would not be so fond of writing to my wife for fear

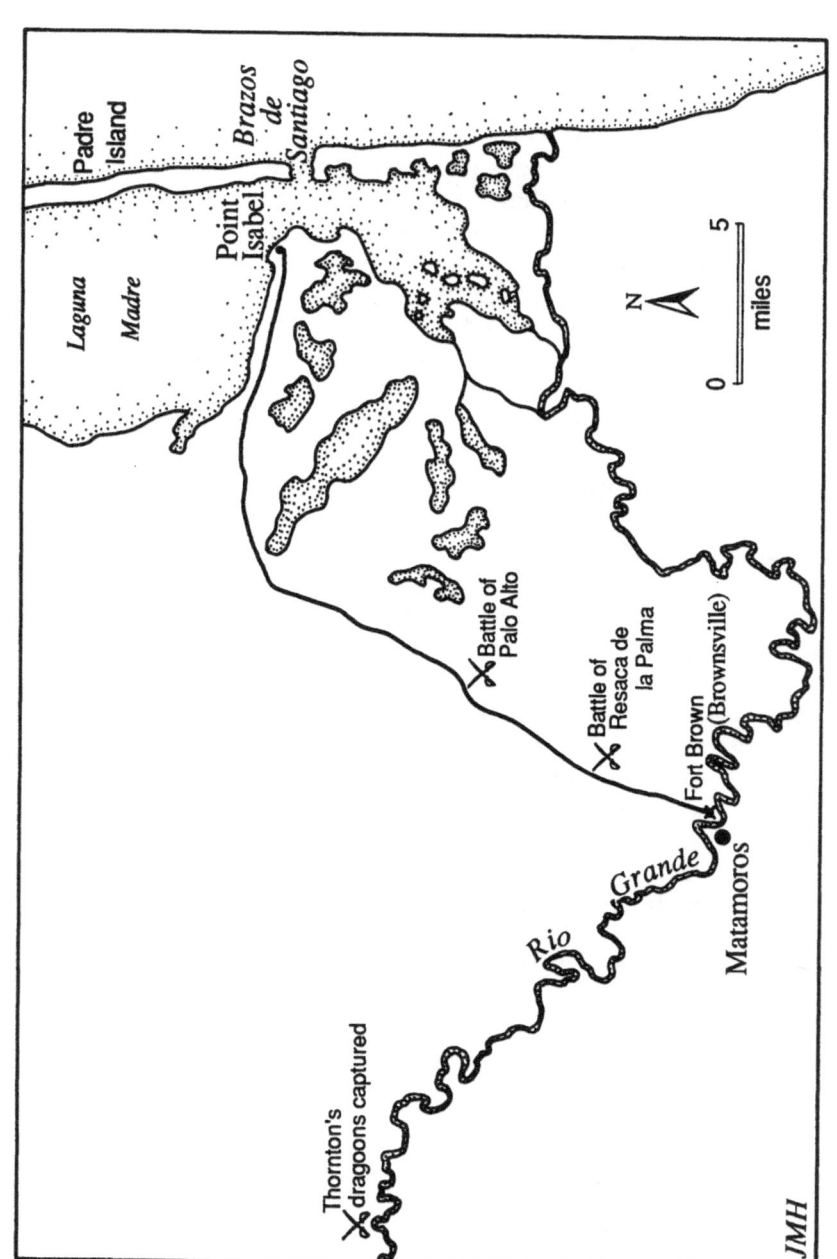

Opening of the War

JMH

that his will think it strange that she does not hear from him. . . .

The probability now is that we shall leave here tomorrow afternoon, be all night at sea, and reach the Brazos the next morning. Nothing at all has been heard here from the army, not one word since it left, nor from the flotilla which left here a fortnight since. We think that the flotilla could not disembark its people and were waiting off Point Isabel for General Taylor to appear. It was reported that there was a small Mexican battery erected at Point Isabel. Everything will doubtless be pacific, but it is possible that the Mexicans opposed Major Brown's landing until General Taylor came.

1. Sue had gone down to New Orleans with her husband, who departed from there for Texas. She remained at New Orleans Barracks, about three miles below the city on the left bank of the Mississippi, later called Jackson Barracks.

Brazos de Santiago, April 8 ✦ Here we are, my own little sweet wife, lying snugly at anchor inside the bar at the Brazos de Santiago. Point Isabel is three miles above, but we cannot go up in this boat, as she draws too much water. We will probably have the *Cincinnati* or *Neva* down for us this afternoon. There was no Mexican battery on Point Isabel as was reported, so that Major Munroe landed unmolested and the place is being strongly entrenched.[1] After he landed here, everything wore the aspect of war for some days. Sutlers, laborers, sailors all were obliged to turn in and perform military service in the way of building breastworks and so forth. General Taylor arrived in due time with his army opposite Matamoros. Two dragoons of the advance guard were captured but were immediately sent back. When General Taylor got on the banks of the river, he had several wagon tongues spliced together to form a flagstaff and the Star-Spangled Banner was hoisted on the Rio Grande del Norte whilst all the bands played "Hail Columbia" and "The Star-Spangled Banner." The army cheered, and all Matamoros, about ten thousand, were on the opposite bank to see the sight. Our flag was answered by the flags of England, France, and Spain from the consuls' houses in the city. And thus did Uncle Sam take the Rio Grande for his boundary line. The river is quite narrow, and the troops can talk across it.

1. John Munroe graduated from West Point in 1814, served in the War of 1812, was brevetted major in campaigns against the Florida Indians, and was brevetted colonel after Buena Vista. He died in April 1861 (Cullum, I, 133-34).

Point Isabel from Brazos de Santiago.

Point Isabel, April 10 ✦ The labors of this army are fast drawing to a close, and very soon it must be decided plainly, either peace or war. Now for the first time in our lives do we see the real soldiers' lives. Watchfulness and labor are our constant pastimes. It is to be much regretted that our numbers are so few and that we cannot frown on our foes as darkly as they do on us. But we are fortifying, and the attack, if there is one, must come from them so that we will be more nearly equalized. . . .

I landed here last evening with my party of men and have been drilling them twice today and shall give them another lesson before night. Dr. Wells, Captain Lee's old friend, invited me to stay at his tent and mess whilst here, so that I am living comfortably and eating the fat of the land.[1] I shall leave here with the train of wagons for the army, which will probably be day after tomorrow. The train arrived today with two companies of dragoons as escort. They stretch three miles, 240 wagons with five mules each.

1. John B. Wells, a commissioned assistant surgeon in 1834, became major surgeon in 1846 and died in 1853 (Heitman, I, 1,017).

April 11 ✦ We have rumors two or three times a day about the Mexicans here. We are prepared for attack at any moment, often sleep in our clothes and the troops two or three times under arms nearly all night, with dragoons holding their horses ready saddled. False alarms are frequent, and both sides appear to be always on the alert. All kinds of reports circulate, some silly and some ridiculous. . . .

Some forty Irishmen have deserted and gone across the river.

The good men are highly incensed at it. The whole army are said to behave admirably well, in the highest spirits, and exceedingly anxious for a fight. They commence cheering at every alarm. Four men attempting to swim the river to desert have been shot by our guards. One belonged to the Seventh. Three were killed and sank, and one was wounded. Good men are always placed on the picket guards and show the deserters no mercy. Those who were killed called out loudly for mercy, but the more they cried, the more the pickets fired. They were said to be shot all to pieces. Our sentinel shot a deserter 'way across the river after he had landed. One of our officers, Lieutenant Judah, shot a Mexican in camp the other night. He told him to stop, but he ran, so he took it for granted that he was a spy.[1] The next day the Mexicans shot a dragoon deserter whom they took for a spy. It served him right. Four deserters were drowned in attempting to swim over. The severity has put a stop to desertion.

But I expect, dearest, that all will go off peaceably enough and Mexico and ourselves will not be allowed to come to any hard blows.

Here I left off this afternoon to go and drill my recruits and during my drill the camp was thrown into a great state of uproar, horses galloping here and there, a detachment of dragoons arriving and so forth, and I made my men stand to their arms, supposing that we were to be attacked and that the enemy were at hand. It was a false alarm, as all of our alarms may be. But the truth of the uproar was this, that our quartermaster general is missing, Colonel Cross. He left the camp of General Taylor yesterday about ten o'clock a.m., was seen afterwards riding about three miles from the camp, and has not since been heard of. All is conjecture respecting him and we hardly know which surmise to believe. He had been sick for some days and may have fallen from his horse. . . .[2]

McLaws is lying asleep in my bed here beside me. His bed is in the wagon train. May I sleep with him? Do I keep my drawers on?[3]

I am writing on the head of a barrel and sitting on a valise. So you see, we make everything tell here. . . .

I have been showing your daguerreotype to nearly everybody. I asked old Giles Porter if I had got as pretty a wife as my father had. But he said he always told the truth and that he never saw a prettier woman than my mother. That was because he did not wish to flatter me. I have just left the old grumbler and told him I was writing to you. So he asked me to send his love. He is a mighty funny old case, ugly as a dried sheepskin. Tell Kitty she may have him. The breed would be first-rate, he tall and scrawny and she thick and fat, and both awfully pretty.[4]

By the way, I did not tell you of some of the Negro servants running away from camp. Gatlin has lost his boy and Major Rains' Sandy has gone too, and several others.[5] All they have to do to be free is to get across the river. Well that I did not bring Mitch.

1. Henry M. Judah graduated in 1843 and was a second lieutenant. A brigadier general in the Civil War, he died in 1866 (Cullum, II, 97). It is difficult to know how many troops were deserting from the American side at this time; Dana is here recounting what he heard, not what he saw. John S.D. Eisenhower, "Polk and His Generals," 37-38 and K. Jack Bauer, *The Mexican War*, 41-42 relate that before the war the army enrolled 8,613 officers and men, and desertions ran to about 1,000 a year. Forty percent of regular soldiers in the army were immigrants, sometimes Irish and often Catholic, who used enlistment as a way out of economic woes. George Ballentine, a Scottish emigrant, was forced out of his native land (like Andrew Carnegie and his family at about the same time) because he was a weaver and power looms were replacing hand looms. Ballentine could not find employment in New York City and enlisted in 1845 in the First Artillery Regiment, which, he wrote, consisted largely of Irish, Scots, and Germans (*Autobiography of an English Soldier in the United States Army* [New York, 1853], reprinted by R.R. Donnelley as a Lakeside Classic [Chicago, 1986], edited with an introduction by William H. Goetzmann). The best-known group of immigrants—most of them not deserters—who fought on the Mexican side was the Battalion of Saint Patrick, or San Patricio, several dozen of whom fell into American hands and were hanged or branded shortly before the triumph of American arms at Mexico City. See Robert Ryal Miller, *Shamrock and Sword: The Saint Patrick's Battalion in the U.S.-Mexican War* (Norman, Okla., 1989). Miller relates that only about two-fifths of the San Patricios were from Ireland; others were born in the United States, Britain, or on the continent of Europe. The desertion rate in the war, he writes, 8.1 percent, was the highest of any American war (for regulars it was thirteen percent, for volunteers six). For other American wars the rates were: Spanish-American, 1.6; World War I, 1.3; World War II, 5.3; Korean War, 1.9; Vietnam War, 4.1 (Miller, 23, 173-75). Miller was able to identify only six members of the Seventh Infantry among the San Patricios.   2. Trueman Cross served in the War of 1812 and attained the rank of colonel in 1838 (Heitman, I, 341). For Cross's fate, see below, letter of April 22, 1846.   3. Lafayette McLaws, an 1842 graduate, was a second lieutenant. He achieved a captaincy in 1851, resigned in 1861, and went with the Confederacy, becoming a major general. He died in 1897 (*DAB*, vol. 6, pt. 2, 120-21).   4. Captain Porter, an 1818 graduate, was promoted to major in 1857. He resigned in September 1861 (Cullum, I, 177).   5. Richard C. Gatlin, an 1832 graduate, was a major in 1861 when he resigned and went with the Confederacy (Cullum, I, 414-15). His close friend Captain Whiting named a son after him.

Shortly after writing the above, Dana and his men were on their way to Taylor's main force opposite Matamoros on the Rio Grande. As he afterward described the journey, "General T. ordered us at Point Isabel to set the train of wagons in motion and to march night and day. It was raining and continued to drizzle all the march. We started about two o'clock in the morning and marched till 4:00 P.M., when we halted at a distance of twenty miles from where we started. We slept here a few hours and at two next morning we set again in motion and arrived here at dinnertime, all caked with mud to our tails and pretty well wet. We started with a squadron of dragoons and my men as escort, and at our camping ground the Fourth Infantry and Ringgold's battery of light artillery were sent to join us."[1]

1. Letter of April 17. Maj. Samuel Ringgold graduated from the Academy in 1818 and served as aide-de-camp to General Scott and in garrison assignments until joining the army of occupation in 1845 (Cullum, I, 174). Together with Lts. James Duncan and Braxton Bragg he developed what was described as "flying artillery"—a battery of four to six guns, usually bronze six-pounders, each pulled together with its caisson by four to six horses. Drill produced extraordinary mobility, and at Palo Alto the guns' efficiency was to cause consternation among the Mexicans. General Taylor might have lost Buena Vista had it not been for the flying artillery (K. Jack Bauer, *The Mexican War*, 54-55, 57; David Lavender, *Climax at Buena Vista: The American Campaigns in Northeastern Mexico, 1846-47* [Philadelphia, 1960], 61, 71, 226-27; and especially Lester R. Dillon, Jr., *American Artillery in the Mexican War: 1846-1847* [Austin, 1975], 9-20, 22-26). For general accounts of the war, see, in addition to Bauer and Lavender, the classic book by Justin H. Smith, *The War with Mexico*, 2 vols. (New York, 1919), based on almost every scrap of manuscript material, American and Mexican, then known, together with Bernard De Voto, *The Year of Decision: 1846* (Boston, 1942); Alfred H. Bill, *Rehearsal for Conflict* (New York, 1947); Ralph S. Henry, *The Story of the Mexican War* (Indianapolis, 1950); Edward J. Nichols, *Zach Taylor's Little Army* (Garden City, N.Y., 1963); Seymour V. Connor and Odie B. Faulk, *North America Divided* (New York, 1971); John E. Weems, *To Conquer a Peace* (Garden City, N.Y., 1974); and especially the fine new book by John S.D. Eisenhower, *So Far from God* (New York, 1989). Excellent short treatments are Otis A. Singletary, *The Mexican War* (Chicago, 1960); and William H. Goetzmann, *When the Eagle Screamed* (New York, 1966). Firsthand description appears in George W. Smith and Charles Judah, eds., *Chronicles of the Gringos: . . . Accounts of Eyewitnesses and Combatants* (Albuquerque, 1968); and Grady McWhiney and Sue McWhiney, eds., *To Mexico with Taylor and Scott: 1845-1847* (Waltham, Mass., 1969). On special subjects, see Walter V. Scholes, ed., José Fernando Ramírez, *Mexico during the War with the United States* (Columbia, Mo., 1950); John H. Schroeder, *Mr. Polk's War: American Opposition and Dissent, 1846-1848* (Madison, Wisc., 1973); and Robert W. Johannsen, *To the Halls of the Montezumas: The Mexican War in the American Imagination* (New York, 1985). Noteworthy chapters by Wayne Cutler, John S.D. Eisenhower, and Miguel E. Soto appear in Douglas W. Richmond, ed., *Essays on the Mexican War*; also see the editor's presentation of lively letters by Andrew Trussell, a Mississippi volunteer, 1847-48. Other titles are listed in Norman E. Tutorow, comp. and ed., *The Mexican-American War: An Annotated Bibliography* (Westport, Conn., 1981). The U.S. Army's archives are described in Elizabeth R. Snoke, ed., *The Mexican War* (Carlisle Barracks, Penn., 1973).

Camp Opposite Matamoros, April 17 ✦ Since I wrote you and indeed ever since I have been here, I have been constantly occupied and at work, so that I have had scarcely a quarter of an hour to myself for anything. The first day I was here I had not duty to do till twelve o'clock, so I spent that time in examining our position and

View of Matamoros from Fort Brown.

reconnoitering the enemy's works. At twelve o'clock I went to work
with the regiment in the trenches of the fortifications which we are
building here, and there we worked constantly till twelve o'clock
yesterday. Then I expected to have a half a day's rest, which I meant
to devote to writing to you, but I had hardly got home, dearest,
when I was detailed with Major Seawell and Mr. Hopson and sixty
men to continue throwing up lines of defense in front of our
brigade, and there we worked till sunset and this, the first time I
have had for writing, is whilst I am on guard.[1]

I can now pick up scraps of time between my duties to drive my
pen, but let me tell you how I am fixed here. I am senior officer of
the guard today. The guard is sixty men, and we are on the edge of
the river with a Mexican picket guard directly opposite to us within
half [a] musket shot. The river is very narrow, and we can easily fire
into the picket if necessary. Our sentinels watch each other all the
time, and if a man attempts to desert, he is immediately shot in the
river. We restrict ourselves to this. If we cannot shoot him before he
gets over, he gets off, for we are not allowed to shoot one after he
touches the opposite bank. We will make them do the same thing,
and if they were to shoot a man after he landed here we have orders
to fire into them with my whole guard.

Our guardhouse is one quite primitive. It is pretty nearly as
good as your father's stable. The roof is thatched with reeds, and a

part of the sides is made of stakes set upright. It is open nearly all round but still is the most comfortable place I have lived in since I have landed in Texas. The men are sitting, lying, and standing all around me. I only wish you were here by my side, my own sweet little Sue, and that instead of writing this I was holding your hand and talking to you. . . .

Yesterday whilst we were working in the trenches we heard that the Mexicans had convened a council of war to decide whether or not they should open their batteries upon us, that there was a great deal of difference in opinion on the subject, but the party in favor of firing carried it and that they were to open the ball in the afternoon. So we ran all our big guns through the embrasures ready for them, and they stood looking at us, but no firing commenced. They know mighty well when they are well off, and there is not the least probability that a single shot will be exchanged between us. They are well aware that the first shot they fire will be ruination to Matamoros and dire calamity to Mexico, and they are not going to give us the chance. Things will be all peaceably settled in a fortnight at farthest, and our officers will be going over to Matamoros to see the girls. . . .

Poor old Colonel Whistler is in arrest again and they say that this time he will be dismissed. He was drunk on the morning when the Mexicans said they would open their batteries. I don't know what the old lady will do about that. She will have to economize in real earnest if the colonel is obliged to leave the service.[2]

Gault, Captain Ross, and Gatlin have all lost their black boys.[3] Sandy was gone some time, but he says that he got lost and some Mexicans carried him to Matamoros. They offered him a wife. He sat at table with the ladies and gentlemen of the town, hired himself out in the country for ten dollars a month, and then ran off and came back. It is mighty easy to lose a servant here, for if he attempts to run away, he either succeeds or is shot. There is no middle ground to occupy. Strong still has Jerry, and he cooks for our mess. Brewer got drunk so often that they were obliged to give him up. Jerry is a mighty poor substitute. However, as we are all living like niggers here in this mudhole, we had as well go the whole hog.

I like this place much better, I think, than Corpus Christi. The main objection is that we are encamped in plowed fields, and in wet weather you cannot put your foot down without taking up five pounds of mud with it. It is ruination to decent shoes. By the way, darling, owing to the expectations of attack when I left Point Isabel, I left my trunk behind me and came forward only with my saddle bags, and in my hurry I forgot to put in an extra pair of drawers. So you may judge that I am pretty dirty by this time, but I will probably get my trunk in a few days now. Everybody goes rowdy here, for we are all hard at work all the time and have but very little baggage. My old hickory shirt I wore a week or more and everybody envied it.[4] Gatlin has one just like it. I have on my blue one now and shall wear it about a week. Economy to the last.

1. Nevil Hopson graduated from West Point in 1837 and was a first lieutenant at this time. He was dismissed for drunkenness in August 1846 and died the next year (Cullum, I, 545).   2. Col. William Whistler, commander of the Third Brigade, alcoholic and incompetent, was later removed. He had been appointed a second lieutenant in 1801 and became colonel of the Fourth Infantry in 1845. He retired in 1861 and died two years later (Heitman, I, 1,026).   3. Richard H. Ross, an 1830 graduate of the Academy, was brevetted lieutenant colonel after Contreras and died in 1851 (Cullum, I, 378).   4. Hickory, a stout cotton fabric, commonly twilled, often striped, was used for work clothing.

April 21 ✦ It is with difficulty nowadays that we can get a chance to sit down long enough to write a word to those we love. We are kept so constantly at work that it is sometime necessary to steal moments from our pillows in order to write at all. My last letter I finished on the nineteenth, and now it is sometime after taps on the twenty-first. Paul Crittenden, Humber, Major Rains, and Strong have just left me alone and I am resolved to write a half an hour before going to bed.[1]

For the last two days I have been constantly at work on our fort. About one thousand men work at it all the time. This morning we went to work immediately after reveille and have been constantly at it ever since, and it has been a broiling hot day too. I don't mind being employed constantly, provided I can only get time to write to my own beloved Sue. . . .

We now lead the real soldiers' life. It will improve us all and make men of us. All here are in the best health and spirits, not a single man has died here. Our men are anxious for the fray, and if they are excited much more by the rascality of the enemy, they will give them the deuce when they do get hold of them. If we come to the fight our men will fight well and no mistake, and when we commence we expect to see some tall walking on the other side. We will make them run to the tune of "Yankee Doodle," the black rascals. The best of them are robbers and murderers, I believe. They say that old Ampudia has got Colonel Cross's watch now.[2] We have not heard as yet whether Arista has arrived or not. They are all alike, braggadocios, and they expect to scare us by big threats. I should think they would feel rather flat that they have threatened now so often and we have treated them with contempt and are not scared yet and what is more have not yet seen them execute a single threat. We will defy all Mexico here when we get our fort finished, which will not take many days, and if Uncle Sam says the word, you will see us take up our quarters in Matamoros.

1. Charles H. Humber graduated in 1840 and was a first lieutenant. After attaining the rank of captain, he died in 1858 (Cullum, I, 609).   2. Gen. Pedro de Ampudia was momentarily in command. For his behavior with Texans at Mier, see below, letter of August 27, 1847. His other claim to notoriety arose after capture in 1844 of members of a filibustering expedition bound from New Orleans to Yucatán. After shooting all the prisoners, his troops beheaded the leader, Francisco Sentmanat, boiled his head in oil, and displayed it in a glass jar.

April 22   ✦   It is just after reveille, my own Sue, and here we have reveille at the first peep of dawn, and instead of men forming half asleep, half awake, in their shirtsleeves or any other, all the troops parade under arms and stand so till broad daylight. At tattoo it is the same thing. Well, it is that early in the morning, and I have just washed myself and combed, etc., and have resolved to seize time by the forelock, for fear that some more work might prevent me from finishing my letter. I do not think that my regiment will go to work today before twelve o'clock, but then it might, so that whilst Strong is snoring away here, I will make sure that my own darling little wife shall get a word from her absent husband. . . .

The *Harvey* was to have remained here for some time to blockade the mouth of the river and keep provisions from going to Matamoros, but the *Monmouth* ran into her in the harbor, and she has gone home for repairs. The river is now blockaded by a couple of naval vessels. The *Monmouth,* you would not know her. She is painted black like the *Harvey,* with false ports, and has two masts. . . .

It is now about eleven o'clock, my own dear wife. You see how I took time by the forelock. I wrote the last page before breakfast, fearing that something might happen to prevent writing after breakfast, and sure enough immediately after we had got through, the regiment was called out to clear away chaparral in front of our defenses, and we have just got in. Now in about an hour we will have to go down to work on the fort and will have to work on it all this afternoon and all tomorrow forenoon. Therefore I must hasten to finish this before the drum beats in order that it may leave here by the first express, and then, you know, at my first leisure moment I can commence to talk to you again.

And now let me begin to tell you of the exciting news here. We have vengeance to take on Mexico for more than one man's blood, and our boys are just in the humor for the business. They feel so indignant at the rascality of the brutes. Well, a few days since, Lieutenant Porter of the Fourth volunteered to take ten men and go some miles up the river in search of news of Colonel Cross. Well he, poor fellow, will probably never return. Day before yesterday, whilst we were at work at the fort, the sergeant who went with him returned with four men, saying that at about twelve miles from here, whilst passing through a thick chaparral, Lieutenant P. and himself were in advance of the party when they suddenly came on some Mexicans who snapped their guns at them immediately, but as it had been raining hard all day, the guns were wet and did not go off. Lieutenant P. immediately called up his men and charged the rascals, drove them away, and captured nine horses and equipments, on which he mounted his men and went on.[1]

It still continued to rain very hard, when about three o'clock in the afternoon he came out of the chaparral and went along its skirts on the prairie. In this way he had not gone long when the first thing they saw was about forty muskets pointed at them. The rascals fired, killed one man dead, and the sergeant thinks Lieutenant P. was wounded. Well, the guns were wet, and not one of them would go off, and the sergeant says that Lieutenant P. ordered the men to the chaparral, where they scattered and that is the last he saw of him. But the fact is the scoundrel ran off and did not stop to look for the rest of the men.

Yesterday the corporal came in and says that he joined the sergeant but insisted upon going back to look for the lieutenant, which the sergeant refused to do. Well, he did go back but could not find him.

Two men came in with the corporal and tell quite a different tale from the sergeant. They say that instead of ordering the men to the bush when the pieces would not go off, Porter rushed on to the enemy and ordered the men to follow him. One of them says that just as he got to the edge of the chaparral, he saw him fall from his horse and that several shots were fired at the place where he fell, and doubtless he was killed.

All the party are in now except Porter and the man who was shot dead. They, poor fellows, never will return. A squadron of dragoons are out in search of the country, and woe betide those Mexicans who are caught with arms in hand. We will have to scour this side of the river of all such vagabonds. The fact is Porter had no business to go out with so small a command in the first place, as he was not ordered but volunteered, and in the next he ought to have taken more precaution with his powder. He would have whipped forty Mexicans if his pieces had gone off. He leaves a young wife and child, poor things. His widow is the daughter of Major Beall of the dragoons.[2]

Well, yesterday afternoon Colonel Cross's body was found or rather his skeleton, four miles from here in the chaparral. He had evidently been captured by some bandits, three or four perhaps, and led off for a mile into the thick bushes where he was basely murdered for his gold stripes, watch, etc. A part of his hair, gray locks, identified him, and one of his shoulder straps and collar torn off near the spot, together with marks of scuffles showed how hard the old man fought for his life. He too leaves a wife and I don't know how large a family. He has a son here, grown, who was his clerk and who has been hunting in all directions for him.

1. Theodoric H. Porter, commissioned a second lieutenant in 1839, was killed on April 19, 1846 (Heitman, I, 800).   2. Lloyd J. Beall graduated in 1830. He joined the Confederacy in 1861 (Cullum, I, 371).

April 23 ✦ Since I closed my letter yesterday we worked all day and again went at it at six o'clock this morning until twelve, when we were relieved by the Fifth Regiment. This afternoon I stretched myself on my bed with the *Albion* in my hand and it was not long before I was fast asleep. . . .[1]

A board of officers held consultation this morning over the body of Colonel Cross and made an official report upon it. His funeral takes place tomorrow afternoon at four o'clock, the escort to consist of a squadron of cavalry and eight companies from this brigade. Our regiment will probably be at work in the trenches so that we cannot go. The exact truth about his murder cannot as yet be ascertained. We believe that he was captured by a party of Mexicans and was being led a prisoner to Matamoros, but when near the river and before crossing, a dispute arose among them whether they should in fact take him to General Ampudia or dispatch him at once. A quarrel ensued, and in a passion a desperado by the name of Falcone rode up behind the colonel and killed him by a blow on the head with his pistol. . . .

Yesterday afternoon whilst our regiment was at work, a parley was sounded across the river, and General Taylor sent Colonel Garland and his aide to see what they wanted.[2] They found a couple of Mexican officers with a letter for General T. from Ampudia. It appears that the country for many miles back of Matamoros is almost a desert and that they are and always have been almost entirely dependent upon the river for their supplies, all their provisions, etc., having to come that way. Well, General Ampudia writes the general that we have blockaded the mouth of the river with vessels of war, that we have ordered off several of their vessels, one belonging to Her Majesty Victoria of England and one belonging to Her Majesty Isabella of Spain, and that he cannot stand it. He also complains that a party of his men whilst engaged in securing a boat which had got loose from them in the river the other night was fired on by our First Brigade guard. General T. answered them today that he had come here and offered them friendship and peace, which they had declined and chose rather to be regarded as enemies, upon which he had ordered the river to be blockaded and that it would remain so, that when their boat got loose if they had have written for it he would have sent it to them but that the guard had orders to fire when they crossed in the night, that he had lost two of his officers and that he could not stand it. . . .

The work here lately has been very disagreeable. The sun is getting to be so powerful. Still, we cannot complain, for the majority of the working days have been cloudy.

It is now Friday morning, my own dear Sue, before breakfast, the twenty-fourth day of the month. I was obliged to stop writing last night because my candle burned out. It is a cloudy morning and we are every moment threatened with rain. I hope we shall get enough of it at last, for since I left you I believe it has rained nearly all the time.

The Mexicans think that rain wets our powder. How mistaken they will find themselves! Last evening they had the impudence to capture two unarmed dragoons who were walking in the woods near the camp. Two Mexicans rode past them and as soon as they had passed wheeled round, presented their pistols, and signified to the men that they must follow them, but fortunately a dragoon scout happened to espy the maneuver from the chaparral where he was secreted, and very soon the officer of the guard was after the rascals with a patrol. He overtook them and the scamps deserted their prisoners, plunged into the river, and swam across. . . .

I only wish our army was full. We could be a great deal more saucy. But we want near a thousand recruits. And whilst we are doing hard service here with small numbers, we are getting badly blackguarded in Congress. This is the reward we shall always get

Fort Brown and the grave of Colonel Cross.

from men who are most perfectly accomplished in ignorance upon military matters. . . .

Colonel Whistler, I understand, leaves today. Poor old man, he is very crestfallen. If they really intend to try him, he had better resign at once and save himself from disgrace, for if he is tried he is probably a gone coon.

1. *The Albion or, British, Colonial, and Foreign Weekly Gazette*, published in New York, offered essays, poetry, political debates, book reviews, excerpts and announcements of books, and reviews of plays.   2. Lt. Col. John Garland had been commissioned a first lieutenant in 1813. He was brevetted brigadier general for Contreras and the Battle of Churubusco and died in 1861 (Heitman, I, 447).

April 25 • We have been in a state of great excitement here last night, which I will tell you about. Yesterday forenoon nothing of interest occurred. We were making preparations for the burial of Colonel Cross's remains. I was detailed as one of the officers on the escort. The infantry of the escort was taken from this brigade.

We formed at four o'clock in the afternoon and marched to the place where his remains lay. We received them with the proper military salutes, and wheeling into column, we moved off to his last resting place with the Dead March. First came the infantry escort of 350 men, marching in a column of sixteen platoons, next the field music and band of our regiment, next came the cavalry escort of 100 men in columns of platoons, all the escort commanded by Colonel Twiggs, and under him Colonel McIntosh, Major Staniford, and Major Brown.[1] Next came the chief pallbearer, Colonel Payne, in full dress, mounted with a large white scarf over his shoulder, tied on the left side with black, next the hearse, which was a gun carriage, four officers on each side with white scarfs as pallbearers.[2] On the hearse, which was drawn by six horses, mounted by light artillerists, reposed the colonel's last remains, rolled in the Star-Spangled Banner. His son on foot and dressed in black followed the hearse, and immediately behind him on jet black horses were two dragoons leading between them another black horse covered entirely with a black cloth, hanging nearly to his feet, fringed and trimmed with white and white reins, black saddle, black holsters, boots and spurs in the stirrups, turned heel foremost. This was the colonel's horse. Then came all the officers of the army, in procession, who were not on duty, closed in rear by General Taylor and his staff.

We marched directly to the river bank, where the other side was lined with Mexican troops. This was the first parade they had had a chance to see of any of our troops. We laid the colonel's remains at the foot of the flagstaff. The service was read and we fired three volleys, which made Matamoros reverberate and told the Mexicans that our powder was plenty dry enough for their tastes. The flag, which had been at half mast for three days, was then run up, and we marched back in quick time, leaving, I have no doubt, a very salutary effect on the minds of the Mexicans.

So soon as we returned home last night, we heard rumors that General Arista had arrived at Matamoros with a reinforcement of fifteen hundred men, and that two thousand men had crossed the river eighteen miles below and two thousand more some distance above us, leaving three thousand in the town, and that it was their intention to attack, so seventy-five dragoons were immediately dispatched down and forty upriver to reconnoiter and report, General T. threatening that if any had crossed, he would open his batteries on the town immediately. We were ordered not to undress but to sleep on our arms all night and be ready at the slightest alarm to spring to the lines and repel an attack. Each man had his post assigned, and the men lay down in excellent spirits, each man with his loaded musket beside him. I did not even take off my coat or boots. This is the second or third time we have had to do that here and still no attack. We slept all night and although we heard the

Mexican horns and bugles across the river blowing all night, none came within cannon shot of us on this side, and what is more, none are coming. They are not agoing to sacrifice hundreds of their men for nothing, have their town cannonaded, and be whipped by inferior numbers in the bargain.

The dragoons from downriver have returned and report that no troops have crossed there. The upriver party have not yet returned, but I expect they will bring in the same report. Still, it was a hired spy who brought the intelligence. Bean was up here last night and made a bet with Hopson of ten dollars to five dollars that there would not be a hostile gun fired by ten o'clock this morning. It is well, however, always to be on the alert, and they will have to be very sharp to catch us napping. I expect that it is probable that the Mexicans have sent a train of mules under an escort to the mouth of the river in hopes to get provisions and the story might have got up from that.

A Mexican colonel was sent over yesterday to ask the general to liberate a schooner which he had captured at the mouth. The general was inexorable and said that he would send an express to Point Isabel with orders to liberate the vessel, provided she had on board neither arms, ammunition, nor provisions. He says, "He'll be damned if they shall have any provisions com up the river until they are willing to be friendly." They threaten to try to cut off our train of provisions etc., but our men say that unless they want to get licked badly, they had better not get between them and the grub.

1. Lt. Col. James S McIntosh fought in the War of 1812. He died of wounds after Molino del Rey (Heitman, I, 669). Thomas Staniford, also a veteran of 1812, was a major in the Fourth Infantry and died in 1855 (ibid., I, 915).   2. Lt. Col. Matthew M. Payne was a veteran of 1812. Brevetted colonel for Palo Alto and Resaca de la Palma, he resigned in 1861 and died the next year (Heitman, I, 777).

April 26 ✦ The dogs of war are now indeed let loose, and a sad tale indeed have we to tell of its commencement. . . . You see on my last page that I told you that forty dragoons had been sent up the river where the Mexicans were said to be crossing in order to reconnoiter and report the facts. These were commanded by Captain Thornton and with him Captain Hardee and Lieutenants Kane and Mason.[1] This party were surprised by a very large number of Mexican troops, hemmed in, and we believe cut off to a man. The guide returned this morning, but not one of them has been heard of, and from Thornton's character we believe that they fought like devils and, rather than give up, fell where they fought.

1. Seth B. Thornton became a second lieutenant of dragoons in 1836, first lieutenant in 1837, and a captain in 1841. He was killed in 1847 on a reconnaissance in the Valley of Mexico (Heitman, I, 959). William J. Hardee graduated in 1838, reached the rank of lieutenant colonel, and resigned in 1861 to go with the Confederate army, in which he achieved the rank of lieutenant general (Nathaniel C. Hughes, Jr., *General William J. Hardee: Old Reliable* [Baton Rouge, 1965]). He was the author of a well-known book about military tactics. Elias K. Kane, an 1841 graduate, eventually achieved a captaincy and died in 1853 (ibid., II, 35). George T. Mason, an 1842 graduate, was killed in the skirmish, (ibid., II, 64-65). See below, letter of April 29, 1846.

4

War

April-May 1846

On the Alert. News of Captain Thornton. Major Brown to Command Our Fort. Texan Volunteers. The Cannonade Begins. Overruling Providence Saves Us. Death of Major Brown. A Trumpet Sounds the Parley. The Shells Continue. Miraculous Escapes. Sound of Cannon Eight Miles. The Mexicans Flee. Dragoons Reach the Fort. The Battles of Palo Alto and Resaca de la Palma. Most Brilliant Victory since the Battle of Orleans.

April 29 ✦ All goes on well here. True, the enemy are getting a little saucy and daring, but we will tell them a severe tale in a day or two if they stop to hear it. We cannot complain so far of them in the least, for they have as far as we can understand been remarkably kind and attentive to our people who are in their hands. They say that we entertain a very erroneous idea of them, that they are barbarous and cannot do a generous deed, but they mean to review their character. We will see soon how they will stand a whipping.

Since I finished my last, my darling little wife, nothing new of great interest has transpired. Our labors have still continued, if anything with increased vigor. We live the real lives of hardy soldiers and see times which try our mettle to a considerable degree. Our fort is nearly complete, and two or three days more will fit it for defense against thousands, and then it will receive its garrison. Our labors, however, for the last three days have not been confined to daylight. On account of the vicinity of the enemy on this side the river we have been required to sleep with armor on, boots, swords, belts and all, the men with their belts on and their arms in their hands, ready to spring up at the slightest noise. The dragoons have slept for the last three nights in the trenches, all sitting in the trench, so that not a man could be seen, so that if the enemy had come expecting to surprise us and find us all sleeping, the first thing he would have met would have been such a volley as he would not have stopped running from till he got home again. . . .

About Captain Thornton's command I told you in my last that they had been captured or killed to a man. . . . Day before yesterday, however, a letter was sent over by General Arista from Captain Hardee giving an account of the affair. He says that their command was fifty-two and four officers, that they had ridden into a field surrounded on all sides by a high hedge, and were talking with an old Mexican, trying to gather some information from him, when they suddenly discovered that they were ambushed and surrounded on all sides by Mexican troops. Thornton immediately gave the order to charge and he led it gallantly on, but the enemy completely hemmed them in on all sides. They were in the field, behind the hedge, and everywhere. After the charge, T. saw that the only chance of escape was over the high hedge, the other side of which was lined with Mexican infantry. He gave the order to leap the hedge, and his horse, which was a very remarkable one, carried him over, but none of the others could go it. After he cleared the hedge, that was the last that was to be seen of him and they supposed as a matter of course that he was killed on the other side. Captain Hardee then rallied his brave fellows and made a break for the river, intending to swim it and come down on the Mexican side, if he could, but he found the banks so boggy that the horses could not get through. Here, then, he had done all that man could do except to obtain an honorable surrender or die on the field of battle in the midst of the enemy, so he drew up his men in line and himself advanced to hold a parley with the Mexican commander. He told [him] that if he could be assured that himself and command would be treated well and honorably, he was ready to surrender as prisoners of war before that condition, but if he could not get the promise, that his men were brave and would sell their lives as dearly [as] possible upon that field. The Mexican general then told him that he would promise him good and honorable treatment to all prisoners who should fall into his hands. Whereupon Captain H. ordered his men to lay down their arms. He states that eight men among whom were two sergeants were killed and Captain T. and Lieutenant Mason were missing and that both had undoubtedly fallen. That himself and Lieutenant Kane (both married) were well and they were living at the table of General Ampudia in Matamoros and treated with as much kindness and politeness as they could desire. They were allowed to send for their baggage and servants, and when they wanted to make some arrangements about their pay, they were told by General Arista that they need not trouble themselves about that, that whilst they were prisoners the Mexican government would advance them half their monthly pay and only on the honor of our government to refund. This was certainly very kind. It is all policy, for they wish to secure kind treatment at our hands.

But to the astonishment of all, a Mexican colonel came over

yesterday bringing a letter from Captain Thornton who says that, so far from being dead, he too is perfectly sound and well, but he says that they took him whilst he was insensible or they should not have taken him at all. It appears that when he leaped the hedge he succeeded in eluding them for two days, and when he had got within six miles of camp, his horse took fright, leaped a precipice, and left him there for dead, and in this position he was found by a Mexican picket guard. So Mason is the only officer who was killed. He was a classmate of mine and a single man.

Yesterday four Texans arrived from Corpus Christi who had actually surprised and routed fifteen Mexicans and captured from them three silver mounted saddles, a carbine, some pistols, and a sword with a German silver scabbard.

But now comes the news of the greatest interest to us. Major Brown has been assigned to the command of this fort, and our regiment has been selected to garrison it, together with two companies of artillery, in all four hundred men, this when there are eleven more companies of artillery here and their proper place is in a fort. We take it as an honorable selection, and the good name of the regiment together with the confidence the general has in Major Brown has undoubtedly got us the place. In two or three days, when the fort will be finished and its supplies of fuel, provisions, and ammunition laid in, we will move into it, and the general with the remainder of the forces will go to look for the enemy, and unless they take good care to keep out of the general's way, he will give them a very hard fight, and if he does not capture a great many of them, he will at least probably give them a bad whipping. We will be very secure here in our fort and will be able to whip as many as they can bring and knock down their town in the bargain. The fort is a very strong one and contains four guns a third larger than those which were at Orleans Barracks, and four six-pounders. It is more than twice as large as Fort Pike inside, with a ditch twelve feet deep and a drawbridge and plenty of muskets, cartridges, and stout men inside. If the enemy were to come, they would not want to make more than one assault. I fear the enemy will be beaten across the river and perhaps Matamoros taken too before the volunteers get here.

May 1 ✦ I am on guard today, darling wife, no mail has arrived or gone for some time. Today everything is bustle and business, and I have scarcely time or opportunity to close this. All is in motion today. General T. moves with all the army this afternoon, except our regiment and two companies of artillery who remain to garrison our strong fort. Our regiment is moving in now. The army is going to look for the enemy and will go to Point Isabel, so I must send this now or it will not go for some time. I am as well as ever and in right good spirits, only don't like to see the troops all going off to meet the enemy and leaving us here where they are not going to come.

Nothing new has occurred since my last. Sleep in clothes all the time, and always on the alert, but the general is now to commence operations, and we will soon see if the enemy will let him find them. The other day three hundred Mexicans attacked four Texans who after killing two soldiers and wounding Colonels Carrasco and Quintarro were themselves killed. All will go well and I trust soon that your dear little heart will be eased by good news of us. The enemy will not hold out long. The army will return in a very few days and will bring mails with them and then I shall hear from my darling.

May 4 ✦ I have a chance to write you but a short letter this time, for our communications by regular channels are altogether cut and we can only get a mail to Point Isabel by good luck if at all. So that it is a great chance whether you ever see these lines. The Mexicans, however, may probably get a glance at them by tomorrow morning. There is here a captain of a small volunteer company of Texans who was sent by General Taylor and who arrived late last night, bringing information that the Mexican forces under General Arista had closed in and encamped on the roads between us and the general. He found his way through them but in doing so had to kill five of their videttes. This morning he tried to return, but the road was so completely blocked that he could not get along. However, he says that he will go through tonight, and I will try to get him to take this letter for me.

Well, now, let me commence and tell you all that has happened since I finished my last at the guardhouse at our old camping ground, that same afternoon the army left with General Taylor for Point Isabel, and the Seventh with two companies of artillery moved into the work, which is a plenty strong fort not yet named. I still remained on guard until next morning. Nothing material happened that night or the next day. We were kept constantly on the alert and laboring to complete and strengthen our fort. The next night also passed smoothly off and reveille was as usual at the earliest dawn and we had just commenced washing, etc., before going to work when the batteries of the enemy opened, and their shot and shells began to whistle over our heads in rapid succession. They had commenced in real earnest, and they fired away powder and copper balls as if they cost nothing and they had a plenty of ammunition. We were all at our arms in a moment and the artillerists at their guns, and soon our big guns began to pay them back in their own coin and with interest. Our shot told on them very severely, as our artillery was much heavier and better than theirs. In the first eight shots we silenced their nearest battery. Having dismounted their heaviest cannon we could see the pieces of the carriage fly into the air, and what men they had in that battery who were not killed or wounded were obliged to abandon it.

The cannonade continued on both sides without intermission on both sides for six hours when both parties stopped, and we concluded that as we had fired away half of our shot (350), we would not answer their guns any more but keep our means for an emergency, and as they did not do us the least injury in that six hours' firing, we concluded that it was unnecessary to throw away any more of our powder and shot unless they materially improved in their firing. Throughout the day and night and also today they have gone by starts and thrown shot and shells a half an hour at a time, thinking they were doing a heap of damage, but we treated all their noise with silent contempt, and our men screened themselves from the shot behind the work and slept on their arms.

The enemy have thrown at us more than twelve hundred shot and sixty shells and out of these all the damage they have done us is the loss of one man. It is wonderful but true that poor Sergeant Weigart is the only man hurt. He was struck by a piece of a shell about a half an hour after the cannonade. It appears to have been a mere chance. He was killed instantly and died with his face to the foe. I was sent out to bury him last night at tattoo. I took the company and executed the duty without even a whisper. We dug his grave in a trench at the banks of the river and laid him quietly in it and a person twenty yards off would have heard nothing of it.[1]

We have dismounted and rendered unserviceable two of the best guns the enemy had, doubtless killed and wounded several who were in the battery, which they were obliged to abandon, and have done a great deal of damage to their town. If we had as much shot as we could desire, we would soon be able to demolish their works and pieces and make them sick of the game. General Taylor will bring us more guns and ammunition when he returns.

As I have told you before, dearest little Sue, this state of things can't last long. It will soon be over. When our reinforcements arrive, the general will probably take Matamoros and then this fort will be a right quiet place. Now there [is no] danger in their cannonade, for our work is so constructed that all their shot pass over us. Their pieces too are so much lighter than ours that they can do the fort but very little damage. And all their firing which has been very expensive to them has as yet done nothing but annoy us a little. We think that the general will immediately march to this place and fight General Arista on the road. The express which he sent up and which will carry this letter back says that they heard all our guns at the Point, and the general sent him immediately to find out about it. Since he could not get back again today, I would not wonder if the general started immediately.[2]

1. The death of Weigart produced confusion, as Dana recalled many years later. "The fire of the Mexican batteries was opened on Fort Brown on Sunday morning, the second day after General Taylor had started with his army for Point Isabel, at the moment when the drums rolled off the end of reveille. The first man killed was a sergeant named Weigart, who stood on the banquette of one of the bastions with his company, facing the fire. A grapeshot struck him in the chin, came out of the back of his head, and he fell on his face down the banquette, dead. The orderly sergeant stepped up to the captain of the company, old Francis Lee, and with a tremulous voice said, 'Shea is killed, sir.' Now, poor Shea was an Irishman with auburn hair like the sergeant's and did not boast of being a good soldier himself but was always ready to stay behind in charge of the baggage and, on hearing his name announced, stood up and called out to the captain, 'No sir, I ain't.' Weigart's body was immediately carried into a hospital tent and had not lain there an hour before a shell from the enemy's battery carried his head off, looking as if they had a special spite against that particular man" (Undated typescript in Dana MSS).   2. The ranger who carried Dana's letter was the renowned Samuel H. Walker, for whom see below letter of August 27, 1846.

May 11 ◆ The enemy can hardly believe it true that we have escaped so well, and I do not blame them for their doubts, for unless we had seen, we would not have believed. Shells are well known to be the most deadly weapons of war, and although their batteries threw eight hundred of them at us, besides two thousand shot, although they fell in our very midst at the very feet of men and burst there, but two were hurt. It is no chance, but it is an overruling Providence.

I wrote you No. 9, dearest wife, on the fourth, which was the day after they had commenced bombarding us. Well, they continued their games night and day for seven successive days. The third day they cannonaded and bombarded very hotly indeed. Very many shells burst inside the fort. They were evidently trying their hardest then.

In the forenoon of that day a howitzer shell mounted the parapet and before he could dodge took off the leg of Major Brown below the knee. An amputation was immediately performed, and he would have done well but that there was no safe place to put him in but in a magazine where it was so hot he could scarcely breathe. Of course his fevers raged, and he died day before yesterday, even whilst he heard the general's cannon pouring death among the enemy whilst marching to our relief. We buried the gallant major yesterday under the flag. He is a very serious loss to our regiment, one which we will not be able to replace. He was a perfect bulldog for the fight.

Well, on the third day after they had tried their best, and as they thought had killed a great many of our men who, by the way, they thought had got out of provisions, in the afternoon they stopped their firing and sent in to us four officers with a white flag. So soon as we heard their trumpet sound the parley, we knew what was coming. They brought a letter from General Arista summoning our garrison to surrender as prisoners of war. He told us that he had a large and well-appointed army between us and our supplies, that the succors we were expecting could not reach us, that he had large forces in reserve, that we were reduced to the last extremity, could not possibly hold out much longer, and that circumstances of humanity dictated that we should save our men from sacrifice. He gave us an hour to consider. Captain Hawkins, who was left in command, immediately convened a council who unanimously agreed that as the enemy had not hurt us and probably could not, that the very idea of a surrender was absurd. An answer was returned to General Arista that we begged leave politely to decline his invitation.

Well, that night we expected that as a matter of course we would be stormed. Our men were delighted, in the highest spirits, and highly incensed at the idea of a surrender to those "niggerly rascals." They swore they would not do it if they had a load of powder left. All put their arms in the best order and made up their minds to shoot as many Mexicans as each man could. If they had only have brought on their assaulting columns that night, they would have been cut all to pieces, but they knew better than that. Mexicans cannot yet be found who will assault a work garrisoned by our troops.

May 12 ✦ A tremendous thunderstorm came up last night, my
own dear wife, and I was obliged to stop writing. Everything got
wet, my candle blew out, and I put things away and went to sleep.
Nothing new of consequence this morning, dearest, so I will commence where I left off.

The fourth day of the bombardment was made still hotter and
the shells were thrown better than on any day previous. They fell
everywhere amongst us and burst in all directions in crowds of
men, and still no one was hurt. A kind of Providence kept us safe. A
shell burst at the feet of Corporal Van Voorhies, another rolled over a
man's back, and another between a man's legs whilst he was eating
dinner, and although they all burst, they hurt no one. A shot went
through Captain Hawkins' tent just over his head when he was
eating breakfast, two through Mr. Page's tent, two through Major
Brown's, a shell and a grapeshot through mine, a shell through
Whiting's, Seawell's, and so forth.[1] In fact all the tents were nipped
in every direction. Fifteen of our horses were killed. A shell fell in
the chest where the band instruments were packed, burst there,
and smashed every one of them. One of the shells went through
three horses.

On the fifth day a man's arm and another man's leg were
broken. The sixth and seventh days were kept up by the enemy as
usual with just as little injury to us.

We all the time husbanded our ammunition for an assault, and
only now and then threw a few eighteen-pound shot where we saw
men, and we killed and wounded at least twenty of them. One of
our shot passed through a house in the town and killed two poor
women. They ought to have been out of the way. Twice a couple of
hundred rancheros were sent up to open musketry on our men, but
they did not dare to approach near enough to do any damage, and
all their bullets fell spent. We placed a few rifles on the parapet and
killed a couple of those fellows, and they went off satisfied.

Last Friday about three o'clock in the afternoon we heard cannonading about eight miles, and immediately knew that the general
was on the move and had met the enemy. The cannonade lasted
until sundown, which showed us that the enemy had made a
tolerably good stand.

Next day we heard nothing at all for so long a time that we began
to be somewhat disheartened, thinking the general had met an
overpowering force and had been obliged to retire. If this had been
the case, we would indeed have been in a bad way. We saw columns
of the enemy in the distance passing down to reinforce their army

The cannonading heard on May 8 was the Battle of Palo Alto. Lithograph after Carl Nebel. Amon Carter Museum, Fort Worth.

which had been attacked. However, about three o'clock in the afternoon we again heard the cannon and musketry within four miles of us. We knew then that the enemy had retreated to a new position and that the general, after having disposed of the dead and wounded of both sides and parked his train, had advanced to give them a second battle. The cannonade and musketry was kept up very hotly for a couple of hours, when we saw retreating columns of the enemy hurrying from the field of action towards the upper ferry, and the way we let in the shot was not slow. There they went, a perfect rout. Horse and foot had thrown away their arms and fled like the wind, trying to strike the river at the nearest points, where they would plunge in to swim over. Many were drowned. Panic and consternation were spread through them. They were wild with fright. They knew not what to do and only sought to fly as swiftly as possible to save themselves from the terrible effect of the fire of our troops, and close upon their heels with shouts appalling to their ears came our dragoons and light artillery, dealing death around them and cutting off from many the last hopes of flight. Our fellows were perfect devils. The heat and excitement of the battle and the flush of one of the most astounding and brilliant victories on record had made them terrible in wreaking vengeance on these savage peoples. All who did not throw down their arms and ask for quarter were cut down without any hesitation.

Soon some of our dragoons came toward the fort. They swung their hats over their heads to tell of their victory. They were the first friends we had seen for eight days. Five hundred of our brave fellows mounted the parapets, threw their caps in the air, and gave them such cheers as made Matamoros ring from the faubourg to the square. You might have heard the cheers two miles. Those shouts told the enemy what had happened on this side the river. The effect was instantaneous. Their guns immediately ceased to fire upon us, and disheartened, disgusted, and appalled, they slunked from their batteries into the town to bear the terrible tidings of their disasters, not knowing what to think was the reason why their fire was not more hurtful to us.

Since then they have been perfectly quiet, doubtless dreading that at any moment we would open our batteries to take the town. We will allow them but two or three days more of quiet. We will then be perfectly ready, plenty of guns and plenty of ammunition. Matamoros will then be summoned to surrender, and if she refuses, which we do not anticipate, she will be forced to do so. I do not think that the Mexicans, after having been so terribly cut up as they have been, will be induced again to take a stand for some time to come.

1. Francis N. Page graduated from West Point in 1841, was a second lieutenant at this time, was brevetted major in 1847, and died in 1860 (Cullum, II, 32-33).

May 13   ✦   I finished telling you yesterday of the cannonade and bombardment of this fort and now I must commence and give you some descriptions of the two battles and the most brilliant victory which has happened since the Battle of Orleans.

You recollect, my darling one, that General Taylor left here on the first of the month with all the army except this garrison, to escort up the train of the army loaded with provisions, ammunition, and other necessities. He had a double object in view in taking all the troops he had as an escort. He knew that the enemy were on this side of the river in force superior to his own. Their object was to capture the train or attempt Point Isabel. His was to protect his train and, if he found them in his way, to give them a fair fight if they were even double his numbers, but he little knew that they were more than three to one.

He arrived at Point Isabel on the second, and the first thing he heard on the morning of the third was the cannonade of our batteries. This put him in a fever at once, and he wanted to start right off to return and fight the enemy if he could find them and compel them to raise the siege of this fort. Reflection, however, and good advice taught him that it was useless to return, and worse than useless, without a fresh supply of provisions, ammunition, and ordnance, and it was also advisable to get reinforcements if possible. He had the highest confidence in this garrsion and knew that it would hold out to the last and repel any attack which the Mexicans were able to make upon it. So he contented himself with sending to us an express of a half a dozen rangers of Texas to get information of our condition and went to work leisurely to load up his train and refresh his troops for the coming storm when the Texan express returned with news of our wonderfully good condition. The greatest excitement prevailed at Point Isabel, and lots of champagne was wasted in health to the gallant command which so firmly held Fort Brown, our stronghold on the Mexican frontier. All the army felt the extreme of anxiety to hasten up to our relief, and they felt confidence in us, and as long as they heard the firing, they knew that we held out.

Well, the general remained at Point Isabel until the morning of the eighth, when at a very early hour, with his train three miles long and barely two thousand men, he took up his line of march for this place. He marched all day until about one o'clock, when evident signs of the enemy were seen, and it was certain from the signs that they were in large force, with a very numerous cavalry and plenty of artillery. Soon the two opposing forces came in sight of each other.

The enemy had chosen a position which at once proved the well-known ability of their General Arista. They were very cunning and tried to get our columns within short range of long nine-pounders by a kind of stratagem. Their cannon were concealed. They held a position on the edge of the prairie at the skirts of a thick growth of chaparral, almost impassable. In this more than half their troops and nearly all their cannon were masked, and drawn up in beautiful order in battle array were the remainder of their battalions, giving a very inviting chance as it would seem for a fair pitched battle in an open plain. They expected that we would advance heedlessly to defeat what troops they had laid out as bait, and then expected to astonish us by a fire from their masked batteries and a sortie from their concealed column. But the general was not in such a hurry. He meant to have his fight, and as they were in numbers three to his one, he advanced very carefully and cautiously. Their left flank rested on the chaparral, whilst their right extended out into the plain. Our general also went to the chaparral, rested his right on it, and threw out his left into the prairie, at the same time holding back from the enemy. The enemy were so much more numerous than ourselves that in this position they outflanked us a good deal, but Lieutenant Duncan's light battery was thrown some way out, which obviated this some.

When all was ready the movement commenced by the army, swinging around on the right as a pivot and throwing the left wing in advance to meet the enemy. When within long shot, the enemy opened his fire from his heavy cannon, which he thought much superior to ours, since he had not heard of our having field guns heavier than sixes, whilst his were nines. You may imagine his astonishment then when two huge eighteens drawn up by six yoke of oxen each (which the general was bringing up to put in the fort) were advanced and thundered to him. Although the effect of them could not be seen, it was ascertained afterwards to be terrible. The firing continued hotly for a short time, doing some damage among our troops but a great deal among the Mexicans. Under cover of the eighteens, Lieutenant Duncan's light battery on one flank and Major Ringgold's on the other advanced, guarded by the different regiments of infantry, to take the enemy on the flanks, or as you would call it, raking. Their effect was terrible. The enemy felt it immediately. The rancheros which compose the Mexican volunteers were not able to stand it, and fifteen hundred of them were put to shameful flight. The enemy's cavalry then saw that to maintain themselves at all, they must charge those regiments of infantry which supported the artillery. Eight hundred lancers formed to charge the Fifth Regiment. On they came with the speed of the wind. Quicker than thoughts the regiment formed in square and with bayonets at the charge awaited the charge as if they had been a solid rock. On dashed the cavalry of the Mexicans, as if they would ride right over the square, but when they had got within about forty yards, the front of the square attacked, poured in its volley of buckshot and balls, and horses, officers, and men of the lancers were brought to the ground. Many more reeled in their saddles, wounded. Some were thrown, and the rest in confusion galloped back to their own side of the field. The same game was tried on Colonel Childs' battalion with pretty much the same effect.[1]

The enemy's cavalry then made two demonstrations to charge the batteries, but all the exertions of their officers, who even beat them with their sabers, could not induce them to do it.

In the meantime our guns had been pouring in a terrific fire.

The enemy fired equally fast from an equal number of pieces, and fired well too, but there as well as here a kind Providence protected us. Not so with the enemy, though. The sun went down on the fight, and it was supposed that both armies would sleep on their arms and renew the battle in the morning. Little did they dream of the immense damage they had done the enemy in comparison to what they had received. Little did they dream of the horrible sights which were on the adverse side of the field. Little did they think that their victory was complete and that whilst they were taking their rest, the enemy, leaving a great part of their wounded, dead, and baggage on the field, were retreating to a new and stronger position. Seven thousand men before two thousand of our little regular army! That night more than four hundred wounded were carried into Matamoros.

Next morning our army arose bright and early, ready to continue the battle and expecting to find the enemy in the same position he had occupied the evening before, but when our fellows looked about, nothing was to be seen of a foe. It was taken for granted that they were secreted in the chaparral in order to catch our men as they came on. But on reconnoitering it was discovered that the Mexicans had evidently left their position in the greatest haste during the night, leaving on the field a cannon which had been broken down by our shot, all their dead unburied, a great many wounded, and considerable baggage.

The battle was a horrid spectacle, corpses mangled most horribly lying where they had fallen in perfect heaps. Our grape and canister shot had literally mowed them down. They strewed the plain, and the wounded crying for assistance were interspersed here and there among the dead. Some were nearly cut in two by large shot, some had their heads off, some had lost arms, some legs, and so forth. Many officers were among them. One officer of lancers had a daguerreotype likeness of his sister on him, another had three letters in his cap to his father, sister, and wife, in which he said that some of the regiments had suffered much for food, that for some days past a number of them had had nothing but salt meat.

The general waited on the field to bury the dead of both parties and to give attention to the wounded.[2] None of our officers were killed in the battle of the eighth. Major Ringgold, Lieutenant Blake, and Captain Page, and Lieutenant Luther were wounded. The first two are since dead. There is but little hope for the third, but the last is doing well.

After the men had breakfasted, the general left his train in park

"Capture of Genl. La Vega by the Gallant Capt. May." Amon Carter Museum, Fort Worth.

with a guard and continued to move on, expecting to find that the enemy had taken up a very strong position in the chaparral. Their whereabouts was found about three o'clock in the afternoon. They had chosen one of the strongest positions possible in the chaparral and in a ravine. Their battery of eight guns were placed with the intention of cutting our columns all to pieces as they advanced, but they did not know then that American soldiers would charge right up to the cannon's mouth. The two light batteries were ordered forward to attack with the dragoons, Fourth, Fifth, and Eighth Infantry. The Third and Colonel Childs' battalion in reserve. Our men spread in the chaparral and advanced on the enemy's lines.

The determination today was to go the whole hog and charge at once, without standing off at shooting distance. As our troops advanced, their fire was terrible. Our buck and ball told with wonderful effect, and the grape and canister scattered death in all directions. So swift was the advance that the enemy had only time to fire two rounds from his batteries before our troops, with yells and shouts, charged in amongst them. Captain May's squadron of dragoons and the Fifth and Eighth Infantry charged right up to the batteries.[3] The Mexicans stood their ground for some minutes like men, fighting hand to hand with sword and bayonet. Now was their last chance. If they gave ground now they were lost, and they knew it. One regiment, the Guarda Costa from Tampico, would not give an inch and were entirely cut to pieces. Our fellows fought like devils. The enemy were borne down on all sides. They were forced back from their guns. The determined courage and valor of our men disheartened them. A panic seized them and, throwing down their arms, they broke and fled in all directions.

A total rout followed. Each fled for life. Horse and foot sought the river by the nearest route. Huddled together, with our dragoons at their heels, many of them plunged into the river. Some were drowned. A great portion were dispersed among the chaparral, and many gave themselves up as prisoners of war. They left everything they had behind them. Everything fell into our hands: nine pieces of brass cannon, a large quantity of ammunition, five hundred pack mules with their saddles and equipment, five hundred muskets, a great deal of baggage, some wagons, all of Arista's private baggage, plate, public and private correspondence, military papers, and so forth, several hundred dollars in specie, horses and saddles, and so forth, General La Vega and twelve or fourteen officers, prisoners besides, about 300 or 400 men.[4]

This is one of the most remarkable and brilliant victories on record. A well-appointed and well-disciplined army of 7,000 men in their own chosen positions, with eight pieces of cannon, utterly routed with the loss of all they had by barely 2,000 men, and look at the immense difference in the loss of the two armies. Our loss was about 150 men in both engagements in killed, wounded, and missing, whilst theirs was in killed, wounded, and prisoners not less than 1,400, all their rancheros dispersed to their homes and their infantry broken up. Out of 3,600 infantry which left Matamoros, only 300 have returned as yet. Their killed alone was upwards of 500, whilst ours was only about 65.

The Mexicans don't know what to make of it. They can scarcely realize their misfortune and cannot account for the best army which ever left Mexico being thus cut up by a handful of men, and they will not believe that they did us so little damage by the bombardment.

But you don't know, my darling Sue, how much we rejoice that all this has happened before the volunteers arrived. The country will see that it is the regulars which can do their business, and had

"Soliloquy of Genl. Vega, after the battle of the 8th of May." Historical Society of Pennsylvania.

the volunteers have been here they would probably have gotten all the credit for our hard fighting.

General La Vega is quite a dashing-looking fellow. I believe he is going to Washington on parole. Captain May took him from his guns. When all of his men ran, he stood there and was taken prisoner. He is astounded and he says that all Mexico will be. He says he cannot account for the decided superiority of our soldiery. He has fought Spaniards, Frenchmen, Mexicans, Texans, and Indians but cannot understand where we can find men who will charge right up to the muzzles of a battery. He says that it is of no use to bring numbers to whip us. It can be done only by the hardest kind of courageous fighting.

In the action of the ninth, our officers suffered much more severely. Lieutenant Inge of dragoons and Lieutenant Cochrane of the Fourth and Lieutenant Chadbourne of the Eighth were killed. Colonels McIntosh and Payne, Captain Howe, and Lieutenants Selden, Jordan, Gates, Maclay, and Burbank wounded.[5] A kind Providence has protected us. When we look over the field of battle and see the large number of the enemy slain, and the number of wounded prisoners we have joined to the 650 which are in hospital in Matamoros, and then look at our own suffering, we have abundant reason to be grateful to God for His goodness. Some officers who were badly wounded, after giving them the best medical attendance here, we have sent over to Matamoros. An equal number of officers and men have been exchanged for Captains Thornton and Hardee and Lieutenant Kane and the dragoons who were captured a short time since, and they are all with us again. The former is under arrest and will be tried for the affair.

And now, my own sweet little Sue, I will bid you good night, and tomorrow if I do not have to close my letter in too much of a hurry, I will talk to you some more. I have so much to tell you of what happens here nowadays that I can't get a chance to talk about other things. I have got to tell you yet all about your letters and how much I am longing to see you and everything else. I hope I shall get a chance tomorrow. It is now very late and I must go to sleep. So now good night, my dear Sue, and may Heaven forever bless you and our little one.

1. Thomas Childs, born in Massachusetts in 1790, graduated from West Point and served in the War of 1812. A lieutenant colonel by the time of Palo Alto and Resaca de la Palma, he was brevetted colonel after these battles. Childs was later instrumental in the capture of Fort Soldado, which was key to the defenses of Monterrey. During General Scott's advance on Mexico City, he commanded the garrison at Puebla. There the large, robust colonel waged a doughty defense against the forces of Gen. Antonio López de Santa Anna, for which he was brevetted brigadier general. He died of yellow fever in Florida in 1853 (*DAB*, vol. 2, pt. 2, p. 71). 2. Jacob E. Blake, who graduated in 1833, was a first lieutenant at the time of his death at Palo Alto (Cullum, I, 435). Roland A. Luther, an 1836 graduate and first lieutenant at the same battle, attained the rank of captain in 1847 and died in 1853 (ibid., I, 502). 3. Charles A. May was commissioned a second lieutenant in 1836. He resigned in 1861 and died three years later (Heitman, I, 698). 4. The capture of General Rómulo Díaz de la Vega became a favorite subject for artists during the war. 5. Zebulon M.P. Inge was a graduate in 1839 (Cullum, I, 571). Richard E. Cochrane was commissioned a second lieutenant in 1838 and was promoted in 1842 (Heitman, I, 313). Theodore Chadbourne graduated in 1843 (Cullum, II, 82). Marshall S. Howe attended the Academy in 1823-27, was commissioned in 1836, and became a captain in 1839. A colonel in the Civil War, he died in 1878 (Heitman, I, 547-48). Joseph Selden, commissioned in 1838 and twice brevetted during the war, resigned in 1861 and went with the Confederacy (Heitman, I, 873). Charles D. Jordan graduated from West Point in 1838 and was brevetted to first lieutenant after Palo Alto and Resaca de la Palma. A captain at the beginning of the Civil War, he was promoted to major in 1862 and retired the next year. He died in 1876 (Heitman, I, 583). Collinson R. Gates, who graduated in 1836, was brevetted captain for Palo Alto and Resaca de la Palma, was brevetted major for Molino del Rey, and died in 1849 (Cullum, I, 515). Robert P. Maclay, a graduate of 1840, attained the rank of captain in 1849, resigned in 1860, and next year joined the Confederacy (Cullum, I, 613-14). John G. Burbank graduated in 1841, was a first lieutenant in 1845, and died in 1847 of wounds suffered at Molino del Rey (Cullum, II, 27).

5

Matamoros

May-June 1846

Consultation with Commodore Conner. Impossible to Press Flowers. We Hook the Mexicans' Boats. The Texas Rifles Hate the Mexicans and Vice Versa. Horrors of the Battlefield. Ghastly Wounds. Making Boats. Meddling with Ammunition. Deputation of the Citizens of Matamoros. The Army Crosses the River. Fall of the City. Stores of Contraband Seized. The city and Its Filthy Women. Volunteers Arrive. General Taylor Strategizes. Debts. Señoritas.

May 14 ✦ We are all hearty and well this morning, my darling one, and nothing has occurred of the least interest since I finished my letter last night. The Mexicans kept up a great tolling of bells, blowing of trumpets, and beating of drums all night. I expect they are dreading lest any moment we will open our batteries on them and cross the river to take their town. They are hard at work trying to barricade their passages to the best advantage. But the general has two heavy mortars coming from Point Isabel, and when our big shells begin to fall into them, they will doubtless be somewhat alarmed. Our shells are very much larger than those they have been throwing at us and, being made of cast iron, are very much more dangerous when they burst than their copper ones, and then we will receive a new supply of large guns which will make this town a very hot place.

We are all anxious to see the general's plans and how the enemy will take it. At present the general has gone to Point Isabel with a train of wagons, a light battery, and a squadron of dragoons. We expect him back today and we would not wonder to see him coming along, a considerable reinforcement with him. Indeed, we would not be greatly astonished to see him come up the river. He is going to consult and cooperate with Commodore Conner, and we understand that the commodore is to bring up the river a steamboat and a large number of launches and barges to assist the pontoon train to cross the army. We hear that the boats are in the river now, and if that is the case, they will not be very long in coming up. The commodore is to bring along a considerable detachment of marines and sailors, and the way we will give thunder to those yellow rascals won't be slow. They have no prisoners at all of ours now and our

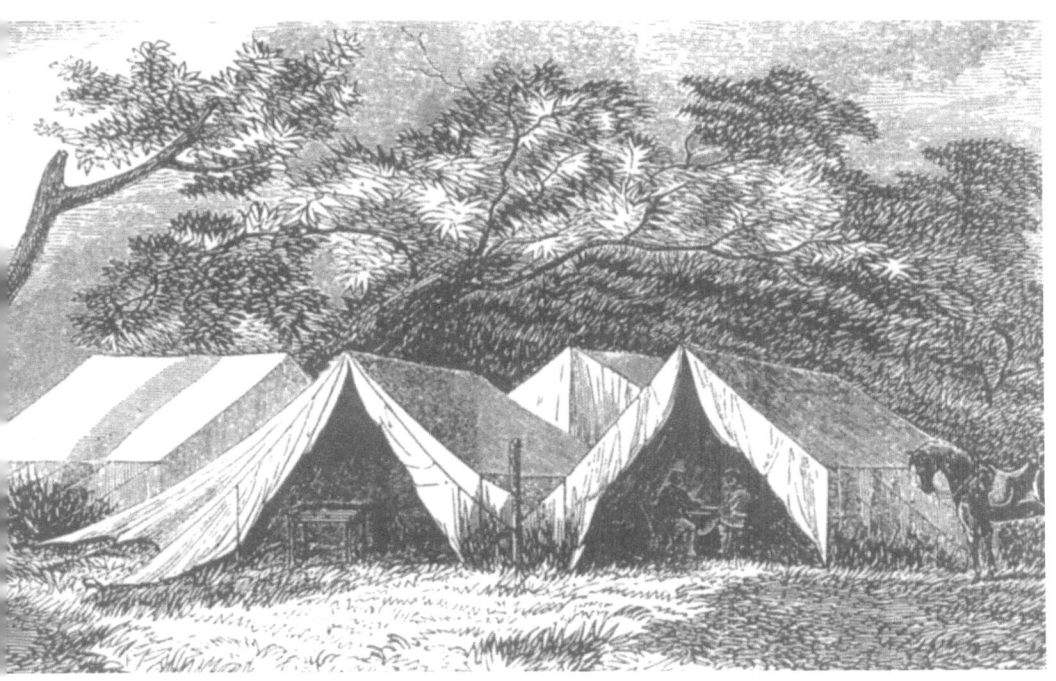

General Taylor's headquarters, near the city of Matamoros.

hands are full of theirs. Commodore C. before the engagements sent word to General T. that the army he was to engage was larger than we thought, that it was the finest army that had ever left Mexico, and that it was the hope of the Mexican nation. It is the opinion, my own dear wife, that as soon as news of the rout of this army reaches the capital, that Mexico will revolutionize and peaceful times will follow. . . .[1]

Henry and his wife are both of them all talk about your flowers and curiosities, my beloved wife.[2] I thought before you wrote about them. I have often wanted to press you some flowers, but could not because my trunk is not here and I have no book to put them in. Many a time when I have passed flowers by the roadside I have wished that I had a book to put them in. I tried to beg some old account book which had been written full, but all gave me the same answer, that they had been left behind with their company baggage. I collected some sea beans and shells at St. Joseph's Island for you. The sea beans I have in my trunk, but the shells were delicate ones and broke in my pocket. I was sorry because they were very pretty ones. Then I have some grapeshot and pieces of shell which have been thrown at us here. I will improve all opportunities, dearest, to get all the pretty things I can for you, and if we go over to Matamoros and are successful, perhaps I will find something novel there for you. . . .

It is hot as very fury here today, almost suffocating, bad weather for fighting. The two battles were fought too on warm days. It makes it mighty hard work.

1. David Conner, born in Pennsylvania in 1792, served with distinction in naval engagements of the War of 1812 and attained the rank of captain in 1835. From 1843 to 1847 he commanded American naval forces in the Gulf and the Caribbean. Slightly above medium height, erect and active and the soul of courtesy, he was an impressive officer. He was not an aggressive commander, and although he carefully brought off the landing of General Scott's army at Veracruz and ably planned the subsequent blockade of that port, he was replaced by Matthew C. Perry shortly before Veracruz was taken. He died in Philadelphia in 1856 (*DAB*, vol. 2, pt. 2, pp. 349-50). Also see K. Jack Bauer, *Surfboats and Horse Marines: U.S. Naval Operations in the Mexican War, 1846-1848* (Annapolis, 1969).   2. William S. Henry graduated in 1835, attained the rank of captain shortly after Palo Alto and Resaca de la Palma, and was brevetted major for his conduct at Monterrey. He was the author of *Campaign Sketches of the War with Mexico* (New York, 1847), a combination of diary and memoir. He died in 1851 (Cullum, I, 483).

May 16 ✦ I do not think, my darling Sue, that our war will last much longer. The people of Mexico will not stand it to be whipped so badly as they have been. Old Paredes, I expect, will soon be supplanted by someone else, perhaps Santa Anna, who will urge a peace and accept pecuniary compensation for whatever Mexico may imagine herself to be despoiled of.[1]

We hooked all their boats from them the other night. Fifty men with muskets went down to the river bank as a guard to the swimmers, whilst six dragoons stripped and swam across to cut loose their boats. It was a daring thing, but no sooner had these naked men got on the other side than the Mexican sentinel, without even firing his musket, ran off as fast as his legs would carry him, and our fellows took the boats. . . .

It will not be long before the Texas rifles get here, a couple of thousand of them, and they are a perfect terror to the enemy. They spare none of them. They merely bring in prisoners enough to keep up appearances and kill all the rest. We can hardly blame them, for they get no quarter from Mexicans. It is a war of extermination between them, and there is scarcely a Texan who does not thirst for Mexican blood. A party of forty-five rancheros met fifteen Texans at the Colorado not many days since, cut the throats of all of them, and threw them into the river. Miraculously, two of them survived and are here now and will take ample vengeance, they say, for the whole gang. . . .

God knows that after this feud is over, if He sees fit to spare me, I would most gladly and joyfully lay aside the sword and seek in a more peaceful walk of life an asylum from the noise and busy bustle of the outer world. The sight of ghastly wounds, the agony of death, its look in every shape, the groans of the expiring and the cries of excruciating pain, the smell of blood and putrid human flesh and the polluted atmosphere, and a woman on the field of battle, with a babe in her lap, unable to weep but wringing her hands and combing the hair of her mangled husband's corpse and kissing his bloody lips, are all sights unsuited to my tastes and shocking to my feelings. The latter case is a real occurrence. A sergeant of the Eighth Infantry who was killed had his wife in the train of wagons coming on from Point Isabel. I did not see her on the field myself, but Dr. Porter told me that he did.[2] I, however, saw her the next morning sitting with a child in her arms, her face buried in its sleeping form, sitting beside a group of dead.

But never had a people [more] cause to be grateful to a kind Providence for warding off dangers than have we. We have heard that poor old Captain Page is dead. Poor fellow, it perhaps is for the best. He could never have spoke or have known a pleasant moment again. The whole lower part of his face—lower jaw, mouth, teeth, tongue, and all—were carried away by a cannonball in the Battle of Palo Alto on the eighth. Colonel McIntosh, it is thought, will recover. He was shot through the body with a musket ball and had a bayonet run through his cheek near his mouth out the back of his neck.[3] You see, our fellows came hand to hand with the yellow rascals and fought them like devils. Lieutenant Jordan of the Eighth got into a crowd of them all alone by some accident. They knocked him down after shooting him in the side, and three of them got on him with bayonets. Lieutenant Lincoln came up and killed two of them with his sword. The third one ran his bayonet through Jordan's shoulder. He is doing very well and will recover.[4] It is well that these things happened, for the Mexicans say that we are not men in a fight but diablos.

1. Gen. Mariano Paredes y Arrillaga, a brave, strutting little man, was the momentarily dominant figure in Mexico. See David M. Pletcher, *The Diplomacy of Annexation*, 172, 174, 273-74, 358-61, 365-73.   2. John B. Porter, assistant surgeon in 1833, and major surgeon in 1846, retired in 1862 and died in 1869 (Heitman, I, 799).   3. John Page was commissioned a second lieutenant in 1818, a first lieutenant in 1819, and a captain in 1831 (Heitman, I, 765). What happened to Colonel McIntosh was almost unbelievable. "I was making my way as well as I could, when I was suddenly beset by six Mexicans. I was completely taken aback, and had not time to reach my holsters to get my pistols. The rascals pinned me, crossing two bayonets in my mouth, one of which I forced out, but the other the scamp pressed in; I felt my teeth go, and the exit of the bayonet at the back of my neck. I fell; they left me for dead. About thirty feet off, a soldier was shot. After shooting him, they beat his brains out with a musket. All this time I was *playing possum*, and

thinking of the chances of my escape. They gave me several *ominous* looks, but I preserved the character of the animal. They all retired but one, who amused himself rifling the pockets of the soldier. I thought my time had come, when he made a few steps toward me. Something alarmed him, and, much against his inclination, he ran away. After carefully satisfying myself the coast was clear, I ceased playing possum, made my way to the troops, and was led out to the road" (W.S. Henry, *Campaign Sketches of the War with Mexico*, pp. 126- 27).   4. George Lincoln, commissioned a second lieutenant in 1837 and brevetted for Palo Alto and Resaca de la Palma, was killed at Buena Vista. At that time he was a first lieutenant (ibid., I, 633).

May 17 ✦ We have been occupied for the last three days in making boats for crossing the river. The general will probably strategize a little, make demonstrations at several points, then effect a crossing perhaps where the enemy least expects it. They are watching our movements very narrowly, and we do not know how they will receive us, but even if they want to give us another pitched battle, which is an extreme case to suppose, the ardor which our men showed at Palo Alto and Resaca de la Palma is a sufficient guarantee for the handling they are likely to receive. By the way, have I told you the meaning of those two names of the battles of the eighth and ninth? They are Spanish, and Palo Alto means the Battle of the High Trees and the other the Ravine of the Palms. . . .

I have been engaged in all kinds of dirty work during the last two or three days. My duties as ordnance officer require me to meddle a great deal with ammunition and arms. Day before yesterday I had to overhaul and examine all the powder and balls captured from the Mexicans, and when I got through I was covered with black dust from top to toe and looked more like a nigger than a white man. I could not care if I never saw another ounce of powder or lead in my whole natural life. It is a glorious profession, that of a soldier, whilst the excitement lasts and success dawns on us, but take it in the long run and it is a mighty unsatisfactory one to many dispositions and seems like time entirely thrown away.

May 18 ✦ I was called off yesterday by the arrival of the train to receive a large quantity of ammunition and ordnance stores. I was kept hard at work all day and then called up again at midnight to issue ammunition to some of the field batteries. . . .

Yesterday a deputation of citizens came over from Matamoros with the alcalde, and the way they did beg the old general was not slow. This is the worst scared set of people on the other side the river you ever did see. These citizens first asked the general to give

"Rough and ready as he is." From a daguerreotype.

them an armistice, but the general told them that he had made an offer of peace when he first arrived here, and as they did not see fit to accept, they should take the consequences, that no cessation of hostilities would be either asked for or granted by him. He then in very severe terms upbraided them with their cruelty, told them that they had killed and barbarously murdered his people and that some of their late deeds were worthy only of a set of naked barbarians. They answered that they could not help it and could not control their rancheros. The general told them then that he could, that he had the power in his hands, and that they should come under it. They then asked him not to move into Matamoros. They said that his army should not be molested from their town if he would keep his troops out of it. This, too, he refused, telling them at the same time that he intended to take their city and occupy it. They then begged him to send over a board of officers who should take an inventory of all the public property in the city, which should be at some future time turned over to him, and that they should engage at the same time that the Mexican army should evacuate the city. To this he answered that the public property in Matamoros belonged to him and they need not trouble themselves about it, that he would move his army in the afternoon three miles up the river where he intended to cross in spite of all they could do, that he should then march down and summon the city to capitulate and that anything they had to communicate before four o'clock p.m. he would be happy to hear. That after that it would be too late, as his army would have been set in motion. In the meantime he told them that they might go around and look at his cannon, his shot, his shells, and his mortars, and his men and make up their minds whether they would fight or not. They went off and did not come back again.

The army left here at four o'clock and encamped at the crossing place, and now we hear that they are nearly all across the river. Some citizens of Matamoros are over this morning who tell us that there is not a soldier or a musket in the town. We feel right sorry here for it because we want our satisfaction for the bombardment. We have now two large mortars with fifty of theirs and ten heavy cannon, all loaded and ready to blaze away when we get the signal from the general but expect that the first thing we shall see will be the Stars and Stripes floating over the plaza without a shot being fired, and so we will lose our fun.

Captain Bliss has just come down from the general and is just going over with a white flag, probably to summon the city. He tells us that the army has crossed. The dragoons swam over on horseback, and Lieutenant Stevens was drowned by his horse. Poor fellow, that is worse than being killed on the battlefield.[1]

The news that Captain Page was dead is contradicted and it is said that he promises to recover,, though he has no desire to live in such a wretched state.

1. George Stevens graduated in 1843 (Cullum, II, 84).

May 19 ✦ Those who have most vilified us must now acknowledge themselves most egregiously in error. They said that we were parlor gentlemen and carpet knights, and the wonders which were worked at San Jacinto could not be looked for at the hands of such delicately brought-up gentry as we. But what do they see now? There is no conjecture about this. It is all reality. San Jacinto is forgotten. The great glories of that day compared with Palo Alto are as a glimmering taper to the full moon, and to the day of Resaca de la Palma like a fixed star to the midday sun. The halo around our arms throws into darkness all that Texas ever did. Our victories are almost incredible. It is seldom that an army can whip three-and-a-half times its numbers, still more seldom that it can rout and disperse them, and almost unparalleled that the beaten force should lose all its artillery and baggage. At Waterloo the French carried off twenty of their cannon. Here, however, it is a more complete rout than has happened with equal odds in the annals of the world, with perhaps one or two exceptions.

The Texans even, devils that they were, are astounded at the daring displayed by some of our troops. When Captain May's squadron, followed by the infantry, charged the enemy's batteries when they were throwing canister shot right in their faces and actually singeing the men's clothes off, a couple of Texan rangers were looking on, and when the batteries were carried, one coolly turned to the other, put his pistol up in his belt, and said, "Well, that spots old Tex!" . . .

I wrote you yesterday on the envelope of my letter that Matamoros had fallen. In fact she may be said to have fallen on the day of Resaca de la Palma, for since then the Mexican force have done nothing but make the best of their way with what little they could carry into the interior towards Monterrey. The general obliged the town to surrender at discretion, with the promise that the rights of persons and civil authority should be respected insofar as they did not conflict with his own military control, as he should occupy the city with his military force. At twelve o'clock our Stars and Stripes were hoisted over the Mexican fort. Our First Brigade encamped for the night in rear of the town, the dragoons, Third, Fourth, and Fifth regiments a little above. We have not as yet learned what disposition the general intends to make of his troops in the city or whether he intends to leave us still in this fort or not. However, I have not as yet been over to Matamoros but will probably go over tomorrow if the day is not very hot. The town is said to be in a great state of confusion, left so by the retreating troops of the enemy. The last columns of the enemy left the city in great haste in the night, after our troops had commenced the movement up the river. All that those columns carried with them was a little to eat in their hands.

May 21 ✦ Yesterday, my own darling wife, I did not get a chance to recommence my letter. In the morning I went over to Matamoros with Whiting and returned at one o'clock, when I was immediately called on to go to work receiving and storing all the heaps of ammunition and public property which they are sending over from Matamoros. I was kept right at work until dark and I suppose that

General Arista and staff leaving Matamoros. Historical Society of Pennsylvania.

they will commence again in an hour or so to send over more. At first we thought that the enemy had made away with nearly all their stores and that scarcely anything would fall into our hands. But we are searching the town, and any quantity of things are being brought to light, hidden in all kinds of places. We had no idea the Mexicans had so much ammunition over there. Boxes and boxes of powder and everything else is brought over. I have already received here, thirty thousand musket cartridges, twenty-five hundred pounds of cannon powder, shot, shells, grenades, and so forth and so forth, innumerable. We found one cannon in a church and one mortar in a well, with a large quantity of shot. Several cannon are in the river with piles of shot and shells. A great deal of ammunition was buried in cellars. Then we have taken about ten barrels of clothing, four or five standards of the Tappadores, muskets, bayonets, public papers, portfolios, regimental desks, public chests, and so forth.

Then it was ascertained that tobacco was a contraband article in Mexico, that the sale of it was monopolized by the government, and no merchant had a right to keep it. It was, then, all public property or smuggled. Consequently the city has been obliged to disgorge all of that article, and the merchants refund all the money they have received for it since the capitulation. It is said that the tobacco and cigars which have been captured are in very large quantity. Wherever public property is found secreted in a house, the house and all in it is condemned. . . .

There are a good many Mexican soldiers in town and some officers, but we take no notice of them. They are not worth the trouble of keeping as prisoners.

The whole town of Matamoros is not so good looking as the third municipality of New Orleans. It is a mean, dirty-looking place, but I believe like the generality of Mexican towns. Orleans from the railroad to the barracks is a very much better-looking place than Matamoros. It is full of fleas and dirt.

The better class of people and all the decent women have left. The women there now are as dark as mulattoes and dirtier and more filthy than Indian squaws. Our ugliest camp woman is better looking than any Mexican woman I have seen yet. They dress very lightly, show a good part of their legs and titties, both mighty nasty-looking sights. They pick the lice out of each other's heads.

May 23 ✦ We received orders last night to march out of the fort, to be relieved by the companies of the First Artillery, and to encamp on this side the river near the fort. We went at it this morning and have been moving all day, and here we are now encamped immediately on the banks of the river right opposite the town. . . . I do not know, my dear Sue, how you would get along to write here now as I am. The bugs are flying around me as thick as bees, against my face, into the candle, over my letter, and all through the tent.

May 24 ✦ My eyes were so weak last night, my dearest wife, that I was obliged to give up writing and go to bed. Occasionally my eyes are right weak now, and I don't know the reason unless it is the hot sun that we have here so much.

It rained here considerably yesterday but this morning the sun is out mighty hot and the birds are singing as joyfully as if there was nothing but happiness in this world and as if war was far, far away from here, and everybody was in possession of their own. But here we are in the country of an enemy, having wrested by our conquest leagues of their territory from them and occupying with our forces one of their oldest and most important towns. The Mexican army of Arista is still rapidly retreating and will in all probability not make a halt until they arrive in Monterrey, three hundred miles from here. . . .

View of the market plaza in Matamoros.

The Mexicans now bring us in considerable marketing but charge very high for all they bring. Still, we are obliged to buy, for we can get no vegetables from no one else. They bring milk, green corn, tomatoes, cabbages, and eggs at 37½ cents a dozen, which is cheap to what we have been paying. They also bring Mexican sugar, some of which I will send you by the first chance I can get. It is something like maple sugar and I think you will find it palatable. At all events, when I can find an opportunity I will send you eight or ten loaves to try. It is much cheaper than maple sugar.

Did you receive the cigars, cigarettes, and cards which I sent you? Are they not queer things to send by mail? By the way, dearest, I wish you would tell me whether you have to pay postage for what I send you, because if you do I won't send you any grapeshot and pieces of shell by mail. Of those cigars, the larger kind, we captured in Matamoros about 200,000. The small ones were without number. They were all distributed among the troops. Each company in the army received about two barrels of them. The cards were the same; about 4,000 packs were captured. They are the only kind of cards which the Mexicans use. It is with them that they play their great game of monte. I marked some of them for you, dearest, so that you could tell the suits. . . .

We have not seen a volunteer yet, though we understand that General Smith's brigade is marching up and will arrive today.[1] We would have been in a bad way if we had have waited for them to raise the siege of Fort Brown. It is three weeks today since the cannonade and bombardment commenced. However, it is not to be expected that a large body of green militia, just raised, can be organized and moved such a distance in a very short time. We are mighty glad that they did not arrive before we had chased Arista and his forces out of the country. We have got all the honor, credit, and renown for our gallant and much abused little army. It remains now to be seen whether they will give us any thanks in Congress about it. I only wish I was out of the way of their thanks and their army, too, free and independent of them all. . . .

The *Neva* came up today. She came along very slowly, as there was just barely enough water to float her and she had to find her own channel all the way. It made the Mexicans open their eyes, I can tell you. A steamboat was a new sight to them. They collected on the banks in crowds and followed the boat up and down as she went along. . . .

The volunteers are beginning to arrive. This afternoon about six hundred have arrived, as perfectly used-up a set of fellows as you ever saw, completely broken down and disgusted, and, I have no doubt, heartily wish they were at home again and had not come to rescue "General Taylor from his perilous situation." They have arrived just in time to see everything in our hands and to find the enemy farther from them than they were when they left New Orleans.

1. Persifor Frazer Smith was born in Philadelphia in 1798, and after graduating from the College of New Jersey (later Princeton University) and studying law, he moved to New Orleans. He raised a regiment of Louisianians for the Seminole War in 1836-38. At the outbreak of the Mexican War, he was commissioned a colonel in the U.S. Army and was brevetted brigadier general in September 1846—he was not yet a general officer when Dana wrote in May of that year. He was later brevetted major general. After several postwar assignments in the American West, he died at Fort Leavenworth in 1858. A very able officer, he was said to unite composure and control with considerable daring (*DAB*, vol. 9, pt. 1, pp. 331-32).

May 27 ✦ I have just finished my morning toilet, washed my face, combed, and put on my purple-colored shirt and am now sitting on my half barrel which I use as a chair and at an old box which I use for a table. I will spend my time in writing to my dearest one until breakfast, and perhaps, if I do not write a couple of pages by that time, after breakfast I will commence again. There is nothing new to tell you of, my dearest Sue. . . . For the last few days we have

Mexican news brought volunteers to the American colors. Amon Carter Museum, Fort Worth.

been leading a mighty quiet life, but little to do and a plenty of leisure, so I was anxious to make the best use of my time and went in search of a book on anatomy. I obtained one from Dr. McPhail, and yesterday I spent the whole day in reading it, and I intend to devote all the time I can borrow from my duties and my dearest Sue to study.[1] There is no knowing how soon, however, my leisure may be broken in upon by a march, and at our next stopping place I may not be able to obtain a book. . . .

Our surgeons have had very hard work here, for they have had not only our own wounded to take care of but nearly all those belonging to the enemy. The enemy will probably lie a good deal about their loss in killed and wounded, but we know pretty near as well, if not better than they do, what their loss was. They have left their hospitals in Matamoros filled with wounded men, several hundred of them, numbers of whom die every day. A great number of them are wounded by cannon shot, which of course is nearly always at least attended with a loss of a part of the body. It is a terrible sight to see those fellows as much mangled, in such great suffering, lying on brick floors with nothing under them but a mat, and in most cases only a sheet over them.

1. Leonard C. McPhail was commissioned assistant surgeon in 1834 and major surgeon in 1848. He resigned the next year and died in 1867 (Heitman, I, 681).

May 30 ✦ The general has sent to New Orleans to buy three light-draft steamboats to navigate this river with, and when they come he intends to load them and then march up and take possession of Camargo, a town on the river a hundred miles from here. We understand that that town and Reynosa, a village halfway from here, have both sent deputations to the general offering to deliver up their towns and inviting him to occupy them. It is from Camargo that the general intends to march upon Monterrey, 150 miles interior from that town. In all, to get to Monterrey we have got to march 250 miles. So you can see we have got some very hard work before us. We shall not meet Mexican forces much this side of Monterrey. It is possible they may try to save that city, but it is more probable that Mexico will be willing to negotiate for peace before we get there. It will not be long now before we can fathom her intentions, and if it is her intention to continue the war, we must put all our muscle into it and overwhelm her at once. If she has not got fighting enough already, we have some of the biggest kinds of whippings in store for her, and if she makes the game last much longer, we will not have the Rio Grande for a boundary but the chain of mountains called Sierra del Madre. That is by far the best boundary we can get between us and such a country as Mexico, for it is only passable at three points, and those three we could strongly fortify.

June 5 ✦ You need not be at all alarmed, my darling, about yellow fever. This is not a yellow fever place. There has been no yellow fever since 1840, and then the river overflowed its banks very much. Now the river is very low. Can't they find something else to frighten you with? . . .

Two skeletons have been brought in today for burial, which

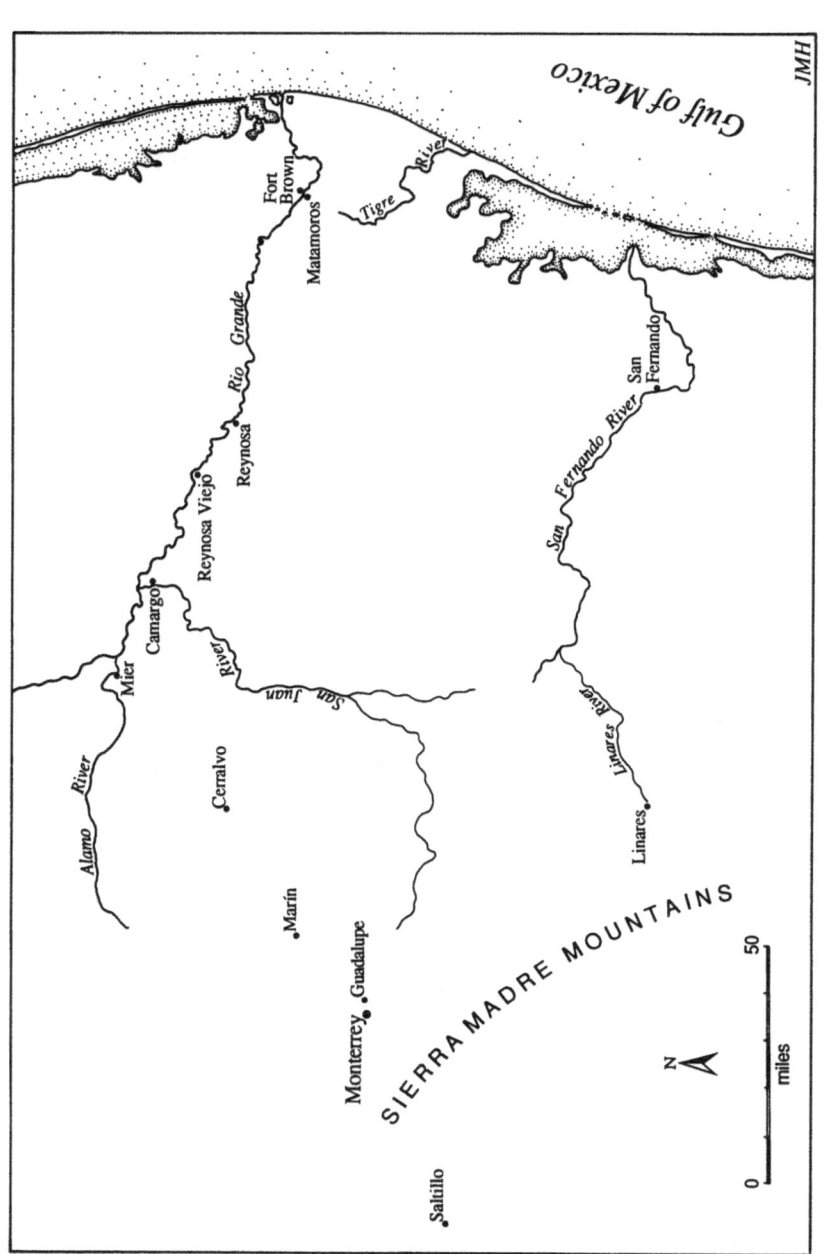

Campaigns of General Taylor

have been recognized as those of Lieutenant Porter and the man who was killed with him.

June 7 ✦ I have been on guard duty all day, and now that the vigils of the night are left to me, I will devote a part of my time to talking with you whilst you are probably fast asleep so far away from me. There being no danger now near at hand, we take the guard duty more easily, and now all of my guard except those who are on post are sleeping around me together with a lot of ragged prisoners. I picked up a couple of volunteers today and one fellow I was [illegible] tying a stick in his mouth to stop his tongue, but he begged off and said he would not say another word. I have no commiseration for the insubordinate rascals and will push them every chance I can get. Our soldiers have had many fights with them, but the funniest thing which has happened yet is that one of Captain Holmes' men whipped one of the volunteer officers over in town the other day. That was going a little too far but I believe they had a regular fight. . . .

The First Infantry left yesterday for Reynosa, sixty miles up the river. This is nearly halfway to Camargo, which will be our principal depot, and where we will commence our march on Monterrey. Our line of operations will be from Camargo through Monterrey and beyond there through the main pass of the Sierra Madre, San Luis Potosí, and so forth. We do not know but that we may yet go through to Mexico [City]. Gatlin says that [he] has got to give a Fourth of July oration in the bishop's palace of Monterrey, and he will take his Christmas dinner in the halls of the Montezumas.

June 8 ✦ Yes, many a long day's march will soon carry me farther from you, and will you believe me, I feel a little impatient for the time to come, for the sooner we start the sooner will we come back and be at peace. Our chief quartermaster has been ordered today by General Taylor to purchase two thousand pack mules in addition to our present train, to help move the baggage of the army. Pretty much all the baggage, I expect, will go on mules, and the wagons principally given up to provisions and ammunition. . . .

We wear all kinds of uniforms here, each one to his taste, some shirtsleeves, some white, some blue, some fancy jackets and all colors of cottonelle pants, some straw and some Quaker hats, and that is just the way, too, that our fellows went into battle. The

Mexicans must have thought that we were real militia ragamuffins. They all had on their full dress caps, pompons and all, and that is the way our fellows will whip them. The shouts which our fellows raised when they charged their center at Resaca de la Palma scared them about as badly as anything. I expect they have often been startled from their dreams since then with those same yells still ringing in their ears.

It would have done any American heart good to have seen those thousands streaking it that afternoon from the field as if their lives hung on their heels and plunging into the river in the excess of their panic. Their shirttails actually stood straight out behind whilst they stretched their good legs to the utmost and fled before our light troops without hats, arms, or anything. We can make a splendid comic almanac out of that week's work. For instance, "a covey of Mexicans flushed by one of our eighteen-pound shot," a very funny picture that will be. Then two hundred or three hundred of their sharpshooters coming up in the night to [illegible] the long shot of our guards, and a trumpeter lying in a hole on his belly, sounding a charge at our walls. That is an actual fact. Among all the dangers of the bombardment we had lots of fun out of those things. . . .

June 11 ✦ I have just paid Burke his fifty dollars. That is good riddance. I wish I had it in my power to settle with all now. I would be glad to not keep anybody's money again. I think that in future when a soldier brings me money I will not take it except with the condition that he shall not have it till he is discharged. Then I can take it and use it to my advantage as I see fit and know just what to calculate upon. Burke's time is up now in a few days. He is a most incorrigible drunkard.

Wise is transferred into another company, but he is on extra duty as a teamster in the train so that I never see him nowadays. I have not seen him for six weeks. I hold ninety-six dollars of his. I hope he will not want it for several months yet, for I must strain every muscle to collect enough to pay over to the government for Sergeant Weigart's heirs in two or three months. I think that if Wise is not in a hurry I can manage it. It was always my understanding with Sergeant W. that he would not wish for his money until he was discharged, and if necessary I will make it appear so. . . .

I met a señorita yesterday at the sutler's store who had a gold cross on her neck which I asked her to sell me, but she could not do it until she asked her "madre." I wanted only to buy it for you as a little curiosity, for you should not put it on after she had worn it. She was about the color of a mulatto and I suppose just as lousy as all the rest of them.

They are absolutely disgusting and sickening in that respect. They are mighty ugly, filthy-looking women, but all have pretty feet and ankles. I understand they are very primitive in their simple manners, think nothing of seeing naked men or of going swimming in the river, quite naked in full view. I have not seen any such sights and will not look at them for your sake. In fact I have been over the river but three times and have found nothing there to attract me in the least.

They have fandangos there every Sunday night. Many of our young officers frequent them and cut all kinds of capers among the girls. From what I hear of them I should suppose they were very rowdy things. Should I be so edified as to happen on one in our marches, I will tell you all about it, but certain it is that I will not go over to Matamoros to seek one. I am pretty much of a sobersides here but keep in first-rate spirits.

June 14 ✦ I have now got a tent again all to myself and am snugly and privately fixed again for as long a time as they will choose to allow us to remain here. How long that will be we still have no idea of. We may march soon, and we may not move for several weeks yet. Everything depends on circumstances, first on the nature of instructions from the government and then on the time which it will take our quartermaster's department to collect the means of transportation. To render our force effective we will have to move with 1,500 wagons and several thousand mules. You can imagine what a train that would be from the fact that now our train is 300 wagons and when stretched out on a march it would extend from the St. Charles to the barracks pretty nearly. The ordinary train which we run regularly between here and Point Isabel of 240 wagons stretches nearly three miles. It is a beautiful sight to see it winding over an extended prairie, the white-topped wagons stretching in the distance as far as the eye can reach. . . .

The *Cincinnati* and the *Frontier* came upriver two days ago and discharged cargoes. The Mexicans all flock to the river bank to see these wonders. I believe that before we came here only two steamboats had ever been up here, and then the people thought they occasioned the yellow fever and forbade any more to come. . . .

You did not say if there was anyone in the Louisville battalion

whom you knew. Did you see any of your old beaux among them?
. . .

If Kate were not so lazy and fat and greasy she might write me occasionally. Ask her if she can't get a costume à la Mexican señorita to show herself to me in when I come home. If she will put it on and let me see her in it, I will bring her one. It comes halfway down the bosom, showing just enough. An inch farther would be too much. Then it is nearly up to the knees, showing a pretty foot and ankle and a good deal of well-shaped leg. These last she might not like to show, but the Mexican women are not crooked-legged. The Mexican señoritas do not wear drawers, and when the wind blows right there is no telling how much one might see, but such things always strike me stone-blind and I never see anything.

6

To Reynosa
and Camargo
June-August 1846

A "High-flung" Fandango. Ready to March. Advice to Kate. The *Neva* and the Quarter-master. Arrival in Reynosa. Monsieur Morblieu. On the March Again. Reynosa Viejo. The Water and Mudholes. Camargo after the Flood. Arrival of General North. Comanches Steal the Horses of the Texan Rangers. Summary Treatment for Liquor Vendors. The Mexicans Perfect Idolators. Mexican Women Bathe Shamelessly in the River.

June 19 ✦ Since I last wrote you, dearest one, I have looked into a Mexican fandango. I heard that there was to be a "high-flung" fandango last Tuesday night, something extra above the ordinary things of the kind at which all the beauty and fine dresses and so forth and so forth were to appear. Well, I thought I would go over among the rest and take a look. So I went with Captain Ross, Porter, and Clitz.[1] I went in, and one look was enough for me. I remained about two minutes and declared my determination to come home, to which all the party assented, and off we came. There were about forty of our officers there and about twenty Spanish girls. I inquired particularly if there was not a mistake in the place but was told no, that was the high-flung fandango. If that was it, I would like to see a common one for curiosity sake. I believe I have felt fleas on me ever since. They are vulgar, disgusting places, and I believe I would rather go to a nigger breakdown.

1. Henry B. Clitz graduated from West Point in 1845 and was a second lieutenant at this time. He served in the Civil War and was brevetted brigadier general in 1865. He died in 1888 (Cullum, I, 135-36).

June 21 ✦ Doubtless we will very soon commence a movement upriver. Every preparation is being made for it. Two steamboats, the *Neva* and *Aid*, have gone up to Reynosa with commissariat stores of different kinds, and the next thing will be some regiments commencing a march for Camargo, sixty miles above Reynosa. . . .

I had my hair cut, dearest one, yesterday, and I have saved a piece of it for you which I will send in this letter. You know I am not good at putting hair up, so I have merely tied it in the middle and leave you to do what you please with it. The man did not cut off so good a piece as I wanted him to, but I expect it is better than any piece you have.

June 22 ✦ Well, we have indeed got orders in this regiment to be prepared to march to Camargo, 120 miles upriver, at a moment's notice. We received the order yesterday afternoon and we only wait for the steamboat *Aid* to come down from Reynosa in order to throw forward supplies for us. She is expected down every hour, and I think it highly probable that we will move day after tomorrow, possibly tomorrow, and maybe not for several days. We are in readiness at any moment. We do not know who is to go along with us, but in all probability we will have two pieces of light artillery and two companies of Texan rangers.

June 25 ✦ We have got no further orders for moving to Camargo and will probably not go now for several days more, although we expected to have been off before this time. The cause of the delay is in the steamboat *Aid*. She returned three days ago from Reynosa, and it appears that she is not a government boat and she asks such an exorbitant price to go up to Camargo that it is the intention now to wait for another boat. Another may arrive any day. She wants $250 a day for going to Camargo and the quartermaster's department, I believe, is only willing to give her $100. . . .

Give my love to Kate, my dearest wife, and say that if she could spare a moment at any time I should always be very glad indeed to hear from her, and perhaps she may want a correspondent to keep her hand in practice. If from her lounge, bed, and book she can spare a moment, let her drop me a line occasionally and I will be very glad indeed to get it. She had better make interest with me, for there is no knowing what I might do in the way of getting her a yellow-legged buck Mexican down here. There is an aristocratic Tonikan chief down here who calls himself Colonel Bob of Texas, and on whose face might be raised a plentiful crop of rich tobacco, and who with his one eye might be induced to look lovingly on a Missouri squaw.[1] Beaux of all sizes, colors, shapes, and tongues are to be had down here, and there is no telling how many admirers a right "well-formed wench" might have here. Now, that is not one of your husband's expressions, my dear wife, but one of your father's.

1. The word "Tonikan" designates an American Indian linguistic family once found in Louisiana and Mississippi.

June 27 ✦ The *Neva* is raising steam and this moment an order has come for three companies of us to go to Reynosa on board of her, where we will wait with the First Infantry for the balance to come before we go to Camargo. It is glorious but very sudden, as we go off in an hour. I am now on guard and am to be relieved and have all my things to pack up and the company to take care of. So I can only write a few lines to set your mind at ease.

It is raining and has been raining for two days without stopping, so we are in great luck, as this will save us sixty miles' march over bad roads.

June 29 ✦ Have you yet got my little short letter bidding you goodby before I made such a hasty start for Reynosa? Were to have gone there in an hour and were in all the hurry and confusion consequent upon such a hasty move. Well, have we not got back quick? You must bear in mind that it is 180 miles by the river to Reynosa, and then say if you do not think we have made a quick trip of it. But I will tell you all about it.

After I finished my little note to you I went right to work to get my things ready for the move, and as Mr. Little was on the sick report had the company on my hands also.[1] Well, I had just time to get ready when the *Neva* came to receive our baggage. So at it we went in a hard rain, struck our tents, and in a couple of hours three companies were on board, bag and baggage ready for a start.

Now, then came into play the efficiency of the quartermaster's department. They sent us the boat for a transport, and after we were all on board the captain stated that the boilers were far from safe and that they had been weak for a long time. Thereupon the jackass of a quartermaster was overhauled and got heaps of cursing for not having this attended to before we took the trouble to get on board. But there we were, all on board and just at that moment when we should have started, forsooth, a doubt is expressed by the quartermaster himself whether the boat is fit to run.

He was required to make a report to the general on the subject, and the general immediately ordered the boilers to be cooled down and a thorough examination to be made of them by three steam engineers, and if there was the least doubt as to the safety of the boilers, the boat should not run. It took till sundown to cool the boilers and then the examination was made, and one of the boilers reported good whilst the other was not safe. Whereupon the general sent us an order about tattoo to disembark again next morning and let the boat go downriver to wait for new boilers.

So yesterday morning, still raining, we again pitched tents in the old places, moved back our baggage, sent back five hundred barrels of provisions which we had placed on board, and here we are again, just where we started, having had all our trouble for nothing except to sleep one night on board the steamboat.

1. Lewis H. Little was commissioned a second lieutenant in 1839 and was a first lieutenant at this time. H was promoted to captain in 1847. He resigned in 1861 to become brigadier general in the Confederate army and was killed the next year (Heitman, I, 635).

July 2 ✦ For the last two days here it has been perfectly melting. During the day the sun is very powerful, making it hot and sultry with scarcely a breath of air stirring. . . . Should we commence our march soon we will probably march pretty much during the night as we now have a fine moon, and the men would not be able to stand it long towards the middle of the day with such a sun over them as we have now. . . .

And you, little modesty, you have never once in your letters mentioned your legs or your titties to me. You have never answered my inquiries about them. I want to know just how they look, how big they are, and how much you weigh. You must always tell me something about these things for you know how much I like to feel them and play with them. When I am home with you, you know I will never allow you to rest. Now mind and tell me about them the very next time you write. . . .

And now let me give you my expenses for last month. I know you will think them too large, but it can't well be helped. I am obliged once in a while to return the compliment of something to drink, and friends particularly at the bars in town when over there. Drinks, cider, ale, and so forth—$2.50; a crystal for a man's watch which I broke—$.50; newspapers—$.50; blacking—$.25; cutting hair—$.25; postage—$.30; washing—$2.50; mess bill and servant—$14.30. In all—$21.10.

Reynosa, July 10 ✦ All is very quiet and peaceable here, and I think the inhabitants rather superior to those of Matamoros and much more friendly to us. The girls here wear long dresses and are of a lighter complexion than they are below though not near so numerous. The place is quite small but much cleaner and neater than Matamoros, the houses generally built of limestone and the town itself built upon a rising of limestone rock. . . .

The officers have a great deal to joke about here among the girls and all appear to enjoy the fun. The other night they had a big dance and had a little of everybody in the town at it. They waltzed and danced till late and drank punch and had all sorts of a frolic. Then they go to the houses and get up little private dances and frolics, anything for fun, and the Mexicans appear to enjoy it very much. Captain Backus and Dr. Laub root around most everywhere. I went with them and shall go again this afternoon. We loaf into any house we happen to fancy and are always hospitably received with a "Buenos días, señor," an apparent welcome. It makes no difference who they are, we go in just wherever we please.[1]

And what do you think the women call Captain Backus? "El padre de diablo," the father of the devil. He has rigged up what they call a "Monsieur Morblieu," a paper figurine which by some contrivance will stand on the floor and dance by itself to music. I never have seen the contrivance, but it appears to be an old thing with the First Regiment. Well, the captain takes this around and makes it dance at the houses and you never did see such a tickled and wonder-struck set of people in your life.

1. Electus Backus graduated from West Point in 1824. He served as a colonel at the beginning of the Civil War and died in 1862 (Cullum, I, 267).

July 11 ✦ Captain Miles has arrived, my own darling wife.[1] He got here after dark this evening on the steamboat *Enterprise*. It appears that after he had marched eighteen miles from Matamoros, the last five in water up to their knees, an express from General Taylor overtook them with an order to strike the river at the nearest point and there wait for a steamboat. Well, he has brought orders for our three companies, the mounted Texans, and two pieces of light artillery to move forward to Camargo, whilst he with his three companies go up in the steamboat. So very early in the morning, my dear Sue, we shall put all of our disposable baggage in his boat and commence our march with seven wagons. I have been making preparations tonight among the men. It is now eleven o'clock, and I have my baggage to pack and select things for the march before going to sleep after finishing this letter.

1. Dixon S. Miles, a graduate of the Academy in 1824, was brevetted major for the defense of Fort Brown. He was a colonel by the time of the Civil War and died of wounds at Harpers Ferry in 1862 (Cullum, I, 266-67).

Rancho Murillo, July 13   ✦   Isn't this a pretty place to be writing from? Captain Holmes has just passed by and laughed at the idea of my sitting here writing in the midst of a march, but I know my sweet Sue will love to have her husband talk to her a little once in a while during the fatigues of an infantry tramp.[1] Well, let me commence and tell you, for I am not going to write much now, for it is far from being comfortable and moreover, like a good soldier, I must soon take a siesta preparatory to the afternoon's march.

We commenced our march by moonlight this morning at three o'clock. The bugles sounded the reveille at half past two and we got up, struck the very few tents, made soldiers' toilets, took our "hasty soup," and at three o'clock moved in advance. Half of Captain McCulloch's company of mounted Texans formed the advance guard and kept about a mile ahead.[2] At the head of our column came the remainder of his company, then the pioneers, two men from each of our companies with their axes. Next came Whiting's company, next the two pieces of [illegible] artillery followed by caissons, next Captain Paul's company, then "C" Company under my command, next the seven baggage wagons, and last the rear-guard of four noncommissioned officers and eighteen men.[3]

We have had a pretty hard march so far, and for the last two have marched in mud and water up to our waists, left so by the late freshets. And I am the only officer left on foot besides Lieutenant Hopson. He had no horse offered him, but I had two offered to me. All the regimental and staff horses were landed from Captain Miles' steamboat, and each officer has one of them, but I am a foot officer. My men have to march on foot with heavy loads, and I prefer to take the rough of the campaign in the midst of them to sauntering easily along on horseback. It is far more creditable and makes the men far better satisfied. It was the same thing in marching from Point Isabel to Matamoros. When I last joined, it was very bad weather, and I was the only officer on foot. Captain Holmes is entitled to ride, as he is in command, but no other officer, and he said this morning that no officer ought ever to think of riding whilst his men were on foot unless he were a mounted officer. I am rather glad they all ride, myself, as it makes the greater contrast.

And how is it now I am the only officer awake? All the rest are stretched on the ground asleep, but I feel fresh enough to start again. I am quite vain of my marching qualities, my darling wife.
. . .

We will probably start from here about four o'clock. It would kill some of the men should we march here in the middle of the day, so we make early and late marches. One of Captain Miles' corporals died of sunstroke on the first day's march from Matamoros.

When we halted here, I pulled off my shoes and stockings to dry them and, by the way, had sense enough to put on woolen socks. Then I laid down in the shade for a half an hour, then put on my shoes and socks again, went to one of the wagons, got my valise, took out my writing materials, and here I am, sitting under a bush in the shade, writing on my knees. Of course it is not a very comfortable way of writing.

I was a tolerably clean man when I started this morning, but now I am far from it, covered with mud and dirt. I have on my old straw hat, those blue-checked pants made by your dear hands, which are torn in both legs and pretty well worn out, and that loose coat you made which you recollect washed white. I don't think there is much danger of a ranchero shooting at me for an officer of high rank. My trimmings don't show much. Both pairs of those check pants I have worn pretty well out.

1. Theophilus Hunter Holmes was born in North Carolina in 1804, graduated from West Point in 1829, and served on the southwestern frontier, in the Seminole campaign, and in the Mexican War; he was brevetted major after Monterrey. Following tours of garrison duty and recruiting, he resigned in 1861 to become brigadier general in the Confederate army. Although his contributions to the Confederacy's cause appear to have been modest, he rose to the rank of lieutenant general. He died in his native state in 1880 (*DAB*, vol. 5, pt. 1, p. 176).   2. Ben McCulloch was born in Tennessee in 1811 and was brought up there and in neighboring Alabama. His family moved back to Tennessee, and McCulloch then learned that a neighbor, the celebrated David Crockett, was going to Texas. He followed and took part in the fighting at San Jacinto, where he was in charge of one of the "twin sisters," the two small cannon in Gen. Sam Houston's army. Thereafter he became an Indian fighter. Of medium height, slender, with quiet manners, he was an unlikely candidate for leadership of a company of Texas rangers. He nonetheless became the idol of his men, and served with Taylor's army during the Mexican War. His exploits caught the attention of such newspaper reporters as George W. Kendall of the *New Orleans Picayune* (below, letter of July 20, 1846). Emerging from the war as a major, he joined the gold rush to California in 1849 and for a time was sheriff of Sacramento. He was soon back in Texas, where he remained until the Civil War, when he joined the Confederacy as a brigadier general. He was the victor of the Battle of Wilson's Creek in Missouri in August 1861 but the next year was fatally wounded (*DAB*, vol. 6, pt. 2, pp. 5-6).   3. Gabriel R. Paul graduated in 1834 and was brevetted brigadier general during the Civil War. He died in 1886 (Cullum, I, 452-53).

Camargo, July 15 ✦ We have this moment arrived here, seven
o'clock, marching nearly all night. Found Miles and his steamboat
just going to shove off, so I will seal this and send it to my own
darling wife and commence to write her more. All are well.

July 18 ✦ I wrote you, dearest one, at our first halting place at
Rancho Murillo. We had then marched nine miles. After I had
finished writing to you there I laid myself down like the rest of them
under the imperfect shade of a mesquite bush and went to sleep.
The heat was intolerable, and we suffered much there on account of
it. It was impossible to get under a good shade, and the perspiration
oozed from every pore. In addition to this, all the water we had to
use was very warm and did not refresh us in the least. At four
o'clock our bugles blew the assembly, and as soon as the artillery
and wagons were hitched up, the advance was sounded and we
again moved on.

My dear wife, those who have never tried marching under a
blazing sun have yet to learn the real suffering consequent upon
excess of heat. It was like marching in a oven. The men suffered
greatly, and it appeared as if they could hardly lag along. Several of
them gave out, and the doctor was obliged to direct them to get into
the wagons. Hopson was obliged to give up and face to the rear with
the wagons. Your hero, dearest, was the only officer left on foot,
and there was no give-up in him. And at the end of the march he
declared himself fresh and ready to go on if necessary, and in fact I
believe myself just as serviceable after my day's hard marching as
were any of those gentlemen who rode their horses whilst their
men toiled along on foot.

We made six miles in that afternoon and halted a little after
sunset at Reynosa Viejo, that is, Old Reynosa, where we made
dispositions to bivouac for the night. This is a little old village on the
Mexican bank of the Rio Grande, and was formerly the only Mexican town of Reynosa, or Queen City, on the river. But the overflow
of the river brought frequent destruction to the property of the
people here, and the town of Reynosa was moved lower down the
river on a high limestone rock. And this place is now called Old
Reynosa, or as the Mexicans have it, Reynosa Viejo, the "j" being
sounded like "h," Vieho.

Well, we bivouacked here in pretty close order, to prevent
surprise mounted our guards. Had our soldier fare served up in
supper form, and the bugles then gave us notice that we might

sleep. So Captain Holmes, Dr. Prevost, and myself stretched our-selves under a tent fly whilst the men strewed along the ground wherever each might fancy his choice place.[1] The night was beauti-ful, bright starlight, and before late came up the moon. We all slept soundly until at three o'clock the bugles again called us to com-mence our march and get ahead as far as possible before the sun began to show his power.

We got our breakfasts immediately, but owing to some delay with the artillery horses, we did not get started till four o'clock. This was a bad beginning and argued that we would have a toilsome march of it for that day. On this day several of the men who had broken down the day before were obliged to get into the wagons, Hopson still trying it on foot.

Well, we were fairly started at four o'clock, Captain Paul's company heading off and mine next to the artillery. We went on at a good pace for three miles when we came to another water and mudhole a half mile across. This appeared to be an old bed of the river. It was not much more than knee-deep, and into it we went, and whilst we halted on the other side of it for the wagons to come up, the day broke, and we had only made four miles. I laid down in the dirt and I really believe it was the easiest way to get clean, for I was perfectly nasty with mud and dirty water.

To add to my misfortunes I had lost the sole of one of my shoes in the last mudhole and still had ten or eleven miles to go. But as I had made up my mind to do the thing up to the handle, I did not get out another pair of shoes out of the wagon, but after cracking a few jokes with some of the men I sprawled off in the road, put my head on my old straw sombrero, and soon forgot all about marches until the bugles again sounded the advance. And we went to work to accomplish the other ten miles we had before us before halting for the day.

After a hard six miles' heat we came to another water and mudhole. This one was waist-deep, and as the sun was now getting hot, it was absolutely exhausting to get through with this. But we conquered the obstacle and halted on the side for the wagons to come up, when we again marched on. The march was now becom-ing very hard. The men began to lag, and I felt a great deal of inconvenience from the loss of the sole of my shoe, for the road was making my foot tender. The sun was getting hotter and hotter and at times was almost intolerable. The march was as really distressing as I ever hope, and horses and men appeared to put forth their last energies to struggle against the debilitating effect of the hot climate and scorching sun. Once or twice I thought it would be mighty comfortable if I could just lie down by the roadside and let them leave me there to catch up in the night. But like all other things this had its ending, and at eleven o'clock we halted at a rancho on the banks of the river and made dispositions to spend the day and night there.

The sun was absolutely like a blaze of fire, and it was impossible to stand under it. Each one picked out some shady spot, and all for once were well convinced that a resting spell at such a time was a blessing indeed. We made ourselves comfortable here for the night and at two o'clock we were to be off next morning. We were only fifteen miles from Camargo and it was desirable to get there before the sun got high. And indeed if Miles had arrived there with only two companies, we did not know but that he wanted assistance.

At two o'clock the bugles sounded. The moon was shining very bright, and I was ordered to lead off with my company. The men had been ordered to put all their knapsacks in the wagons. The road was good all the way, and I was determined that since I was to lead off, we should see Camargo at an early hour. Hopson reported himself sick and got into a wagon at the start.

Well, at the call to advance I started my company off at a pretty brisk pace, followed by the rest of the column. When I thought the men had walked off some of their stiffness, I quickened the pace imperceptibly until I made it so rapid that the artillery horses were often obliged to trot to get up and the companies in the rear were as frequently obliged to follow suit and go into a dogtrot. We soon outstripped the mules, and the wagons fell nearly a half a mile in rear with the rearguard. I kept up that same pace and it tickled the men so that they were all laughing and talking and in fine spirits, and all agreed that it was less tiresome to march fast in the cool of the day than slow.

At sunrise we halted for half an hour to get water for men and horses, and from the rapid march it was ascertained that we had gone twelve miles without a halt and that Camargo was only three miles ahead. Here we were then, having nearly finished a day's march and the sun just rising. All were pleased except Whiting, who said that his men would break down, but I thought I was best able to judge as I was on foot and he on horseback. So I concluded when we started again not to slacken the pace.

Well, we got here at seven o'clock and found Miles and all the rest of them mighty glad to see us but not expecting us till next day. We had marched forty-five miles in three marches in fifty hours, and that in the middle of one of the hottest months. . . .

View of Camargo on the Rio Grande.

We are now encamped, my dearest wife, in the plaza, or public square, of Camargo, K and I companies on one side, C and F on another, and D and E on another, whilst the guardhouse, hospital, adjutant's office, and so forth occupy the fourth. The church is on my side of the square and is by far the prettiest one we have yet seen, although its style of architecture is ancient and odd. It is also the only one we have seen with a finished steeple. It is quite a picturesque building and like all Mexican churches has three bells of different sounds in its steeple. These ring regularly, four times a day, at daylight, at twelve, at sunset, and at nine o'clock.

The alcalde's house is also on our side of the square. We face the side occupied by the guard and so forth. The report which reached us about the total destruction of the town was false, but it is in a most deplorable condition. Many of the best houses have fallen, and a great many others cannot stand long. The water was five or six feet deep all over the town, and many of the poor people are altogether ruined. Before the late freshet Camargo was undoubted-

ly quite a pretty place for a Mexican town. The plaza is now a glare
of white sand, and before the river rose we are told that it was a very
pretty square and covered with grass. It is said that the people
intend to build their town three miles above here on the other side
of the San Juan (called San Huan). They have a higher piece of land
there. The town itself occupies a very pretty and picturesque situation, right on the high bank of that little river, and as it glides
beneath us some forty or fifty feet it would appear almost impossible that the stream could rise that much. The San Juan empties into
the Rio Grande about three miles from here.

The population of this place before the freshet was five or six
thousand. There are two or three thousand here now. It has some
fine houses but none over one story, and like all Mexican houses,
flat and tiled on top such as you hear of at Jerusalem in olden times.
But like the other Mexican towns we have seen, all the houses on the
suburbs are made of cane and thatched with straw. The best house
in town is not so good as our kitchen at Orleans Barracks, and none
have wood floors or glass windows, and in fact most of them have
no windows at all.

1. Grayson M. Prevost, assistant surgeon beginning in December 1845, resigned in 1848
and died in 1896 (Heitman, I, 806).

July 20   ✦   Another awfully hot day, my dearest wife, and no relief
by a refreshing breeze. A few gentlemen have been sitting at my
tent all the forenoon until eleven o'clock, talking about a little or
everything. Well, at that time they left one by one, and I was just
about to come and have a little talk with you when Kendall of the
Picayune came in and sat for another half hour. . . .[1]

It appears that old Polk is really determined on swallowing
Mexico without any grease. If he will give us the means, we are just
the boys to do it.

1. George Wilkins Kendall was born in New Hampshire in 1809 and, after employment as
a printer in Burlington, Vermont, and in Washington and New York, went to New
Orleans, where with Francis Lumsden he founded the first cheap daily newspaper in the
city, the *Picayune*, in 1837. After establishing his paper, he joined the ill-fated expedition
to Santa Fe sponsored by the independent state of Texas and soon found himself
marching as a prisoner to Mexico City, where he was incarcerated for a time in a prison for
lepers. Upon his return he wrote his *Narrative of the Texan Santa Fe Expedition*, 2 vols. (New
York, 1844); published by Harper, it sold forty thousand copies. When hostilities began
along the Rio Grande, he rode with the Texas rangers. He witnessed most of the battles of
Generals Taylor and Scott and was wounded in the leg during the storming of Chap-
ultepec. Kendall and his New Orleans associates reported the war by modern methods,

sometimes outstripping government dispatches with their ingenious system of couriers and steamers known as "Mr. Kendall's express." He even arranged to have his ships met by other vessels containing compositors and printing equipment, so that his accounts were ready to be run within minutes of their arrival. His stories were extensively copied. After the war he spent several years in Europe, part of which time he devoted to preparing *The War between the United States and Mexico* (New York and Philadelphia, 1851), illustrated with lithographs by the German artist Carl Nebel. He married in Paris and moved to Texas, where he had a ranch in the county that bears his name. He died in 1867. See *DAB*, vol. 5, pt. 2, pp. 327-28, and especially Fayette Copeland, *Kendall of the Picayune* (Norman, Okla., 1943). For Nebel, and generally the problem of illustrating the war, see the excellent book by Ronnie C. Tyler, *The Mexican War: A Lithographic Record*. The Kendall volume sold for the then phenomenal price of $38 to $40, with plates and text, suitable for framing, at $34.

July 29 ✦ General Worth has arrived here and assumed the command of the forces stationed here until the arrival of the commander-in-chief. . . . The general was aground in the river for two days, so that he arrived here in a mighty bad humor. He has for the present given the Seventh Infantry the command of the town. All the rest of the troops will move about two miles out to a general encampment. Matamoros is to be garrisoned by but two companies of regulars and a battalion of volunteers. Colonel Clarke has been appointed governor of the town.[1] He will have his hands full to keep it in order. We have now up here at present all of the Fifth, Seventh, and Eighth regiments of infantry and eight companies of artillery and two companies of mounted Texans, about eighteen hundred men, enough to whip any force of Mexicans which might have the daring to attack us here. . . .

There is quite a strong force of Comanches in the country somewhere on this side the Rio Grande. They have been committing depredations on the inhabitants, and they are all scared to death. . . . A company of Texan rangers was sent out from here the other day to look for those Comanches, and whilst the rascals were all asleep at night without a guard, the Indians stole forty of their finest horses. The best of the joke is that they were on their way back to report that there were no Indians to be found. . . .

General Taylor has full powers out here to try for life and death. We have already commenced a summary course with the citizens who have been following the army, selling liquor and so forth. As fast as they arrive here, very much to their astonishment they are seized by the guard of our regiment, their liquor destroyed, and themselves put on board the first conveyance for Matamoros. Our guard yesterday captured fifteen barrels of whiskey. The consequence is that we make this a pretty sober place, unlike

Matamoros, where every other house is a gambling house and liquor shop. . . .

I am glad indeed to see the superior and more dignified bearing of our troops. They appear to have a supreme contempt and disgust for the militia organization and discipline. Wait till we get them to Monterrey, then we will have them in a tight place. We hear that all of the Louisiana volunteers have been discharged and are being sent home, six regiments of them. I believe too it is a good riddance. I hear the Kentuckians and Tennesseans highly spoken of.

1. Newman S. Clarke served in the War of 1812 and became colonel of the Sixth Infantry in June 1846. He was brevetted brigadier general for the siege of Veracruz. He died in 1860 (Heitman, I, 307).

July 30 ✦ There is a great mortality here among the babies. Many of them have died since we have been here, and I believe it is whooping cough. They are always carried to the church dressed in all ridiculous ways and there they have a great mummery over them. I have been in to see several of them. They are always brought on a pillow and are covered with crosses and artificial flowers. The Catholic priests who are with our army here say that these people are perfect idolators, that they just go through ceremonies and forms without understanding the first principles of their religion. They are very different from the Catholics of our country. I expect the priest and their images are all the God they know.

August 1 ✦ My darling Sue, I wish I knew how you were off for money. You know that if I had the means I would send you plenty at all times. It would do my heart good to keep your purse running over all the time. I hope I may be able to do so one of these days. When once I get free of these troublesome debts I will not have to be so mean, will I? My expenses this last month have been heavier than usual: watermelon—$.20; hatband—$.25; servant—$1.50; postage—$.50; drinks—$1.15; board on steamboat to Reynosa—$3.00; mosquito bar—$2.50; peaches—$.50; candles—$.35; lemon syrup—$1.50; suspenders—$.50; mess bill—$14.45; washing—$2.50; total—$28.90.

August 2 ✦ I have been this morning to church to see the Mexicans celebrate high mass, and it was well worth while to go and see it. They have a great deal [of] mummery about it, but it is all very imposing upon these poor people, who are no better than idolators. A great many of our soldiers go and get down on their marrowbones with the Mexicans. This appears to please them very much. They have no pews or benches, but men, women, and all kneel and squat down on the brick pavement just as you have seen it represented in ancient pictures. The women do it very gracefully. They are all decked out in their best on a Sunday, and all classes go together and are mixed together on the floor, some in silks with mantillas which cost fifty dollars and others in homely attire, but all clean and tidy.

They all wear shoes and stockings when they go to church, and when they squat on the floor they are very careful you shall not see even their feet, but they will bathe before us in the river and show themselves perfectly naked to the waist and sometimes lower. They just strip off and think no more of showing their titties than they do their faces, entirely bare. They do not even put their hands over them. Some of them are beautiful indeed, hanging 'way down to their waists. They can all swim like ducks, but all the water and soap they use will not kill the "buggers" for them. We see the most disgusting and revolting sights every day of these people looking in each other's heads. They are taught it from their infancy up.

7

To Monterrey

August-September 1846

General Taylor Comes Up. The Louisville Legion. Quantity of Transportation Allowed Us. Our Women Go Home. Organization of the Army. We Cross the San Juan. The March Begins. Mismanagement by the Quartermaster. Arrival at Mier. The Story of the "Mier Prisoners." Punta Aguada. Cerralvo. Visit with General Worth. Difficulty of Finding Books to Read. Picket Guard. Sue's Arrival at Covington. Marin.

August 9 ✦ General Taylor came up yesterday with his staff. I have not seen him yet but understand that he intends to move in three weeks on to Monterrey. The volunteers, I believe, are coming up from below both by land and water, and we shall soon have a large force here. We shall probably move on to Monterrey with a force of eight thousand men in the first column, about half regulars and half volunteers. We don't know yet who will get there first, we or Paredes. . . .

The whole army is in fine health and spirits, that is, so far as the regulars are concerned. I do not know much about the volunteers, for there are none here, though I suppose a good many of them are sick and still more of them disgusted. We hear that an Ohio regiment is to be left to garrison Matamoros and an Indiana regiment to garrison Barita. I suppose there will be four broken-down volunteers for one regular.

August 17 ✦ It is a nice comfortable day, and everybody seems to be filled with life. It is easy to see by the bustle and noise that we are close on to marching day. Everything is being got in readiness, mules, wagons, pack saddles, baggage, shoes, and so forth. . . .

Some of the regiments look remarkably well, and among them the Louisville Legion. They wear uniforms and look far better than the Louisiana troops did. A number of these here have uniforms. . . .

And now, dear Sue, I will give you an idea of how much baggage we can carry by telling the quantity of transportation allowed to us. Every eight men have one pack mule, and every three officers ditto. These are to carry tents, poles, baggage, cooking utensils, and everything. So you can see we can carry scarcely anything. Our mess has purchased a pack horse to carry our messing things, for it is quite impossible for us to get along with one mule to carry everything. And the farther we go, the rougher will be our life. We will live like real soldiers on nothing but hard fare to eat, hard ground to walk on, only blankets to sleep on, and lots of watchfulness. It will be a fine life to make us hearty and strong. And by the time the war is at an end, we shall be a mighty rough-looking set of fellows, worse than those you saw at New Orleans Barracks.

We are all in fine health and in excellent spirits at the prospect of starting soon. For the sooner we commence the work, the sooner will it be finished. As yet though we can see no end ahead of us, and it is possible that we may conquer to the City of Mexico itself without bringing the war to an immediate termination. There is no telling, though I suppose that so soon as Mr. Polk gets a tight hold on California and New Mexico that he will propose terms of peace.

August 20 ✦ All our women go back from here as we cannot provide for them any longer. They are a great pest in the field anyhow. I believe the greatest part of them are going 'way through to New Orleans, and I hope we will not see any of them back again so long as we are campaigning.

By the way, I have not told you, I believe, that Colonel Smith (the late General Smith of the Louisiana volunteers who was appointed colonel of the mounted rifles by the president) is assigned by General Taylor to the command of the Second Brigade, and the whole of the regular infantry is now organized into two divisions, each composed of two brigades. The First and Second Infantry form the Fourth Brigade. General Twiggs commands the First Division of regulars, composed of the regiment of dragoons, Bragg's and Ridgely's batteries of light artillery, and the Third and Fourth brigades of infantry. General Worth commands the Second Division, composed of Taylor's and Duncan's batteries of light artillery and the First and Second brigades of infantry. I believe the volunteer force is not yet organized into brigades and divisions. The remnants of the Louisianians, a company of eighty men under Captain Blanchard, are allowed to serve in our brigade. They are all from that state who would consent to serve for twelve months.[1]

1. Braxton Bragg graduated from the Academy in 1837 and was a captain at this time. He resigned from the army in 1856. He enjoyed a notable career as a general in the Confederate army and died in 1876. See Grady McWhiney, *Braxton Bragg and Confederate*

Defeat (New York, 1969). Randolph Ridgely graduated in 1839 and was brevetted captain after Palo Alto and Resaca de la Palma (Cullum, I, 543-44). He died in an accident after the Battle of Monterrey; he was riding through the streets of the city when his horse stumbled and fell. George Taylor, a graduate in 1837, was brevetted major in 1845 and died in 1853 (ibid., I, 533). Albert G. Blanchard, a graduate in 1829, resigned in 1840 but was a captain of the Louisiana volunteers. He served in the Confederate army during the Civil War (ibid., I, 352).

August 21 ✦ Now, my own dearest Sue, I must finish this letter so as to be ready for work immediately after breakfast, for today we get rid of all our surplus stuff, and tomorrow we cross the river and encamp on the opposite side. We are about starting on our new campaign, and it is just one year today since our regiment sailed from New Orleans in the *Alabama* for St. Joseph's Island, one year in the field. Now I really hope that another year will not be spent in that manner. . . .

I am anxious, my own dear wife, to hear of your safe arrival in Kentucky before I leave here or at all events before I leave Cerralvo. I shall feel much easier when I know that you are safe among your friends with Kate and our little Mary. I hope, dear one, this is the last trip you will have to take upriver without me. Wouldn't it make us so happy if you and a nurse and little Mary and I could have an abundance of money and could spend a summer in travelling all over the country to all the summer places and all the great cities, to Niagara, White Mountains, West Point, Saratoga, and so forth? I hope, dear, before we get old I shall be able to show you some of those places. Our two trips downriver were both so happy that I know we would enjoy traveling by steam very much.

But Mexico is about the last place I want you to travel to. It is a mean, miserable, dirty, good-for-nothing place, at least so much of it as we have seen. When we used to look across the river at Matamoros before we captured it, we thought it was a mighty pretty place, but we were very much disappointed after we crossed over. Monterrey is said to be about double the size of Matamoros.

August 24 ✦ Here we are across the San Juan and all ready for our march towards Cerralvo. We crossed day before yesterday in the afternoon, and the probability is that we shall start very early tomorrow morning. Our march will probably last five days, and we are to halt a day's march this side of Cerralvo, where the First Brigade is with General Worth. I do not know the reason why we are to halt there unless wood and water are more convenient and abundant than at Cerralvo. General Twiggs, all the dragoons, and three batteries of artillery have come up by land since my last letter, together with a train of 150 wagons, and we hear that the Second Infantry has arrived at the mouth of the river. . . .

A quartermaster, Captain Sibley, has just ridden by and tells me that we march this evening.[1] So I suppose we will march until about ten o'clock tonight. This is the soldier's life, my dearest wife, a blanket, a piece of pork and a biscuit, and ready to move at any moment.

1. Ebenezer S. Sibley graduated in 1827 and served as a lieutenant colonel during the Civil War. He died in 1884 (Cullum, I, 307-8).

August 26   ✦   You can see that we are now on our march towards Cerralvo, and our first day's march has been far from an agreeable one. So far from it that we have been obliged to halt here for a day in order to reorganize our train and arrange our transportation differently. Our baggage train failed us entirely yesterday, owing to some mismanagement or other, probably on the part of the quartermaster's department. The brigade took up its line of march yesterday morning at three o'clock in order to get through with its day's march before the heat of the day came on. But owing to delays at starting we did not make twelve miles before nine o'clock when we arrived here, the day extremely hot, the sun well up and blazing, and our men suffering a good deal, and many of them ready to give out. So here we halted to spend the day and night and were in hopes that our baggage, which we left behind to start at daylight under escort of a company of dragoons, would come up in an hour or so after we halted. But no, it did not come, and we suffered somewhat from heat, there being a very great scarcity of shade and our tents being with the baggage.

Well, we waited all day in hopes the train would be up every moment and when the sun got low we stopped thinking about our tents for a shade, and thought we would be mighty glad if we could get our blankets to sleep on for the night. But even in this we were disappointed, and officers and men were obliged to make the best of it upon the naked ground. The confounded train did not get in until late at night, and none of us had any bedding. I fared better than some for Little had a horse blanket along, and on that he and myself stretched ourselves. And with the stars above us and ants stinging us all night, we made out to get a pretty good night's rest.

The consequence of all this is that we could not start this

morning but had to lie by here in order to make a different arrangement with the train. We will now take a wagon to every two companies and go on our own hook with our baggage along with us, and let the quartermaster go to the deuce with his train and take care of it the best way he can. . . .

Day before yesterday, my dearest wife, I saw a cousin of yours at Whiting's tent, James Prather. He is a private in the Louisville Legion. He says that soldiering is no fun, but he means to go through with what he has undertaken. He has plenty of spunk on the subject and appears to be quite a promising chap. He had just marched up with his regiment from Matamoros. He had to ride in a wagon the last two days of the march, having lost his shoes in a bog.

Mier, August 27 ✦ Here we are at Mier, my own beloved wife. When I left off writing to you yesterday at our last halting place it was because we were summoned to our soldier's dinner, and after that our company was detailed on guard. I tell you we do not fare so badly in the field as you might imagine. We get chickens, eggs, mutton, and milk at all our halting places, and with them, although we cannot find vegetables, we get along pretty well.

Our march of today was a pretty good one and as comfortable as any march could be at this season of the year. In fact the day is much more cool, fresh, and pleasant than any we have had for some time. We have got more into the high and hilly country and have a fine and invigorating breeze. But let me tell you, my dearest little wife, of our day's march. I know you will like to hear how your husband gets along day by day on his march of invasion.

Our reveille bugles and drums sounded this morning at one o'clock, and we were all ready for a start in half an hour. But the train and all did not get prepared for a start before half past two, when again stretched our columns and wagon train out on the sandy road, the dragoons in rear, and at it we went with a steady, regular pace to accomplish our day's march. I expect this company of Louisianians whom we have attached to our brigade never saw quite so much regularity before. They are a fine company, as well behaved so far and pretty nearly as precise and well disciplined as the regulars. Our old Sergeant Nugent is one of them.

Our first halt for the men to get water was after we had marched five miles. It was in a deep ravine where it was evident that in rainy seasons there must be quite a river. The sides of the ravine were perpendicular and about fifty feet high of hard clay, and the sight was quite grand and picturesque, not only in the scenery itself but our columns winding through the place. I wished that my dear little Sue could be with me to admire it.

Besides this place we passed other scenery which was quite pretty, the commencement of the hilly country. Our next halt was made at another ravine with water three feet deep in it. This was quite pretty. Here we saw a Mexican with a pretty girl in his lap on horseback crossing. Our horsemen all crossed the ford, but the infantry made a circuit of half a mile and were then able to cross on dry rock bottom. As we advanced, the country became more hilly and rolling and the roads more stony and harder on our wagons.

Well, after a tolerably good march at eight o'clock we came in sight of Mier, situated on top of a hill. As we rose over the brow of our hill, it seemed as if we could throw a stone at the town across the valley, but we found that it was not so, for it was a good two miles before we reached it. It looks very pretty as it is approached, and we could tell even at a distance that it was the nicest town we had yet seen in Mexico. Here we are encamped, right outside the town. There are some quite nice stone houses here, all nicely white-washed, two churches, and so forth. The town is built on the summit of a hill of rock, so that its streets are naturally paved. Two little streams meander through the town and empty into a large creek called the Alamo, which runs like a mountain torrent.

And indeed we shall before long see real mountain torrents, for we have now left the muddy Rio Grande and tomorrow's march will take us about fifteen miles interior from it. Mier is the place where the Texans and Mexicans fought their last battle in 1842. It lasted all day. The Texans fought in the houses of the plaza against two thousand Mexicans, many of whom were killed. At last the Texans, three hundred, surrendered and suffered a long and severe imprisonment. These were what are called the "Mier prisoners." Once they attempted their escape from their guard and partially succeeded, for which Santa Anna ordered them to be decimated, that is, every tenth man to be shot. To ascertain the victims a horrid lottery was got up. A bean for every man was placed in a hat, all but one-tenth the number white. Then the Texans were obliged to draw for and every man who got a black bean was shot. The man Walker whom the papers made so much ridiculous fiction about was one of these prisoners. We have many of them here among the Texans. They all swear vengeance against Ampudia, who was the general who captured them.[1]

The people here are whiter than in the other towns we have visited and much better looking.

1. One of the Mier prisoners, Samuel H. Walker had been a leader in the attempted breakout of the Texans that resulted in their decimation. He had joined General Taylor's army and to Dana's annoyance received a considerable newspaper accounting. Walker, however, was a fighter and had been one of the rangers who had contacted Major Brown during the siege before Palo Alto and Resaca de la Palma. He had informed Taylor that the major was able to hold out so that the general was then able to take his time returning from Point Isabel. Walker was killed by a Mexican lancer in 1847 while he was with General Scott's forces on the way to Mexico City. See David Lavender, *Climax at Buena Vista*, 67-68, 126-27.

August 28   ✦   Now my own darling little one, we are another day advanced on our march. We have now but one more march to make to our halting place, Punta Aguada, where we are ordered to remain till further orders. It is evident that General Taylor does not intend to let General Worth have the whole of his division so far away from headquarters for fear he might make a fool of himself like Harney.[1] Worth does not stand very high at the headquarters of this army. Punta Aguada is a village twelve miles from here and twelve miles this side of Cerralvo, where General Worth now is with the First Brigade.

Our march today, dear one, has been a very toilsome one. Our bugles called us up as usual at one o'clock, but after we started at half past two, some of our wagons got jammed in a crossroad, which delayed us an hour. Then when we had got well started again, one of our wagons upset and another broke down. This delayed us again, so that when the sun rose, we had got only two miles or perhaps three. So that our march of fourteen miles which we have come today had to be mostly performed under the heat of the sun. However, after a heap of toil, we are here in a nice piece of ground beside a beautiful torrent, a branch of the Alamo which rushes by us tremendously with pure water, the cleanest we have seen since I was in Missouri. It is very deep and rapid, and so soon as I finish writing I shall take a nice bath in it and put on a clean shirt.

I have three hickory shirts now. They are first-rate for marching in.

Today our road was all uphill and downhill, with rocky and stony roads, and the marching was really hard. A great deal of the road was red sandstone. But today we have had the first view of the great chain of the Sierra Madre. We can see them forty or fifty miles off, dark and blue, the peaks towering high up towards the skies and extending for many miles from northwest to southeast. It is a grand and beautiful sight. I wish my darling one could take a look, but I would not have her to come the way that I have come to see any sights.

We are all well. So far only four of us have marched on foot, Whiting, Gault, Clitz, and myself. All the rest of them ride, the shirks.

1. A second lieutenant beginning in 1818 and rising through the ranks to colonel in June 1846, William S. Harney became a brigadier general in 1858 and retired in 1863. He died in 1889 (Heitman, I, 502).

Punta Aguada, August 29 ✦ We arrived here this afternoon, my own dear wife, from our last halting place fourteen miles back. We had a toilsome march of it, and all felt pretty well worn out when we arrived. I for one was mighty glad to come to a halt, for my legs were well-nigh marched off. Here by orders we are to remain until we receive more. It will not be more than a week at the farthest. We received communications today from General Worth from Cerralvo, twelve miles in advance of us. Two days since he sent an express to General Taylor, requesting that we might join him. . . .

We are encamped, my beloved one, right on that same beautiful mountain stream which I told you of yesterday. After I had done writing to you, I went and took a bath, and it was certainly the most delightful one I ever had in my life. The water is clear, deep, and rapid and of most delightful temperature. I only wished that you were there with me that we might go in together and have such a fine time. I walked half a mile down the stream from the camp to a private spot where no one was near, and holding onto a limb of a tree, I laid there for some time in the current. Here I will be able to bathe in the stream every day.

September 1 ✦ Since we have been here, we have been at work all the time, clearing all the ground in the vicinity of our encampment, a large parade and so forth, and as soon as we can complete this work, we are to go to drilling again. This does well enough for volunteers and recruits, but for old soldiers it is utterly absurd for the short space of time for which we are to remain here. Whilst the men are marching they might be allowed to rest and lounge in the intervals of their tramps, but we have nothing to say and have only to obey orders.

I have found time today to have me a regular field bunk made out of four rough stakes and some bread barrel staves. On this bunk I have covered with about six inches of long grass on which my blankets are laid. It makes a very comfortable bed. At all events it raises me out of the dirt. It being very narrow, though, there is no room in it for rolling. I believe, however, that I keep pretty much in one position all the time I am asleep, and I have no doubt I could sleep very well on a rail.

There is another great comfort too, in my bed, as it serves to write upon. Still, my table is very low. My camp table I was obliged to throw away when we left Camargo, as well as my chairs, because we could not carry such useless things. My camp cot I cut the sacking out of to roll my blankets in. My trunk I left at Captain Crosman's office, and Mr. Jenkins' clerk, Binney, promised me that he could get it for me and keep it safe.

September 4   ✦   It is but twelve miles to Cerralvo, so that for this move we have but one day's march. When we arrive at Cerralvo we shall have the whole of the Second Division regulars there, about sixteen hundred men. I presume it will not be long now before the general himself will come on. He will probably wait at Camargo to see the First Brigade of volunteers started off, and then he will join us himself. It is impossible with our means of transportation to move a very large force at once on Monterrey until we get into a part of the country which can be made to subsist the army. We have mills along for grinding corn, and when we begin to find corn in abundance for horses and men, we can begin to get along with less transportation. Wherever we can find plenty of corn, we can subsist our troops on cornbread and beef and will not have to transport the immense amount of bread, pork, and forage which we are now obliged to carry. Even our horses and mules cannot be fed in the country we have been through, and we are obliged to carry along corn and oats for them in very large quantities. Here the corn is beginning to be found, and our quartermasters have succeeded in obtaining about one thousand bushels from the Mexicans at one dollar a bushel.

This is a strange kind of war which we are waging. All other nations whenever they are at war not only help themselves to whatever they want wherever anything is to be found but they lay every town under contribution as they pass. But we pay high for everything the enemy's people are willing to bring and protect the inhabitants not only against the annoyances of our men but against the Indians. The people of Mier actually asked for a force there to guard them against the Comanches, and a hundred men were sent up to look after them. All this does very well if Mexico chooses to come to terms, but if she does not do so soon, we ought to put the rigors of war upon them and spoil as we go, make the country support us, and every city and town contribute largely towards the support of the war. It would be a good thing if General Taylor could send home a few millions to our government.

Cerralvo, September 8 ✦ We had a very pleasant and easy march up here, my dearest wife, twelve miles and a half and the road very good. Day before yesterday at one o'clock we had our reveille, and at two we were on the road. When the day dawned, we had marched seven miles and a half without stopping, with a fine, bright moon to march by. Then we had a small mountain stream to cross, which detained us a little while, but at half past seven o'clock we had arrived here, and all hands felt fresh enough to go much farther if required.

I went to Dr. De Leon's tent and found him just going to breakfast, so I sat down with him and helped him to dispatch it, a couple of boiled eggs, some nice baked bread, some rabbit, and a cup of coffee.[1] We do not get butter at all now. The Mexicans do not know how to make it, and our sutlers find it impossible to follow us farther with anything but tobacco and absolute necessities. . . .

The air in this part of the country is pure, fresh, and bracing. This morning was quite cool, like the approach of fall weather. We must be much higher here than we were at Matamoros, and the climate in this mountainous district more nearly approaches that of our native land. If we are in the mountains in winter we shall have a cold time of it.

Cerralvo is quite a pretty town with a great many large and fine trees in it. The houses are all of stone, and the church has one of those three-story steeples which puts us in mind of our own churches at home. The people here are not so good-looking as many we have seen. A mountain torrent winds through the town, crossing the streets at many places and supplying abundance of pure water and delightful bathing. The town is very near the foot of those mountains I told you of. The chain is two or three miles from here, and it would appear that we could shoot a bullet to the tops of them from here. They are very rugged, irregular, and picturesque. This chain is the Sierra Alva and is a spur of the great chain of Sierra Madre. The last on a clear day can be seen in the distance some fifty miles off, their peaks and summits towering to the sky. That is the great Sierra Madre, at the foot of which is Monterrey. It appears almost incredible when we see those mountains so distinctly on a clear day that we shall have some days of toilsome marching to enable us to reach them. Mountains make distances very deceptive.

General Worth told me last night that our first two days' march from here would be very laborious, as torrents ran through the roads in rains and in some places large boulders lay in our way, at which we might have to unload our wagons and help them over. Last evening I went and spent an hour with General W. Very few pay him such long calls nowadays. I had only intended to make a call of five minutes or so, but we got to talking of old times when I was a little shaver, and time passed very pleasantly. I believe he does not lack much of being a little cracked. He is very much inclined to make a noise about nothing and a fuss out of trifles.

The farther we go now into the interior and the farther we get removed from our baggage, the more scarce becomes reading matter. We can take so little along with us that books are almost out of the question. I made out at Punta Aguada to get hold of the *Gambler's Wife*, which I have just finished, and now I doubt if I shall be able to find another book. In reading the *Gambler's Wife*, when reading on the character of the heroine I could not help often thinking of Orphy. But I do not give Orph credit for the same depth of feeling which Maud possessed. . . .[2]

I have just been warned, my dear wife, that our company is detailed for a picket guard tomorrow. We belong to a picket which is posted a mile and a half on the road to Monterrey. We go on tomorrow morning and are relieved again next morning. So I will finish my letter now and leave it go by the first opportunity, for on the picket I could not write, having nothing but the bare ground and the shade of a bush to live in. General Worth has several pickets out in different directions. General Taylor does not think it necessary to give so much attention to such matters, but General Worth always makes mountains out of molehills, and one would think now the enemy and old Ampudia himself was within a mile of us, ten thousand strong.

1. David C. De Leon became an assistant surgeon in 1838 and a major surgeon in 1856 and resigned in 1861 to go with the Confederacy. He died in 1872 (Heitman, I, 366).   2. Orphana Sanford was one of Sue's sisters, Elizabeth Caroline Grey's *The Gambler's Wife* (London, 1844) was a novel of two sisters, May and Maud Sutherland, the former a lily-of-

the-valley, the latter a rose. The former was affianced to a young man grievously injured in a jump during a hunt, and after his death married her distant cousin Arthur Balfour and lived happily ever after. Maud, however, possessed feelings that were too strong, "and those she loved she adored passionately; but her affections had been confined to her father, mother, and sister: as they never contradicted her, it was difficult to discriminate whether her love for them or her self-will would gain the victory, if set in opposition one with the other." In this description Dana apparently saw similarity to his sister-in-law. It was the fate of Maud Sutherland to marry Harry Percy, a marriage that never should have been—"the two beings who had broken down every boundary of faith, honour, gratitude, and affection to unite themselves with one another." The death of a newborn infant brought Maud to her senses, and she returned to her father's house to die. The gambling husband arrived back just in time, and thereafter gave his inheritance to the poor and sought solace in evangelical religion, which he preached to the residents of a distant place.

September 12 ✦ So you are all safely arrived at Covington at last. You don't know how glad I am to hear of it, for it seems an age since you started from Orleans Barracks, and it has appeared to me that you made mighty slow progress. I am glad you have arrived at your journey's end and glad to hear that you met with so pleasant and gratifying a reception among your friends. I did not think that your Aunt Harriet would give you so warm a welcome, but it is probable that she did not then know that I also had entered a suit against her husband. . . .

Our whole invading column is here now, with the exception of a regiment of Texas horse which will join us at Marín, halfway between here and Monterrey. We are more than six thousand strong, of which there are three thousand regulars. General Butler is here with his field division of two thousand volunteers.[1] We have eighteen pieces of cannon and a mortar, and when we are joined by all of our mounted forces, we shall have twelve hundred horse. Some part of the road between here and Monterrey is very bad, and the first two days' march from here to Marín will be especially toilsome, but all of the pioneers of the army left here this morning to put them in a good order for cannon and wagons. They will keep a day ahead as far as Marín. There are about a hundred pioneers in all, and they are covered by a squadron of dragoons and a company of Texans. They left here at daylight this morning and by this time are probably digging away at some part of the road. . . .

When we arrive at Monterrey the general will pursue a different policy with the people. The army must subsist on the country on account of our long lines of communication. We will pay for what we get, but the civil authorities will be compelled to furnish everything we want, or if they do not, we will take it and punish them in the bargain. We have already commenced on the corn. The bread is made of half cornmeal, half flour, and it is nice, I can tell you. The army grinds its own corn. We have mills along, and a dozen of them are kept going all the time. They grind about two thousand pounds a day here. We look upon it as a luxury, for we can now have whenever we want them: corn bread, hand bread, flour bread, mush, grits, or tortillas. Our mills are quite large, and we have enough to keep us supplied with bread when we can get corn, and that we can always find in this country, for if necessary we will take it away from the people, and if they starve they will know better than to war with us another time.

1. William Orlando Butler was born in Kentucky in 1791, served in the War of 1812, and practiced law until the outbreak of the Mexican War, when President Polk appointed him major general of volunteers and assigned him to General Taylor's command. For bravery at Monterrey he received a sword from Congress and another from his native state. He then joined the forces of General Scott and before the treaty of peace succeeded Scott in command of the army in Mexico. That same year the Democrats nominated him for vice president on a ticket with Lewis Cass of Michigan. Although he was a slaveholder, Butler opposed the extension of slavery. He sided with the Union in 1861, but he was too old to serve. He died in 1880 (*DAB*, vol. 2, pt. 1, pp. 371-72).

September 15   ✦   I had intended, my darling Sue, to have written you a few lines the day before we left Cerralvo, but we were all out on inspection, the whole division of sixteen hundred men, when the biggest kind of a storm came up, and not only ourselves but everything in our tents got wet, and as we started next morning at four o'clock I could not find a chance to write even a word. Well, when we halted yesterday it was pretty late, and our mule train with my valise did not come up till night, so that I could not write, of course. Today it was twelve o'clock when we halted, and I have just now got hold of my valise, and now retreat is beating so that my lines must be very few, but let them set the sweet little heart of my darling Sue at ease about her husband, knowing that he is in fine health and spirits.

Every mile I march, dear one, the less I think of the hardship, I am getting used to it. The enemy have been constantly reported in our front. A body of four thousand were at Marín, fifteen miles in front where we shall be tomorrow, but General Taylor sent us word that they have evacuated the place, and he is in all probability there now. He is a day in advance of us with the First Division, and General Butler a day in our rear with his division of two thousand volunteers, each occupying at night the ground the other leaves in the morning.

A mail has just arrived, but there is nothing for me. I don't know why.

After General Taylor encamped here last night, a small skirmish took place. Captain Graham was sent out with his company of seventy dragoons as a picket in advance. They came suddenly on a body of four hundred of the enemy's cavalry, delivered their fire on them, which the enemy returned, and then cleared the track for Marín. The cowardly rascals, whipped by one-sixth their numbers! Two Mexicans killed, two wounded. One American horse wounded.[1]

We are ten days' march (twenty-five miles) from Cerralvo and seventeen miles from Marín. We are to go through by a forced march to join the First Division tomorrow. We start in the morning at three.

1. Richard H. Graham, an Academy graduate of 1828, was a first lieutenant at this time (Cullum, I, 570). See below, letter of September 26, 1846.

Near Marín, September 17   ✦   I sent you a letter, a short one, from our last halting place fifteen miles back from here. I wrote it night before last and gave it to a reporter of the *Picayune* who is along, for if there happened to be a chance of getting a letter off, he would be sure to find it out in order to send his reports. Whether he got the letter on to Cerralvo or not I do not know. I understand that an express is to leave here this afternoon, and I will try and finish this in time to get it off.

We reached this place, dearest wife, about eleven o'clock yesterday. We left our last stopping place fifteen miles from here at four o'clock. We found General Taylor encamped with the First Division a mile and a half from the town on the Monterrey road on the banks of the San Juan, the same river we were on at Camargo. It is about thirty yards wide here and only knee-deep at present.

The scenery on our march yesterday was absolutely beautiful. We passed through the mountain pass of the Sierra Alva, and as soon as we got through it, the Sierra Madre looked upon us in all its grandeur. The view came suddenly on us just as the sun was rising, and the sight was so grand, so beautiful, that all exclaimed at once. The tops of the mountains actually appeared to reach the sky, and their sides of crags and rocks appeared to be right perpendicular. Their outline is very sharp, and every peak is sharp. They are more grand and picturesque than any mountains I have seen, and I have seen the highest ones in our country. Although these mountains are ten miles off, it appears as if we could throw a cannon shot into them, and we can see the steep and craggy rocks which form their sides as plainly as if they were within a stone's throw.

Tomorrow night the army will probably encamp in the gorge through which our route lays to Monterrey. It is right before us, and the opening of the pass is about five miles off. The pass through which we came yesterday was quite easy, but on either side of us, we wound our way along like a huge snake, was now a large high hill and now a deep, almost bottomless chasm. These are great places for defense, but our enemy are too much afraid of us to try it.

Soon after we came through the pass of the Sierra Alva, we arrived at a little village called Ramos, situated on the crystal waters of a pure and swift mountain torrent. It was a pretty, neat little place of about three hundred inhabitants but entirely deserted except but by one old man. This was the second deserted village we had passed through, and it looked right sad, I can assure you, and gave us a better idea than we had had for some time of the horrors of war. The Mexican troops have just been through this country and have driven all the inhabitants away before them. They oblige them to leave their homes and all they hold dear to keep them from trading with us and from seeing how well we treat them. All we saw in these two villages were a few half-starved dogs, chickens, and pigs. The enemy played the same game here, but General Taylor came so suddenly on them that they did not have time to finish their work, and about one-third of the inhabitants of Marín still remain here and are getting all their corn ready for sale to us. They are obliged to do this whether they want to or not. We make them bring their produce and pay them a fair price for it.

Marín is a very pretty town of three thousand, built entirely of stone, and it is built on a flat tableland with a stone base. The streets are entirely level and clean. It is situated just on the brow of this tableland, and from this down on this side is a steep descent in a very large, level plain which stretches to the foot of the mountains. Through this plain meanders the San Juan, and there we are encamped.

We are expecting General Butler's division every moment now, and we all understand that the army is to march for Monterrey tomorrow morning. The distance is only twenty-two miles and we will take two days at it. Ampudia is playing his same old game at Monterrey and is driving all the people out of the city. Isn't this hard, that thirteen thousand people in one city should be obliged to leave their homes and all their property to be taken hold of by strangers?

View of Marín and advance of the American army.

Well, my dear Sue, you can see that the four thousand troops who were said to be here were not found when we arrived, and the expected battle did not come off on this plain. And so it will be at Monterrey. The farther we march, the farther off does the battle get, and the smaller grow the Mexican forces. Distance always magnifies danger. When General Taylor arrived at the brow of the hill here, the column saw clouds of dust in the mountain pass ahead of us, and the inhabitants tell us that it was General Ampudia with a column of one thousand men and two cannon leaving for Monterrey in great haste. Last night, and the night before our advance, cavalry pickets and those of the enemy were within a half a mile from each other, they watching us with evident anxiety. . . .

But I hope that soon we shall be at peace and long, long for the happy day when I shall again hold my own sweet and beloved Sue to my fond heart. God grant, darling one, that the day may not be very distant. How different will be our feelings when treading our homeward way to what they are on our march of invasion. But we have many, many miles before us and many behind us. We are now 115 miles from Camargo and 100 miles from Saltillo, and if we receive orders to retrograde from Saltillo, we have 215 miles to march back to Camargo and from there 300 miles in steamboats to the mouth of the Rio Grande.

8

Monterrey Is Ours
September-October 1846

March en Masse from Marín. Arrival at Walnut Springs. Four Hills on the Saltillo Road. The City a Perfect Gibraltar. General Worth's Second Division Assigned to Take the Hills. Lancers Repulsed. We Take the First Hill. Then the Second. The Third. A Captured Nine-pounder and Our Howitzer Hurl Consternation into the Bishop's Palace. The Star-Spangled Banner Waves. Terrible Losses of First Division before the City. Second Division Enters. Hot Fight, House to House. Devastation Rains on the Plaza and Threatens the Cathedral. Ampudia Surrenders. General Taylor Gives an Eight-week Truce.

September 24 ✦ Monterrey is ours.

I can hardly describe to you with my pen what difficulties, dangers, and labors we have gone through to gain it. We have been fighting hard, hard for four days. The place is a second West Point in strength, and the Mexicans have defended it to the last, but we have fought them too hardly, and they were at last obliged to give in and capitulate. We have carried all their strong places by storm except two, and we have them now penned up in those with all our murderous weapons pointing them in the face. We have reduced them to such extremity that they are willing to agree to most any terms. Ampudia himself is frightened to death. The articles of capitulation have just been agreed upon. General Taylor allows their army to march out of the city with the honors of war, carrying with them their muskets, swords, personal baggage, and six pieces of light artillery. All the rest is surrendered to us. In our assaults we have taken from them large quantities of ammunition and thirteen pieces of cannon.

But our fighting has been bloody and hard. In the First Division, death was scattered with horrid freedom, but it is their last fight. They are ruined, and commissioners are treating for peace. So soon as I can get the first opportunity, I will tell you all. Now I am dirty, wearied, have nothing at hand, and have not had even a cloak to sleep in for several nights. Until you hear from me again, make yourself entirely easy, darling. The danger is all over.

Our killed and wounded cannot now be accurately estimated. Captains Lewis Morris, Barbour, Field, and Lieutenant Irwin,

Third Infantry, and Captain McKavett, Eighth Infantry, Colonel Watson of Baltimore volunteers, are among the slain. All are married. Captain Scott, First Infantry, also. Captain LaMotte is either killed or badly wounded, I don't know which. Major Lear and Lieutenant Richard Graham are mortally wounded. Many officers are wounded, among them Gatlin and Porter, neither of them very badly. I understand that General Butler is also wounded, as well as Major Mansfield and Captain Williams of the engineers, and so forth.[1]

But all is now well. Thank God for our favors. Be easy, dearest Sue, and until I can write again be perfectly easy.

1. Lewis N. Morris graduated from West Point in 1820 and was brevetted major for Palo Alto and Resaca de la Palma (Cullum, I, 204). Philip N. Barbour graduated in 1834 and was similarly brevetted (Rhoda van Bibber Tanner Doubleday, ed., *Journals of the late Brevet Major Philip Norbourne Barbour . . . and his wife, Martha Isabella Hopkins Barbour, written during the war with Mexico—1846* [New York, 1936]). The original of Barbour's journal is in the West Point archives. George P. Field, also a graduate of 1836, was lanced to death at Monterrey (Cullum, I, 453). Douglass S. Irwin, an 1840 graduate, was killed during the street fighting (ibid., I, 618). John M. Scott, an 1835 graduate, survived, was brevetted major, and died in 1850, (ibid., I, 483-84). Joseph H. LaMotte, an 1827 graduate, also survived, was brevetted, and resigned in 1856 (ibid., I, 319). William W. Lear was in the War of 1812, was commissioned second lieutenant in 1818, and became major in 1842 (Heitman, I, 621). Joseph K.F. Mansfield was brevetted lieutenant colonel for Monterrey and colonel for Buena Vista. A major general of volunteers in 1862, he was killed at Antietam (*DAB*, vol. 6, pt. 2, p. 257). Dana recalled Mansfield's gallantry during the siege of Fort Brown: "The first night after the cannonading of the Mexicans commenced on Fort Brown, a sortie was made from the fort to bury the dead and to burn some shelters which were within rifle range of the fort and had been occupied by the enemy, and in that sortie Captain Mansfield was the engineer officer accompanying it" (Undated typescript in Dana MSS). William G. Williams, graduate in 1824, was mortally wounded at Monterrey (Cullum, I, 262).

September 27 ✦ It seems an age since I was last able to sit down and have a good little talk with you, and since I wrote you from Marín how very much have we all gone through! How many labors, fatigues, privations, and dangers have we experienced! And alas, how many whose hearts were then beating high with hope and pride now fill a bloody grave. But with the favor of Heaven, I hope I have now seen my last battle. Peace must soon return to us, and God grant that we may never again have to lift our arms and point our swords against another people. . . . Fort Brown was not anything to what we found here, and Palo Alto and Resaca de la Palma hold not half the bloody graves which are filled by American soldiers in and around Monterrey. . . .

But, my darling wife, I must commence where I last wrote you

Monterrey. The volunteers approached the city between the citadel (in the center) and the forts on the left; the regulars under General Worth moved round to the right.

at Marín and tell you regularly, so far as I know, all that has happened. Our division since the fighting commenced has acted separately and independently from the rest of the army, so I know not exactly how the other divisions have been employed all the time. But with the exception of the first day (the day of their slaughter) I believe they have remained pretty quiet.

Our division has been actively engaged all the time. We have taken the city, and we now occupy it. The remainder of the army are encamped where we first stopped before the city, three miles from here. . . .

On the eighteenth of this month, dear Sue, at six o'clock in the morning, our army of six thousand men and eighteen pieces of cannon commenced its march "en masse" from Marín for this place. We marched that day twelve miles, passed through two very pretty villages, crossed several very beautiful mountain streams, and at night, after having chased away a squadron of the enemy's lancers, we encamped at San Francisco, twelve miles from here. We spent the night there very quietly, and at six o'clock on the nineteenth we started again for this place where we had begun to believe that Ampudia had seven thousand men. The scenery from Marín here is grand and beautiful. The nearer we came to this place, the more beautiful it is, and here it is absolutely superb.

In our line of march General Taylor was about two miles ahead of our division on the road, and after we had marched about five miles ahead we heard the report of heavy cannon in our front and at once concluded that the enemy had come out of Monterrey to meet us and General Taylor was engaged with the First Division. Our columns cheered. All were in fine spirits, and we pushed forward very fast to take part, as we thought, in the first battle before Monterrey. After we had gone ahead about three miles farther, we had orders to encamp in a place called Walnut Springs, where we found the First Division already encamped in front of the hostile city. Here we found out the cause of the artillery firing. As soon as General Taylor arrived at his camp, he and his staff under escort of dragoons and two companies of Texan rangers went out to reconnoiter the enemy's positions and the city which we were to attack. As soon as these reconnoitering parties got within reach of cannon shot, the enemy opened upon them from a very large fort in front of the town with four twelve-pounders. The very first shot struck within a few yards of General Taylor, but no one noticed the firing, and the reconnoitering parties kept out for about two hours and then returned.

These reconnaissances were conducted by Major Mansfield of the engineers and Captain Williams of the topographical corps. Both were indefatigable in this all-important and dangerous duty. They were out under fire all the time, and one night they kept out alone, creeping up in the dark to ascertain the most practical methods of forcing the enemy's positions with least loss. Poor fellows, one of them is now wounded, the other fills a soldier's grave.

That Mansfield is one of the most noble specimens of gallantry and heroism and chivalry I have ever met with. He is unacquainted with a feeling of fear and is persevering to death. After he was wounded, he tied a handkerchief round his leg and led the murderous charge on the enemy's works where the First and Third Divisions suffered so severely. (M. was our engineer at Fort Brown and was brevetted.)

Reconnoitering was kept up all the day of the nineteenth. The

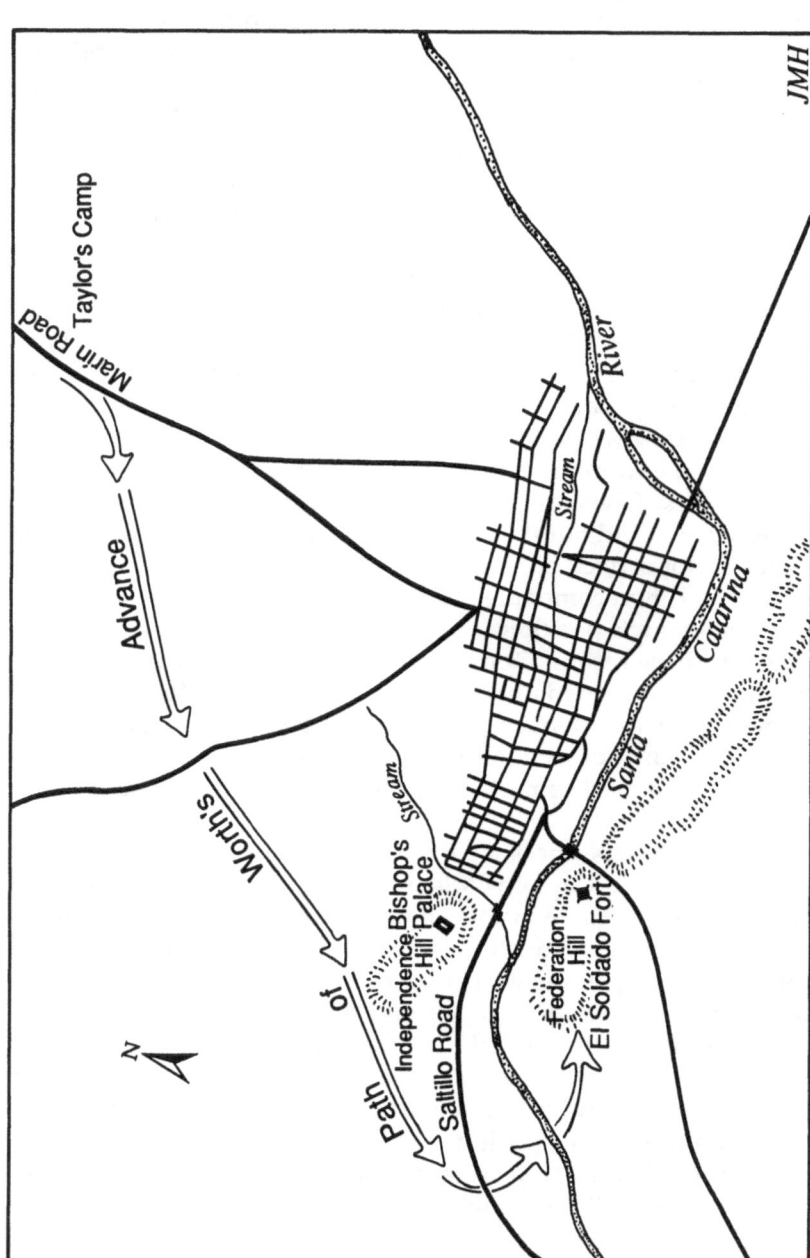

Battle of Monterrey, September 19-24, 1846

The Bishop's Palace, from a drawing by J.P. McCown.

enemy plied their heavy cannon, but they did no damage. At night we all went quietly to bed with the understanding that nothing was to be done until Monday morning, the twenty-first, when our division under General Worth was to storm the enemy's works.

I can hardly make you understand, dearest wife, the strength, the immense strength, of this place and how admirably and with what military judgment it had been fortified by the enemy. If we had been in it with one thousand men who were resolved to die at their posts, fifteen thousand could not possibly have captured it by assault. But we had six thousand men, and Ampudia had seven thousand regulars, two thousand citizens, and forty-one pieces of artillery. In front of the city there is a large permanent fortification with a citadel of great strength inside. This fort was built of hewn stone with deep ditches and formidable flanks, and it had in it fourteen pieces of heavy ordnance with a garrison of one thousand men. This work in itself was a perfect barrier to any enemy, but this was not all. It was supported by two redoubts of four guns each. This was the front of their city.

Now, in rear it looked still more formidable. Just behind the city on the Saltillo road are four very high hills, some of them commanding the road, others the city, one the big fort in front. On the top of the hill nearest to the town, in rear and commanding the city, stands the palace of the archbiship, a very large and strong building of stone. This they had fortified with great strength and had surrounded it with a stone fort mounting four pieces of cannon. This was garrisoned by a strong force and could be assisted from the city with several thousand men. This they considered one of their strongest holds. On the next hill in rear of this, with very high and steep sides, its pointed top commanding the palace and the Saltillo road, they had another force with two pieces of cannon, and on the two next high points in rear of these, they had also fortified themselves, with a heavy cannon on each. Here we could plainly see that the rearmost of these heights was the key to their whole position.

These four hills were their strong hope. On these they depended for the safety of their city. On these if they fought at all they would fight hard, for if these were taken, their retreat was cut off, and it would be madness for us to enter the city so long as these heights were in possession of the enemy. Here, then, we thought, must come off the grand struggle. Here was the post of honor and danger. These heights were to be successively stormed and carried by assault at the point of the bayonet before we could do anything with the city.

Who was to do this? Who were to pass round in rear of the enemy, cut off his retreat, oppose seven thousand men with two thousand, the former on the mountains, we in the valleys, and who were to undertake to assault in succession four such heights with steep sides and so strongly guarded? Our division, the Second, was a solid mass of regulars except one company of Louisianians; our commander, General Worth, was known to be a desperate man, and we thought it would be us.

Now, in addition to all these strongly fortified places for the protection of their city without, the city itself was a perfect Gibraltar. The whole city on the river side in rear was surrounded by a stone wall higher than the head, with ditches outside, and filled with loopholes for musketry and embrasures for cannon. The three plazas of the city were walled with loopholes and embrasures, and towards the center within six hundred yards of the plazas every street was crossed here and there by strong walls for musketry and cannon. In addition, every house was a small fort, for the tops are flat and walled above as high as the breast. When we look at the place, it appears hardly possible and scarcely credible that we could have driven any kind of an enemy out of it, so impregnable does it seem. But here they were, the poor miserable cowards, from nine thousand to twelve thousand of them, cooped up here in this strong place waiting quietly for a far inferior force in numbers to come and attack. But I understand that their confidence never wavered until we commenced beating them. They fully expected to repulse us this time, and so they would have done if they were half the men the American soldiers are.

Well, on Sunday morning the twentieth, we were all waiting at our camp at Walnut Springs till the dispositions for the offensive war on the following morning should be made known to the army. But all at once about two'clock the bugles of the Second Division sounded the assembly, and after we got under arms, we received our orders. They were for General Worth to take the division together with five hundred Texans, in all about two thousand men, to make a circuit of eight miles through the fields and hills in the right of the city, to strike the Saltillo road before daylight on the twenty-first, and after having cut off the enemy's retreat and secured our position in his rear, to do the work on that side of the city.

Here, then, we were really in for it. The work was ours. Everyone would hold his breath as he looked at the heights and saw the work before us, but it was to be done, and we all knew that if two thousand men could do it, we would suceed. At one o'clock we all bade our friends goodby and left the camp to commence our movement. We were all in good spirits, and the whole army which was left behind were strung along the road as we passed, looking with curiosity at what they considered the forlorn hope. The volunteers wanted to see how men looked who were marching out to battle. Poor fellows, little they thought that tomorrow's sun was to be the last for many of themselves.

We marched through cornfields and so forth for about six miles, making a circuit all the time and drawing nearer to the heights in rear of the city. About an hour before sunset, our advanced guard composed of mounted Texans had a skirmish with some advanced cavalry of the enemy, and after the skirmish a shell was thrown at them from the top of the hill in rear of the bishop's palace. But soon after this a very hard rain came on, and we were soon all wet through to the skin. It soon turned so dark that you could not see your hand before you, and the cold was keenly felt through wet clothes. We marched forward two miles farther, and there on the wet ground on a hillside with no cover, wet clothes, on a cold and cheerless night, no supplies, and as dark as pitch, we lay on our arms with nothing but our coats and not even able to take exercise to keep warm. On account of the near neighborhood of the enemy, we

Cavalry charge on the morning of September 21.

were halted as we had marched, in close columns, stacked arms, and were instructed not to leave our posts but to lie down, each man where he stood. That was the most cheerless, comfortless, unhappy night I ever spent. It was hard to inspire us with satisfaction for the certainty of battle on the morrow. The night, however, did not hurt any of us materially, although it was exceedingly disagreeable, and it was impossible for us to take that rest which was necessary to recruit and invigorate us for the fatigues which tomorrow was to bring forth.

At the earliest dawn on the morning of the twenty-first we were again in motion, an advanced guard of about 100 rangers ahead. We marched for a half an hour when we came within range of the guns on the heights in rear of the bishop's palace, and they commenced on us with both shot and shells. They fired on us until we began to get too far for much execution, and then they held up again. The shot and shells came very near, but all the damage done that time was one soldier of the Fifth Infantry lost his leg, one horse killed, and one of the wagons injured.

Scarcely had the hill ceased firing when we came suddenly on a regiment of the enemy's lancers formed in the road behind the point of a hill. Orders were immediately given to form line of battle in double-quick time, and whilst we were doing it, the enemy charged the rangers at a gallop. Four rangers were badly lanced and the splendid horses which the people of Louisiana sent. Walker was run through the neck. He will get over it, though. The Texans emptied several of their saddles for them, and by this time the Eighth Infantry had advanced upon the enemy as light infantry and Duncan's battery opened on them, and before the line of battle was fully formed they were put to flight, leaving their colonel and some twenty men dead.

We pursued rapidly, and after advancing a quarter of a mile, we were formed in line of battle, with two fronts where the Saltillo road joined the road we were on. Here we remained for a half an hour or so, thinking that this cavalry regiment was only the advanced guard and that the enemy would be out in force to fight us in order to keep secure its line of retreat. But soon a piece of heavy artillery commenced playing upon us from the rearmost height (now nearest to us), and the very first shot came right in our midst but hurt no one. We saw that that was no place for us, so after standing that close, shooting for near an hour, we drew off a little farther, just out of range, not, however, until Captain McKavett of the Eighth had been killed dead. A nine-pounder ball went right through his breast.[1] It is a dreadful feeling to stand off at long shot and be fired at by artillery without being able to do anything or to raise any excitement. One of these shot passed between the bayonets of the company next to me and struck in the road ten feet from me, but no one was hurt except those I tell you of.

After we had gotten out of reach of this last hill, which was the highest and most difficult of the four, we stacked arms in line of battle and laid ourselves down to eat and sleep and ready to catch the enemy should he come to make his retreat to Saltillo.

I forgot to say that the regiment of lancers which we had driven off in the morning never got back to Monterrey. We cut them off the city, and they were obliged to keep the road to Saltillo.

I was just getting into a doze after having made a lunch on hard bread and bologna sausage when the Seventh was called to arms. The order was that Captain Smith of the artillery battalion had gone by a circuitous route to storm the rearmost height with four hundred men.[2] We were to support him, and both together were to carry the hill by assault. The orders were to be cautious but to carry the hill. We did not take the same route as the artillery battalion but went straight towards the foot of the hill, through high corn. The enemy had not seen Captain Smith yet, but as soon as they perceived our movement, they commenced on us again from two cannon with round shot, but they overshot us, and we went ahead pretty fast for when we got near the base of the hill they could not use their cannon on us any longer. We had a very rapid river to ford, nearly waist-deep, and just as we got on the bank of this we were in full view of them, and they sent the grapeshot after us. How we got off I cannot tell, but no one was hit. The twigs fell about our ears like hickory nuts shaken from a tree.

We put into the river, and the depression being now too great for them to use their cannon any longer, the infantry rose, about five hundred of them, and poured in their lead as fast as they could send it. They were high up the side of a steep hill and we right under them in the water. Their bullets showered on us literally like hail. They struck the water all around us, between us, before and behind, everywhere. It appeared impossible that we could escape being shot. That was by all odds the hottest fire I have seen, and I have seen it pretty warm. Several men stumbled and fell in the water around me. I thought they were shot, but no, they got up again and laughed.

Our blood was now getting up, we were excited. We all hallooed and yelled, but I tell you we made tall tracks to get under cover of the rocks at the foot of the hill. It was every man for himself and devil take the hindmost, for we were to halt as soon as we got under cover and wait till we saw Captain Smith advancing up the hill. Well, we got under cover, and would you believe it? I hardly could. Not one man was hit in crossing that river. Providence certainly covered us with a shield.

We sat under cover to wait for Smith. We certainly had made a most excellent diversion in his favor, for the enemy had not yet seen him and were wholly taken up with us. It was hard, holding our fellows back. They wanted to go right up, but we were under orders, or we would have done so. We laid there for some time, waiting impatiently to hear of Captain S., but he from where he was hidden could see what we could not, that the troops on the hill had been reinforced by a column of one thousand men. He sent this word back to General Worth, and soon the Seventh Infantry came up with two hundred Texan rangers on foot with their rifles.

We raised a tremendous shot, and up the hill we went with a rush, the Texans ahead like devils. Terror soon found way to the hearts of the foe. On we came like an irresistible wave. Nothing could stop us, and the enemy saw that if they remained at their post, they would soon feel again the American steel. So their fire began to slacken more and more, and when we were about two-thirds the way up the hill, they were in rapid retreat to the next one. We took possession of their first height and found there a nine-pounder brass cannon.

When we were on top of the hill we saw right before us and a little lower than we their second height. There was a stone fort on it and the top of the hill was covered with large tents. They commenced playing upon us immediately with another nine-pounder from this place. We were flushed with victory. A tremendous shouting and yelling was raised and all cried out, "Forward!" The sight was too tempting, and we must have the second hill before sunset. Colonel Smith, who was in command, gave the order to charge, and on we rushed again like a torrent on the enemy.[3]

The effect was the same. We routed them from their fort. They fled like good fellows, scarcely stopping to look behind once, and left in our hands the two heights, two brass nines, and a very large amount of ammunition. We could see as soon as we obtained these positions that we had the key of their posts. We placed our colors on the hills and cheered like real Americans. The rest of the army could see it from beyond the city on the other side, and in the morning we had the congratulations of General Taylor, but the same letter brought us doleful tidings from the other part of the army. The sun went down with the guns from the bishop's palace playing on our hills. The Seventh was left to hold the places which had been carried, whilst the remainder of the division returned to General Worth. I was ordered to take a detail and serve the cannon on our hill against the palace, so I prepared all for the morning's work and spent another most rainy, chilly, and comfortless night.

1. The shot came out under his breast and carried all his vitals with it. Henry McKavett was an 1834 graduate of the Academy (Cullum, I, 455-56).   2. Charles F. Smith, an 1825 graduate, was brevetted colonel during the Mexican War and became a brigadier general in 1861 and major general the next year. He died that year (*DAB*, vol. 9, pt. 1, p. 247). General Sherman said of him that had he lived, General Grant would have "disappeared to history" (Cullum, I, 357).   3. Col. Persifor Smith.

September 29   ✦   I was obliged to stop short, my own darling wife, day before yesterday because my regiment was ordered to change position to the plaza. This is the very first chance I have had to touch a pen since, and an order has just come to me, saying that hereafter a mail will leave here every Tuesday. So as this is Tuesday afternoon, I must cut very short. Once a week now is all that we can send. Camargo is 140 miles from here. Mail goes by express. I fear I am telling you too long a story altogether, my own darling one, about the fighting. I will commence in my next where I left off and tell you the rest. We have taken from the enemy this time thirty-three cannon and an immense amount of ammunition. They are all gone now, and we are quiet again. I will tell you all in my next.

October 4 ✦ I believe I left off, dear Sue, at the night of the twenty-first, leaving the Seventh Infantry to garrison the two captured heights taken from the enemy through that cold and rainy night. I was ordered to take charge of the captured cannon and ammunition and use them to the best of my judgment. So I prepared everything to open a fire on the bishop's palace at daylight.

After spending a most comfortless night, rolling in the dirt alongside of Whiting, I got up about an hour before day, was at my gun and in readiness with match lighted to give them the morning gun so soon as it was light enough to be sure of our fire. But just as day began to show itself on the horizon, there arose on the side of the third and steepest height a yell such as can only come from the hearts of soldiers such as ours. Cheer succeeded cheer in perfect roars, yell succeeded yell, and these were followed by the heavy fire of musketry and the din of arms. These things certified to us that the balance of our division were taking advantage of the earliest dawn to storm the third height.

I immediately opened on the enemy with my cannon and kept up a fire as fast as we could load. The sides of that hill were very steep and the hill very high. The enemy tried to stand and repulse the assault. They had it hot and heavy for about a half an hour, but it was of no use. Our brave fellows intended to carry that hill, or they would cover it with American bodies. The sun of the twenty-second rose in a thick fog, and three out of the four strongly garrisoned hills of the enemy were ours, and our guns were ready to bear upon the bishop's palace, the last and most formidable of their strongholds on this side of the city.

They had fortified this with the greatest care, and their highest hopes appeared to have been placed in it. Its walls were two stories high and very thick and filled with musketry, and the stone fort at its base had three heavy cannon and a howitzer throwing heavy shells.

Still, we held the key to their whole position. We had attacked them where they had least expected us, and their fate appeared to be sealed in the storming of the third height. . . .

Well, here we stood, looking at the castle and thinking over the best method of taking it. Here was the deuce, the hardest tug of all. We knew that it was a strong place. We expected to experience a considerable loss in taking it. They could keep up a deadly fire on our advancing columns whilst between them and us were thick stone walls. It was concluded to assault, and our troops were formed under cover of the fog on top of the third height, down which to the bishop's palace was a gradual slope.

Twice did our brave soldiers advance to the assault, and twice were they obliged to retire from the terrible fire, finding no way of entering this strong position of the enemy. We saw that we must have recourse to artillery before we could render the castle practicable to assault. So a piece of our light artillery, a twelve-pound howitzer, was after a good deal of labor got up on the third height by Lieutenant Roland of Duncan's battery and was placed behind a small stone wall which they threw up there, and this piece and my nine-pounder were ordered to keep up a hot fire on the palace.[1]

The first shot I threw went right in among them inside their fort, and the effect of the howitzer was terrible. The two first shells it threw burst right in the fort, and the third burst in the very center of the castle. It was evident they could not stand this long, and we saw horsemen pass into the city, probably carrying messages, and not long afterwards we saw a regiment of cavalry advancing toward the third height. Our three regiments of infantry were in rear of the howitzer and sitting down behind the brow of the hill, so as to be covered from the fire of the guns from the palace, so that not more than two hundred men, deployed as skirmishers, could be seen by the enemy. So the regiment of lancers advanced bravely to charge the cannon, and the garrison at the same time made a sortie. This was just what we wanted, a perfect godsend for us. When the cavalry had advanced halfway up the hill and the infantry began to rattle their musketry, our twelve hundred fellows rose with a shout and rushed on to meet them, and you never saw such a surprised set of fellows in this world as were those lancers to see so many soldiers rise, as it were, out of the rocks. They checked their horses at once, looked. Our fellows rushed on and poured in their fire whilst I threw cannon shot among them. They turned their horses' tails and struck off like quarter racers for the city, leaving some twenty or thirty of their fellows on the ground.

Our men then took after the infantry. The long legs were the best. The Texans were invaluable and brave as lions. They pursued so hotly that they entered pell-mell with the enemy into the palace

Storming of the Bishop's Palace. Amon Carter Museum, Fort Worth.

before they could close their doors on the position for defense. The Mexican tricolored flag was hauled down, and soon the Star-Spangled Banner waved over that dauntless band who had carried a fort and castle which ought to have held out against double our numbers.

The sun of the twenty-second set clear, and the guns from our height and the bishop's palace, which had before been used against us, were played with fatal effect upon the doomed city. Thus far we had met with most brilliant success in our division. Not one effort had failed, and what was best of all, we had met with but little loss compared with the service rendered.

Not so with the other part of the army. It had stormed three of the enemy's batteries in front of the city and had met with that terrible loss, three hundred or four hundred men killed and wounded. True, they succeeded in the end in carrying the work, but the enemy had so many fire on them afterwards that they were ordered to retire, and they remained pretty much inactive during the remainder of the affair.

So it appeared that the Second Division had in reality done all

Street fighting on General Worth's side.

that had been done, and it still appeared to remain with it to take the city. Well, on the morning of the twenty-third, after having driven the enemy from their nearest barriers and cleared about one-third of the upper part of the city by means of the cannon on the hills, General Worth gave orders for the whole division to prepare to enter the city and take with us our light batteries and a ten-inch mortar which General Taylor had sent round for us to use. After getting all in readiness and having first sent in some light troops, we entered by a half a dozen different streets, and driving the enemy gradually before us, we pushed about two o'clock to near the center of the city, and here we were brought to a stand for fighting. For the tops of the houses were filled with Mexicans and they poured their bullets like hail upon us in the streets. In one place three men of our company were wounded (one of them mortally) in less time than you could count three. We had nothing to do but fight them their own way. So after constructing ladders we left our artillery and a strong force to keep the streets whilst we took to the tops of the houses. This is the time when Gatlin was wounded by a musket ball through the arm.

The enemy fought very obstinately here, and we had to fight them by inches and advance upon them from house to house. They fired with great accuracy, too, and wherever they saw a man they threw their bullets thick and very close. Do you remember Ficker-son, who was at Fort Pike? He rose once and was just taking aim when he was shot right in the eye. It killed him instantly. He never stirred.

Our Texan riflemen told well upon the enemy, and by night we had advanced to within a musket shot of the cathedral. This was their great center. Here they appeared to have determined to make their last expiring struggle. This was the very citadel of all their positions. It was the main plaza of the city, and they had barricaded and fortified it most strongly, and we had got them pretty well penned up to this and their large fort in front of the city. They were nearly whittled to a point. We had advanced upon them step by step, and now we appeared to have them nearly within reach and would crush them at once. Soon after dark our mortar began to fire and threw these very large shells, each weighing over a hundred pounds, all night. The shells all burst beautifully right in the plaza, scattering death and devastation on all sides and making them tremble lest one should go into the cathedral where they had all their powder and blow them all sky-high.

All this was more than they had bargained for and more than old Ampudia, coward as he is, could stand, and the morning of the twenty-fourth brought us a white flag with a letter from General Ampudia to General Taylor saying that, having done all he could to protect his people, the liar, and maintain himself in his positions, that he, having failed, proposed to capitulate on condition that he should march out with all the "materiel and personnel" of his army. This General Taylor flatly refused and ordered him to lay down his arms and surrender his army as prisoners of war. This was refused on the part of General Ampudia, but it would not have been refused long if General T. had insisted. But what did we want of all those contemptible rascals to take care of, and how would we have fed them? It was better to let them go, more especially as we thought it more than probable that terms of peace were about being negotiated between the two countries and it was but following up the generous and forbearing policy of our government.

So General Taylor offered them these considerations, gave them an hour to think of it, and if they did not return a favorable answer in that time, he would again break loose on them in the fix in which he had them. He would allow them to march out to Saltillo with their muskets, swords, private baggage, and six pieces of artillery, that they should surrender to him all their forts, the city, and all public property, that he would grant them a truce for eight weeks, that they should draw a line through a mountain pass thirty miles in our front, Linares, and San Fernandez on the Gulf, and cede to us all the immense tract of country on this side of that line, that they should not pass over that line during the cessation of arms, and all prisoners to be given up.

Ampudia, seeing that there was no getting off, was glad enough to accept these terms, and the articles of capitulation were signed. And we had the satisfaction of seeing double our numbers of Mexican troops defile before us in disgraceful retreat, giving up strongholds which one thousand of our men would have held against the whole of them. They left in our hands an immense amount of public property, thirty-three cannons, a quantity of ammunition of all kinds which we had no idea they possessed, very much more than we ourselves have in the country, commissary stores of all kinds, clothing, arms, and in fact everything.

1. John F. Roland, an 1836 graduate of the Academy, attained the rank of captain in 1847 and died in 1852 (Cullum, I, 503-4). James Duncan, an 1834 graduate, was captain at this time, was brevetted colonel for Monterrey, and died in 1849 (ibid., I, 446-47).

9

Life in Monterrey
October-December 1846

The City is Full of Oranges and Limes. My Quarters. Texan Volunteers Commit Dreadful Outrages. Father Rey, Our Catholic Priest, Holds Forth in the Cathedral. The Convent. Naked Women of Camargo and Reynosa. Whiting at Work on a Painting. A Spree for the Regiment. Big Bunged Eye. Organist Plays Waltzes in the Cathedral. Whiting Does More Pictures. Mexicans Refuse to Sell to Our Train. Desertions. Rascals of the Louisville Legion. A Hellish Outrage. Row in an Eating House. A Guard Takes a Long Shot and Brings Down a Prisoner. Farewell to Don Manuel. Packing.

October 5 ✦ I am on guard today, my dearest wife, and in what time I am unemployed by my duties I will pick up snatches and employ them in talking to you.

First, let me tell you how I am living just now. The day after the articles of capitulation were signed, General Worth's division went into quarters in the city. The Fifth and Seventh Regiments took possession of two large, fine houses belonging to rich people who had probably gone into the country to wait till the fighting was over. But all the officers of our regiment lived in one very large room. It was fully capacious enough but was not so very agreeable, living all together. There was a library there, two cupboards filled with china, decanters, and so forth, a lady's workbox, some artificial flowers made of hair, and a good many things which showed that wealthy people [lived] there. The yard was filled with oranges and limes. In the evening some three or four of us got out a decanter, china bowls, tumbler, sugar dish, and so forth, and made some fine punch, for which we were much obliged to the hospitable owners of the house.

Oranges were very abundant, and some eat now I suppose eight or ten a day. The city is full of them, and all of our people help themselves whenever they want them. One of Whiting's sergeants brought him a couple of hundred the other day from General Arista's garden. They sell them here four for five cents.

Our regiment only stayed two days in this house when we were ordered to take possession of the main plaza of the city, so soon as it was entirely evacuated by the Mexican troops. We marched up on the afternoon of the twenty-seventh and slept all night in the street, or, more romantically speaking, we bivouacked for the night.

On the morning of the twenty-eighth, the last division of the Mexican army filed past us, and the city was cleared of them. We then set to work to select quarters for officers and men. We took possession of two sides of the plaza, and I had a room in the second story of a house all to myself. Gault, McLaws, Gardner, and Clitz lived on the same floor.[1]

Out of my room a door opened on a small porch. In my room I found a table, several straw-bottomed chairs, a wardrobe, and cot, and I was quite comfortable, but I was destined to another move. My company was not comfortably quartered, and the council chamber of this state (Nuevo Leon) was taken for it. It is a very large and handsome room with large pictures in it, tables, chairs, and so forth. Under this were two very nice rooms, quite private, and in cold weather could be far more comfortable than the room I had. Little and myself were told that we might take these rooms.

They were owned and occupied by one of the aristocracy of the country, one Don Manuel Somebody. He was a very rich bachelor. He temporized with me for two days, promising to move, when at last I got out of patience, thinking there was but little chance of his going, and I took a wagon and six men to his house, told him to show me his baggage and I would load it for him and have it carried wherever he should designate. All he said was "Mil gracias," for he knew he had to go then, and I moved over.

On the floor of the council chamber was the only carpet I have seen in Mexico. The men took it up, and I have had it put down in my room. I have now a nice little square room with three doors, two opening on two different streets and the third into Little's quarters. It is nicely carpeted. I have a table with a drawer in it, three large mahogany armchairs, and a cot, besides a washstand. Am I not quite comfortably fixed? I hope I am settled now for some time, unless we take the road homewards.

As I sit in my room now and hear our wagons rattle by on the paved streets (which, by the way, are much better paved than many of our cities), I can imagine myself in New Orleans or New York again. Were it not for the old-style fabrication of the Mexican house and the great, great void in my heart owing to the absence of my beloved one, the delusion would sometimes be almost complete. How happily, I have thought, how more than happily could we live, my dearest one, even in this little room so far from our friends and our native land. God grant that we may 'ere long meet somewhere, better away out here than be separated longer by a cruel and almost useless war.

All the best houses belong to the wealthiest citizens of the place [and] are taken for the uses of the army. Some are filled with mirrors and [illegible]. Occupied or nor, if one is wanted, the alcalde is called upon to have it vacated immediately. General Worth, General Butler, General Smith, all have fine houses. Arista had just finished for himself here a perfect palace. The grounds in rear are most beautiful, such as you may have seen in pictures of Italian gardens in older times, filled with vases, images, streams, baths, oranges, lemons, limes, flowers, and so forth. This we have made a hospital of. I suppose we have in use at least a hundred private houses in the city.

Our division alone is in the city. The other two are still at the camp at Walnut Springs. Some of the Texan volunteers are quartered in the city. They have committed some dreadful outrages since the capitulation. In one night they killed seven Mexicans because one of their comrades had been killed in a row. This afternoon an old Mexican soldier, a lancer who had been left behind to wait on a cavalry officer, was following this officer, both mounted and in uniform, on their road to Saltillo, when one of these lawless scoundrels shot the harmless old fellow dead in the street. General Worth is searching high and low for the offender. It is one of the most barbarous, cold-blooded murders I have ever heard of. The man who would do such a thing is a second Cain. It will tend to excite the Mexican soldiery to acts of cruelty when they can get a chance. They will understand though the difference between troops of the line, as they call us, and volunteers. . . .

So you had a dispute with your uncle about my looking at the naked girls at Camargo.[2] Everybody looked at them, dearest one, and no one could go to the river without seeing them. If men were in swimming, the women would not mind it but would come right in too. They think nothing of such things, but I would look at them as I would look at so many wild beasts, orangutans, for they had no more beauty. And as to kissing them, one look was almost enough sometimes to turn one's stomach. These are only the lower classes who are so public. They are quite dark and most excellently ugly. Did you tell your uncle, dear Sue, that your legs, titties, and so forth were the only ones I liked to look at closely? I would get a spy-glass for them but not for others. He is teasing you, but it is something new for you to talk to gentlemen about such things. Weren't you ashamed? Tell your uncle from me that I do not want your young and guileless heart to be all undeceived in relation to this wicked world.

1. Franklin Gardner, an 1843 graduate of West Point, was a first lieutenant at this time. He joined the Confederate army in 1861 and died in 1873 (Cullum, II, 83-84).   2. Sue was staying with her Uncle Alex and Aunt Lucy in a large house on a farm near Covington.

October 12 ✦ Our Catholic priest holds forth here in the cathedral every morning and preaches a sermon every Sunday, that is, the last two. I have been to hear him both times. His name is Father Rey. That is the way his name sounds, if it isn't the way it is spelled. He is a French Jesuit, but I believe he is a very good man.[1]

The cathedral is a very large and beautiful building. The front is most elaborately ornamented with sculpture. There is a steeple on each front corner, in one of which is a large clock or dial which strikes the quarter hours. In the other steeple are hung nine large bells, enough to wake the dead in the vaults below. Inside the church is very rich. The whole is a collection of massive pillars surmounted by a series of groined arches. There are seven altars with as many images, crucifixes, pictures, and so forth. Three of the altars are surmounted to the heights of twenty or thirty feet with gilded carving. There are four pulpits and a fine organ, but since we have been here there has been no one to play on the organ. The floor is divided into panels which can be taken up. Each panel is the size of a grave, and they say that they take these panels up and bury their dead underneath. This is the place where the enemy had the principal part of their ammunition stowed.

Just opposite to my quarters is a convent.[2] Here are five more bells. The inside of the chapel of this convent is the most chaste and pretty church I have seen in Mexico. It is really a pretty little place. It has five altars, many fine pictures, and other ornaments. In the main altar is a full-length carving of the Savior standing, bearing his cross. Images of the Virgin are abundant everywhere. There is a large bridge in town, in the center of which is a large image of the Virgin. At her feet is a lantern burning every night. The courtyard of this convent is surrounded by a gallery, and this gallery is hung round with many large-sized pictures, very old, and some of them very fine ones, principally portraits of saints and monks, full-length. There are several very old priests in this convent. The old prior looks as if he had been used to mighty good living during his life, to judge from the size of his paunch and jowls. . . .

Has your uncle been plaguing you about the Mexican women yet? I expect you took it all in sober earnest. Certainly, dear one, you are the very first one I would come to tell of it if I looked at naked women, and if I thought you would have cared a straw, I would not have noticed one. I never looked any more than I would have done if I had been walking with you. You know, dearest, how I do those things. Many women used to go bathing in the river before and among the men, and many went down especially to look at them. Among others that beast Hopson used to spend half the day at the river bank. I saw but few in passing and never saw one naked lower than the waist. And every one I saw was truly disgusting, almost sickening. They were the low people, very dark and exceedingly ugly. I have heard talking of pretty girls, but they are mighty scarce in Mexico and none in Camargo. I would see one of these women naked with just the same feeling that I would see an orangutan. To one who is desirous of seeing naked beauty, those sights would not repay the trouble of lifting the eyes. I have heard it said that they sometimes went in entirely naked, though I never saw it. I have seen them swim, though, in crowds, like so many ducks.

I would never look at a woman's ankles, dearest Sue, if I thought you would object. I told you this, you know, at Matamoros, but I know you would not. Tell me, dearest, what you think.

There were two very pretty women at church last Sunday, right fair and white. They were evidently not Mexicans but Castilian ladies. Everybody was looking at them, but I just gave them a passing glance. If there is anything I hate, it is this rudeness of staring at ladies, for I do think it excessively rude, and some can do it most brazenly.

Those sights of naked women have not been seen, I believe, since we left Camargo. At least I have heard nothing of it. There appear to be very few women here. I believe the greater portion of the female population left the city before the fighting commenced and have not since returned. Poor Terrett, he was a man of a troublesome degree of modesty, and at Reynosa whilst he was in bathing once a couple of women came down and sat on the bank close to him, looking at him with perfect innocence. He was in a great quandary how to get out, and they kept the poor fellow in a long time. At last they stripped right off and went in alongside of him. Terrett left the place in perfect disgust and towering indignation, swearing that Mexican women were no better than beasts nor half so modest and that he would never go near the river agan by daylight whilst he was in Mexico.[3]

Captain Backus tells a story: whilst he was riding near the river at Reynosa one day, a woman came up to him out of the water, perfectly stark naked, stood and talked with him and had not even the decency to put her hand before *it*. I don't know what Terrett, poor fellow, would have done in that case. I expect he would have made tall tracks! I think I should have hauled out pencil and paper to take a sketch, though perhaps a Mexican female would object to having her affairs put on paper.

1. President Polk feared the Mexicans might wage a religious war and consulted three American Catholic bishops, who turned the problem over to the head of Georgetown College, with the resultant appointment as civilian chaplains of Fathers John McElroy and Antony Rey. The two Jesuits accompanied Taylor to Monterrey. Father Rey left the city early in 1847 for Matamoros, but bandits murdered him near Marín (K. Jack Bauer, *The Mexican War*, 85).   2. This was the Convent of San Francisco.   3. John Chapman Terrett, a second lieutenant in 1839, became first lieutenant in June 1846 and was killed at Monterrey (Heitman, I, 951).

October 13   ✦   I have been occupied, my own dearest wife, with the proceedings of a court-martial this morning, so that I only have time to finish this for the mail. Poor Dick Graham of the Fourth died of his wounds last night. Major Lear is still doing well. A bullet passed in at his mouth, crushed the bones of his face, and came out at the ear.

October 18   ✦   I have just come in from the cathedral where I have been listening to a sermon preached by our priest. He appears to be a very good man indeed and gave it to the men hard today about drinking and excesses. There has not been as much drunkenness and rioting here as at Matamoros, but still several murders have been committed on both sides, mostly by Texans. Last week, too, one of the men of my company was run through by one of the sergeants whilst he was taking him to the guardhouse, and the man died next day. . . .

Our volunteers are crabbing off in great numbers. All who can lay hold of any excuse call for discharge, some because they are not of age. Some big, stout, robust lubbers are discharged for disability. They find war is not as funny as they thought. . . .

Whiting has commenced a painting of the scenery here. It will probably make a very beautiful picture when it is finished. The view is taken from the top of a house in the plaza and looking towards the hills which were stormed by our division.

There are few places which nature has made more beautiful than this, situated as it is just at the entrance of the principal pass through the Sierra Madre. In the background and apparently very near are these stony mountains with their sharp and ragged peaks strongly relieved against the sky and their steep sides presenting nothing but steep precipices of crags and rock uncovered by any kind of growth. The nearer hills are less grand and more beautiful, sloping gently and covered with a small growth which is now green and which I rather think preserves its greenness throughout the year. If I could only take views from nature, how glad I would be to go to the top of some of these hills and draw and paint for my own darling Sue. . . .

October 19   ✦   I hope for the best and try to think that my dear Sue is well and contented among her friends. And you must now be at Louisville, I think, but I am afraid to send my letters there for fear that before they reach you, you may be at Covington again. If I only knew to whose care to direct, I would send this to Louisville. But I have no doubt it will go safely by way of Covington, though it may take a little longer.

October 20   ✦   For the last three days I had been rather low spirited and unsettled, and yesterday, feeling a little desperate, I suddenly came to the conclusion to work off the blues by giving a spree to the regiment. It cost me $3.50. Wasn't I foolish? It was so, but we had a right jolly, pleasant time. Your health was frequently drunk and our dear little Mary's. They all said that I gave the blowout because I did not hear from you, and Van Dorn and Ross said they would write you about it.[1] The spree came off at tattoo. The night was cold, and the drink was brandy punch, boiling hot and plenty of it.

1. Earl Van Dorn, an 1842 graduate of the Academy and a second lieutenant in 1846, was brevetted captain after Cerro Gordo, became a major in 1860, and the next year joined the Confederate army, in which he served as a major general. A personal enemy shot and killed him in 1863 (*DAB*, vol. 10, pt. 1, pp. 185-86).

October 26   ✦   I had intended to have commenced this letter yesterday after church, but yesterday morning I got up with a big bunged eye. I had taken cold in some way or other in my right, and it was entirely closed. Today it is almost as bad but it is a little open. I am almost ashamed to walk the streets with it, for fear people will give me credit for having been to an Irish wedding. Yesterday in church General Worth looked very closely in my face as if to

Monterrey, from a housetop in the main plaza. Lithograph after Daniel P. Whiting.

Monterrey, from Independence Hill behind the Bishop's Palace.
Lithograph after Daniel P. Whiting.

inquire how that was done, but I looked quite as saucily back again. . . .

But alas, my dear wife, I fear that the Mexican señoras and señoritas were far from being impressed favorably with the comely appearance of your "cara esposo" (does that mean better half?).[1] I combed my hair over my eye and tried to look my prettiest, put the most heart-reaching effect into the glances of my good eye, but alas, the old bunged eye would stick out, and the pretty girls would look at me as much as to say, "You evidently have a much higher idea of your good looks than anyone else." Poor things, they little thought that I had a daguerreotype in my pocket which was prettier than anything they could show, and that I wouldn't give a copper for the favors of the prettiest mixture of Indian, Negro, and Castilian which Mexico can produce.

1. It means "dear husband."

November 1 ✦ Whiting has finished his picture, and it is a very beautiful one. It is the first one of a series which he intends painting for publication. He will send it back by Captain LaMotte on its way to the engraver at Washington. I have no doubt that W. will succeed admirably well in this undertaking, and I feel very sure that he will make himself quite independent. I believe he will realize ten thousand dollars if he carries the thing out. How happy I could be if I had such a chance. Then indeed I should feel very sure of leaving the service before long. General Worth has excused Whiting from all duty to enable him to take these views and has authorized him to take a public horse to go out in the hills with. The view is taken from the top of a house in the main plaza and looking toward the bishop's palace. His next will be from the first captured redoubt, looking at the bishop's palace and repeating the battle scene when it was taken. It must be that this series of pictures will sell admirably well and Mr. W. will undoubtedly realize a large sum from them.

November 8 ✦ I received two more letters from you, my darling one, by last night's mail as late as October 2, and one of them has pained me not a little. I have not been able to drive it from my mind, and I have felt about it as I have no doubt you feel sometimes when you have a good cry. But I trust it was merely a passing thought with you. Still, it appears to trouble you, and you ask me with apparent earnest to tell you if I have kissed any of these women, and say you feel sure that I would do no worse. But "have I done that"? Can you, my darling Sue, is it possible for you to make yourself for one instant believe that I have done or indeed would do such a thing? . . . Did you mean what you wrote? Have you forgotten what you wrote? I will enclose the letter back in this in order that you may review it. . . . About the native women bathing, my dear Sue, all who expose themselves so are of the lower order, and I have never seen one stripped lower than the waist, and then the sight was truly disgusting, a pair of long, flabby, sickening-looking bags of skin hanging down to their waists. If I have written to you about beautiful bosoms it was all in jest, only to tease you.

November 9   ✦   Whiting is still hard at work at his drawing. He has been out for five days, sketching among the hills. Three days I went with him to keep him company.

November 15   ✦   I have just returned from church, not Father Rey's church but from the mass of the Mexican priests. The organ was in operation again today and the organist plays delightfully. He is one of the best I have ever heard and a Mexican at that. He played during the service a couple of very lively waltzes, I should think very difficult to execute on the organ, but he played them without a fault.

November 16   ✦   Whiting has progressed a good way with another picture, which will be a very beautiful one. The view is taken from where our column stood in the road under the cannonade of the two hills where Captain McKavett was killed. The column will be represented in the picture and will of course make it more interesting. . . .

Did Mrs. Lee write to you that Julia Clark was married at last? She wrote to Mrs. Holmes that the girl had married a Mr. Ord, brother to Lieutenant Ord, Third Artillery.[1] He has got a heap of wife, if that is all he wanted. I should be afraid he would get smothered one of these warm nights. What a taste his must be!

1. Edward O.C. Ord, whose brother married Julia Clark, enjoyed an illustrious military career (*DAB*, vol. 7, pt. 2, pp. 48-49).

Heights of Monterrey, from the Saltillo road. Lithograph after Daniel P. Whiting.

Valley toward Saltillo, from Monterrey. Lithograph after Daniel P. Whiting.

November 23 ✦ Yesterday afternoon, dearest Sue, General Worth's empty train returned from Saltillo, bringing us information of the state of things in that quarter. The people were quite hostile in their feeling and would not furnish corn for our horses and mules at any price. Confound them, now it ought to be taken for nothing, and they ought to be made to pay a heavy military contribution in the bargain to help support our army in other ways. It is a very erroneous idea and one ruinous to us to spend so much money among these people. We ought to make them feel the weight and bear the burden of the war. . . . General Taylor himself returned from Saltillo this morning as fresh as when he started. . . . The general captured about 350 barrels of flour at Saltillo . . .

November 29 ✦ By last night's mail I received at last three letters from you, and I assure [you] they did me a heap of good and cheered my heart not a little. Three weeks had elapsed since I had heard from you, and I was becoming very impatient and anxious to get more letters. I knew well that you would be suffering much about the time the rumors of battles were reaching you, and I longed to hear of the receipt of my little letter which I hastily wrote in the midst of confusion on the afternoon of the capitulation. I bought that sheet of paper from an old Mexican woman, gave her a bit for it, and got her to lend me a little ink and an old stump and wrote that little scrawl on her window sill. . . .

Major Hawkins has not yet arrived up here. He is waiting below for orders. I believe it is not intended to keep him here. Henshaw has gone down to Matamoros on private business.[1] I would not be at all surprised to hear of difficulty between him and Hawkins. Henshaw wrote that piece about Hawkins wishing to surrender Fort B., and he acknowledges it, sticks to it, and says he will publish worse than that and will prove all he publishes, and says he will give Hawkins any kind of satisfaction he may demand. If they will go to work down there and cut each other's throats, it will be a happy thing for the regiment. We would get rid of two nuisances at once, and it would make me a first lieutenant. . . .

We have had a good many desertions from among us since we have occupied this city. This regiment has lost about twenty men and among them two sergeants. The Mexicans have emissaries here who have been offering high honors, offices, and money and horses to men who will desert. We have been watching them pretty sharply, but none have watched closer than the honest and well-disposed men. And a few days since, some of the honest men pretended to wish to desert and obtained proof and information against several Mexicans of high standing here and one Spanish officer and one Frenchman. These have all been arrested, and we have them now in the guardhouse in irons. . . . Among the prisoners is a son of the alcalde. The old man (who has supreme control over the Mexicans here) went to the general to beg for his release. The general got furious at him, shook both fists in his face, told him to shut up his mouth or he would hang him on the spot, and if he did not have this tampering with our men stopped immediately, he would have him and his son strung up without trial. The Mexicans are much frightened about it, and the families of all who have been acting in this mean and underhanded way have suddenly left the city.

The volunteers here have also been behaving shamefully. The fact is the army wants more active employment. General Taylor has been exceedingly enraged against these rascally volunteers. One regiment, the Louisville Legion, was ordered to the rear (Camargo) in disgrace a day or two since. They have been committing a good many murders among the people. A band of twenty-five of them went out regularly to work to murder Mexicans because one of their men had been killed in a drunken outrage among the Mexicans. The officers are, many of them, as bad as the men. Colonel Rogers and other officers of the regiment interceded so hard with the general to save their regiment from disgrace that he has countermanded his order on condition that they shall detach the culprits, officers and all, and offer them for punishment.[2]

Many outrages have been committed on respectable females, some of the most hellish, devilish kind, and heart-rending in the extreme. Some volunteers the other night, for instance, entered the house of a very respectable family, obliged the husband to leave the room. Some held him outside whilst two remained inside. One held a pistol to the lady's head whilst the other fiend incarnate violated her person. . . .

The consequence of these things is a great many families have left their homes and gone into the interior and a great many more will leave. The common people are also scared and many of them have left. They believe that we are going to send some of them to the United States for slaves, and we cannot persuade them to the contrary. The Mexican government and their generals and influential men spread these things among them and encourage them to believe all these foolish stories.

Last night quite a row took place in an eating house near here which resulted in the death of one man and wounding of another. Some Tennessee volunteers were at this eating house and were having a drunken row, breaking all the crockery and so forth. Our guard went to put a stop to it on the application of someone. When the guard entered the room, the volunteers fired and wounded one of the guard, a man of my company, in the arm. But they killed one of their own number, a young man named Forrest from Nashville, who was the noisiest of any of them. The guard were much more forbearing than many guards would have been and did not fire on them. The general will hang some of these people yet if they are not more careful. Or if he does not, it will be because he will have them shot.

1. John C. Henshaw was commissioned a second lieutenant in 1839, was promoted in 1844 and again in 1847, and was dismissed from the army in 1856 (Heitman, I, 524).
2. Jason Rogers graduated from West Point in 1821, became a captain in 1828, and resigned in 1836. He was lieutenant colonel of the First Regiment of Kentucky Volunteers. He died in 1848 (Cullum, I, 219).

November 30 ✦ Whiting has nearly finished a third piece of painting. These paintings will doubtless be a great source of profit. It is a most fortunate and lucky hit for him.

December 7 ✦ Yesterday, my darling wife, I was on guard and had intended to have written you some. But I was so busy and troubled so much with prisoners and other rowdies that I could not get a chance to sit down quietly and write. When a guardhouse is made a depot for all the prisoners in the army, it is not a very comfortable place. We get lots of volunteers in our guardhouse, and some of them receive pretty harsh treatment. Soon they will have it pretty much to themselves. Yesterday one of my patrol shot a soldier of the First Infantry, and he died in the afternoon. He was trying to escape from the patrol and they took a long shot at him and brought him down. . . .

Now, my own darling Sue, I must close my letter, for it is getting very late, and I must get hold of that military law tonight for awhile. One of the prisoners to be tried is the companion of the man who was killed yesterday. After his companion was shot, he went home, loaded his musket, and came out to shoot the men of the guard who fired at his companion. I sent my patrol to catch him, and he snapped his musket at them. Then I caught him, put him in irons, and put charges against him, and he is for trial tomorrow.

December 12 ✦ Today is a great festival day here among the Mexicans. It is the day of the Lady of Guadalupe, the saint patroness of the nation. They have been having masses and ringing bells ever since daylight. I went to church immediately after breakfast, and it was perfectly crowded. There must have been three hundred women there, of all classes and descriptions, some pretty, many ugly, some richly dressed and others in homespun or something worse. I did not see any naked, but there were some who looked as if they would appear tolerably well naked. . . .

This evening I am going to bid farewell to old Don Manuel, the owner of this house. He is a doctor here and has a large apothecary store in the same building. He is a good old fellow and is worth some $600,000. He has been a senator at Mexico [City] under the Federation, a friend of Poinsett and Waddy Thompson.[1] He is also a well-educated and well-informed man. He has taken a good deal of interest in Whiting's paintings. This evening W. bade his goodby, and the old man made him a long and affecting speech. He embraced him and hugged him for some time while his eyes filled. He told him how glad he was of having made an acquaintance and hoped that in battle the balls would always be turned aside. He said that if the war continued, he foresaw nothing but the ruin of his native land but that however deeply he lamented and deplored its fall, he would not remain to see it. Should the war continue, he will abandon $200,000 or $300,000 worth of property here and go to France until things get quiet or forever. Whiting asked him for his address in order that he might send him a copy of his pictures, but he told him that he dared not give it to him. He would be misrepresented and perhaps called a traitor to his country. He is a right good old fellow and one of the very few Mexicans I have seen whom I could like or respect.

Now, my own darling one, I must go to packing up and preparing for starting early tomorrow. As I have but a little valise to pack in, it requires some calculation to get all my things stowed away. Isn't this soldier life with all its change, vanity, romance, and wildness a mighty blackguard way of living after all?

1. Former ministers of the United States to Mexico. See Waddy Thompson, *Recollections of Mexico* (New York, 1846), together with *DAB*, vol. 9, pt. 2, pp. 473-74; Dorothy R. Parton, *The Diplomatic Career of Joel Roberts Poinsett* (Washington, D.C. 1934); and J. Fred Rippy, *Joel R. Poinsett: Versatile American* (Durham, N.C., 1935). Poinsett brought back the Mexican flower that bears his name.

10

The Long March

December-January 1846-47

First halt out from Monterrey, December 13 ✦ We are playing "sodger" again at our [illegible] game, and it is really delightful for variety sake. It feels as if we had got out of a prison, getting out of the city.

It is night here, a bright, starlit night. We have made our march, and all are resting from the fatigues of the day. But our company is on guard, together with a company of the rifles. There are four officers of us, so that we will only have to keep up three hours each. My watch is in the morning, but before taking my soldier's nap I have remembered not to forget what I have been thinking about all day, having a little short talk with my darling one before going to bed. You can see by my writing that I am very uncomfortably fixed for writing. I am sitting flat on my bed, tailor-fashion, with my valise on top of my pillow for a table. I have borrowed a little piece of candle long enough to last a half an hour from the sergeant, and I have got it stuck on the point of a pen whilst the other end of a pen is stuck through a buckle of my valise. Of course it is a very unsteady candlestick, and every time I move, it wiggles a little. However, it is a good friend and I will not complain of it, for it is like a long trumpet through which I can talk to my loved one.

We had our reveille this morning at half past four o'clock, and I got up and prepared my little soldier baggage for the wagons, ate my frugal fare, and then took my last look at my comfortable quarters, my nice carpet, cot, table, and so forth, and old Monterrey itself. . . .

Well, at half past five o'clock, the general was sounded and at six the bugles called the advance, and we were really off again on another long tramp. All the women about the city turned out to see us off and not a few of the curs. My first start was rather a bad one

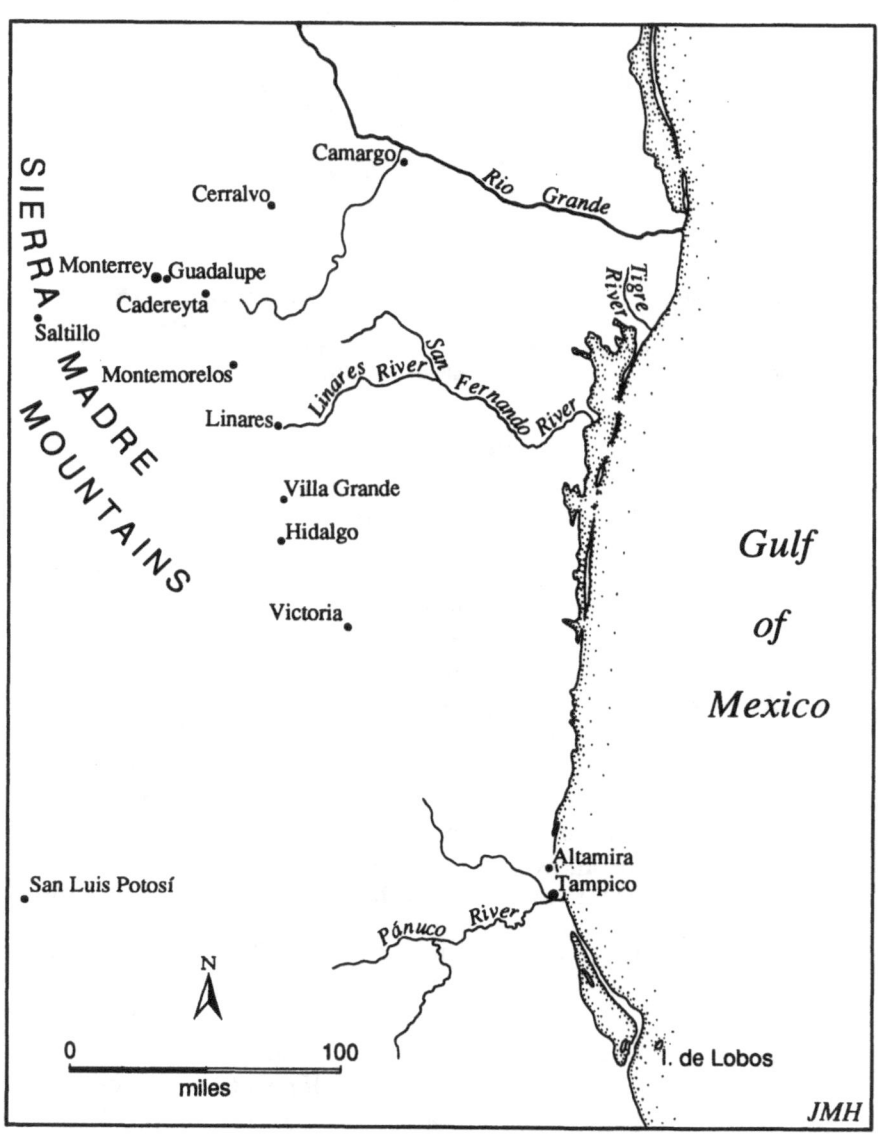

The Long March

for I went to strike one of these brutes, which was in my way, with my scabbard, and I broke my broad belt. However, I fixed it up after a fashion, and my poor crippled belt had the satisfaction of a canine requiem.

We crossed the river at the border of the city with dry feet over a little temporary bridge which had been put there for us the night before and took up a winding course down the mountains facing to the southeast. We went at a pretty brisk pace over a rolling country for four miles and a half when we reached the little village of Guadalupe, quite a nice little place with a church and seven shops in it. Here we came to a halt for a while and were joined by the corps from the camp which came by a crossroad. We reorganized our column and all hands moved forward together in columns on our route, intending to move today not a great deal farther because, to use a sailor's phrase, we would be obliged to "heave to" for our supply train, which had not yet left Monterrey. But the first day's march is almost always a short one as things do not get fairly started, and in future we will make full-length marches, fifteen to twenty miles a day.

We are very fortunate in getting on guard tonight, for we are not fatigued and worn by a long march, whereas it would be hard to be on guard when nearer to a hostile country and after having made a long and hard day's march. Well, our camp is eight miles from Monterrey tonight, and we have again crossed the same mountain stream which we started with this morning. But this time we had no bridge, and we not only had to cross with wet feet but wet tails. The water was delightful, clear, rapid, and just cool enough to be pleasant after having marched in a hot sun through clouds of the lightest dust. Many of the officers have been bathing in the river since our halt.

Tomorrow we will probably halt at Cadereyta, about fifteen miles from here and quite a sizable town. From here where we look back at the beautiful mountain scenery around Monterrey, and so deceptive is it that those mountains appear hardly any farther than they were when we left the plaza this morning. The scenery as we go is full of interest, and every now and then we make the march interesting by stealing sugarcane and eating it with a heap of dust along the road.

Third encampment from Monterrey, December 15 ✦ I could not write you as I had intended from last night's halting place, and I will tell you why. We had marched twenty miles and crossed four streams, the sun burning like fire all the time. So when we halted, you may be sure we were pretty tired and I took the remainder of the afternoon to rest, intending to continue my letter after dark. But after dark Bean came out to see me with a Spanish gentleman he is staying with, and they did not go home till late, so that I was obliged to postpone my little talk with you until tonight. . . .

Well, didn't we make a long march yesterday? It was a hard one, too, and we were all tired out. The sun was burning hot and the roads parched and covered by clouds of light dust which our columns kicked up. We commenced our march yesterday at six o'clock. I had then been up watching on guard since midnight but still did not feel sleepy. We marched very rapidly, still through beautiful mountainous country. Here was the Sierra Madre on our right, distant about twenty miles, with another chain on our left about the same distance, whilst our line of march laid down the valley between them. We crossed two or three pretty deep ravines and arrived at Cadereyta at twelve o'clock, fifteen miles from our camp of the morning. Here I thought we were to have stopped, but on we went, right through the town. This is by far the prettiest, nicest, and cleanest town I have seen in Mexico. The population of it and its environs is twelve thousand, and it does look like a really nice place. And the men who were looking at our column as it passed were apparently of a higher order than the generality we had seen. I did not see any girls. They kept very close.

Well, we continued our march till near two o'clock and halted five miles this side of Cadereyta on the banks of a stream we had just forded. Here I bought some oranges, and after I had peeled one nicely I found they were bitter. The scoundrel who sold them to me had told me that they were "mucho bueno y mucho dulce" (very good and very sweet), and if he had have been near when I detected the lie I believe I should have flailed him. However, I made up for my disappointment by eating sugarcane. . . .

We did not commence our march this morning till eight o'clock because we had to kill beef. At eight we were off, and the sun was mighty hot and the road awfully dusty. Moreover, the route since we left Cadereyta is totally devoid of interest. Our faces are turned towards the Sierra Madre, and our road lies through an immense prairie with high chaparral on each side of the road, hot, dry, dusty, and covered from view. We crossed several streams and about eleven o'clock passed hacienda P [illegible], a large plantation belonging to some wealthy fellow (there, you see, I have dropped

Napoleon Jackson Tecumseh Dana, his wife Susan, and their daughter Mary. The above faded daguerreotype, probably taken in 1847 after Napoleon's return from Mexico, is the only likeness available from the Mexican War period. Civil War Library and Museum, Philadelphia

Dana in Civil War uniform. U.S. Military Academy Archives, West Point, N.Y.

Sue in later years. U.S. Military Academy Archives

Dana in old age. U.S. Military Academy Archives

Zachary Taylor. Society for the Preservation of New England Antiquities, Boston

William Worth. J. Paul Getty Museum, Malibu, California

Winfield Scott. Special Collections Division, The University of Texas at Arlington Libraries, Arlington, Texas

A page from one of Dana's Mexican War letters. U.S. Military Academy Archives some spermaceti on my letter). Well, we kept up our march till one o'clock and encamped here on the banks of quite a large stream, having marched twelve miles. We are now about fifteen miles from Montemorelos and forty from Monterrey. Tomorrow we will make an early start and go to Montemorelos, where we expect to find more troops and where we will probably wait for the brigade of volunteers to come up.

December 19 ✦ Here we are again, my own darling Sue, halfway between Cadereyta and Monterrey, retracing our steps mighty fast, a regular countermarch. The day after I wrote the last we arrived at Montemorelos after a hard day's march, and there we found the Second Infantry and laid out ground for a large camp and made ourselves comfortable to stay there three or four days. Montemorelos is a mean little old place, one of the poorest I have seen.

Well, the next day General Taylor arrived and General Quitman's command of five regiments of volunteers, and the order was to start this morning all hands on our route to Victoria.[1] But at sundown an express arrived from General Worth saying that Santa Anna was advancing towards Saltillo.[2] So all of our division including the Second were ordered to countermarch at quick marches, leaving General Quitman's command with one light battery to keep on to Victoria. We left yesterday morning and retraced our steps seventeen miles. Today we have come through Cadereyta again, twenty miles, and we are now only sixteen miles again from Monterrey, which we thought we had seen for the last time. Such is the soldier's life.

1. John A. Quitman was born in New York state in 1798 and after moving to Ohio became a lawyer in 1821. That same year he settled in Mississippi, where he engaged in politics, eventually participating in the controversy over nullification, an idea that he supported. He served as a brigadier general and a major general during the Mexican War, and General Scott chose him as military governor of Mexico City. Returning to the United States, he visited Washington and proposed to President Polk a permanent occupation of Mexico. During the controversy over the national compromise measure of 1850, he spoke openly of the possible secession of his state from the Union. He took interest in the expeditions of the Cuban revolutionary leader Narciso López and at one juncture resigned his office of governor of Mississippi because of indictment by a federal grand jury for violation of the neutrality laws. He was later elected to Congress and died in 1858 (Robert E. May, *John A. Quitman: Old South Crusader* [Baton Rouge, 1985]).   2. For Santa Anna, the principal general and Mexican leader of the era, see Frank C. Hanighen, *Santa Anna: The Napoleon of the West* (New York, 1934); Wilfrid H. Callcott, *Santa Anna: The Story of an Enigma Who Once Was Mexico* (Norman, Okla., 1936); and especially Oakah L. Jones, Jr., *Santa Anna* (New York, 1968).

December 21   ✦   Yesterday, dearest one, we marched from our last encampment sixteen miles from Monterrey and halted at Guadalupe, where we pitched our tents and sent in to Monterrey for orders. But we got none there but found that General Taylor had left for Saltillo that morning. The city was almost deserted and no troops in it except the Fourth Infantry. All the people were moving out in fright because they thought that Santa Anna was coming to attack the city. . . .

But just at tattoo last night, all was settled. General Taylor returned back to Monterrey, having met on the way Colonel May with a squadron of dragoons, who told him that it was all a "flash in the pan," a false alarm, and that Santa Anna was not coming. So here all this fuss has been about nothing. General Wool marched one hundred twenty miles with twenty-four hundred men, General Butler sixty miles with eight hundred, and we countermarched sixty miles with fifteen hundred men, all because General W. raised a stampede.

General T. sent us an order to remain where we were till after breakfast this morning and then come over here to his old camping ground and encamp. So here we are and have a beautiful camp containing some twenty-five hundred men. After we got our camp fixed, I could not rest, loved one, until I had borrowed a horse and ridden to town to rummage the post office for a letter. And sure enough, there I found the letter you sent by Lieutenant Bennett, who sent it from Cerralvo.

And so you are really at New Orleans. I trust you may be happy and comfortable there, but I must say that I do not see exactly how you will manage. However, if you find yourself disagreeably fixed, you must make whatever shift you wish, for you know that I will approve whatever will be for your happiness. I really hope you will be able to stop my letters at New Orleans, for if not many will have passed by you on their way to Kentucky. I hope you will be comfortable and happy at the barracks, but I fear lest it may be otherwise, as there is no one there to take care of you or to look after you. How will you be able to provide yourselves with what you want? How will you even get your letters from the post office? What will you do for a physician, should you require one? I regret you did not receive my letters in season to stop you in Kentucky.

I hope you have got money enough. I do not know yet whether you received the check for twenty-five dollars which I sent you, for the letter which you dropped at Louisville I have not yet received and perhaps the last one from Covington. I also sent you forty dollars on the first of this month. . . .

This afternoon seven companies of a Kentucky regiment arrived in the greatest haste from Cerralvo on the same errand that we came. I have just been told that Mr. Bennett is among them, and I will see him tomorrow.

Camp first night out from Monterrey, December 23 ♦ On our last march along here, the sands were exceedingly dusty. Clouds of dust came along on line of march, and we were almost choked by it. But now the case is quite the reverse. It rained all yesterday afternoon and last night, and during our march today we have had a fine drizzle all the time, so that the roads instead of being dusty have become very muddy and heavy. And as I have had in addition a pair of heavy boots on, marching is a little harder. . . .

Yesterday, dear Sue, I saw Mr. Bennett, from whom I learned a good deal about you, about your arrival and situation at the barracks and so forth. . . . I rode into Monterrey with Mr. Bennett yesterday morning. I went in for the purpose of overhauling the letters in the post office to get out the one I had directed to Covington. I succeeded in my search and put my letter together with another half sheet which I wrote for you in a new envelope for New Orleans Barracks.

December 24 ♦ We are in the same place where we were encamped before on the second night from Monterrey, on the banks of a stream called Río Ramos. We are five miles beyond Cadereyta and nineteen miles from where we started this morning. When we left the camp this morning at daylight, the weather was still lowering and heavy, but the roads were fine, beaten down hard and even by the cavalry and light artillery which marched ahead. So the way was not near so toilsome and disagreeable as it was the last time we marched it. About eleven o'clock the sun came out hot, and it has been hot ever since. And now in a couple of days we will probably have dusty roads again.

Camp three miles beyond Montemorelos, December 26 ♦ Well, we left our encampment near Cadereyta very early yesterday morning before day and made a very hard and distressing march for

twenty miles. When we had completed our day's tramp our recruits, and indeed a great many of our old soldiers, were pretty well
beaten out. . . .

Wasn't that a great way to spend our Christmas Day, dearest
one? Different from the last one, where we had a plenty of eggnog,
cake, and so forth and nice comfortable homes in the bosoms of our
families. We were really bright and happy and cheerful then, but
now dread war separates us and makes us comparatively wretched.

It was well-nigh dark when we got our tents pitched and had
our suppers. After that we had all got our beds rolled down and
were quietly talking over the events of the day and the prospects for
the future when Captain Holmes happened to think that he had a
bottle of whiskey and told me if I would agree to make an eggnog he
would produce the ingredients. Of course I easily agreed and after
the necessities were brought forth Captain Ross and myself set to
work to make the eggnog.[1] You know, I never did succeed in
beating the white of an egg, and this time too I could not make the
froth stiff enough. However, we succeeded in turning out for our
Christmas frolic a tolerably good glass of eggnog apiece for Holmes,
Ross, Hanson, Little, and myself. It was the first eggnog I had been
treated to since that night when you made us some at your father's
house, and it tasted mighty nice. I could easily have drunk another
glass if I could have found it, but it is hard to will such things in the
midst of a wilderness and especially a Mexican wilderness. . . .

I slept mighty soundly last night and did not wake up until the
sound of our early reveille aroused me. We were on our march as
early as usual at the earliest dawn and at sunrise were getting our
wagon train over the big hill. At ten o'clock we passed through the
ugly little town of Montemorelos, forded the river this side of it, and
are now encamped three miles this side of the ford on our way to
Victoria. Captain Holmes and Little are both snoring away, taking a
nap and making up for lost sleep. . . . General Taylor passed
through here last night, and we understand that he received dispatches from Camargo, but we do not know the nature of them. He
has gone on ahead of us to overtake General Quitman before he
reaches Victoria.

1. Richard H. Ross, a graduate in 1830, was brevetted twice during the Mexican War, and
died in 1851 (Cullum, I, 378).

Rancho Las Vegas, December 27   ✦   Last night I cut my letter No.
64 quite short because Little was about going into Montemorelos

and I wanted him to take it along, thinking he might find an opportunity to send my letter to Monterrey. Well, he carried my letter together with one of Whiting's into town, and when he got there he found that an express had left for Monterrey just an hour before he arrived. So he was too late for that, but the interpreter at the quartermaster's tent told him that he knew of a person who was going to Camargo today and that he would take care of the letters. So he left them with him. . . .

Our reveille beat at the usual hour this morning, and at early dawn we were on the road again in line of march. Our track today was new to us, as we had not traveled it before. To us it was "terra incognita," but we heard that we had a very long stretch of thirteen miles without any water. The country we passed through today was very different indeed from that we have passed in coming from Monterrey. The face of the country entirely changed as we crossed the river at Montemorelos. Our road this morning brought us to within eight miles of the Sierra Madre and led us down the range, the mountains decreasing in height. But our road itself was nothing but hill and vale, up hill and down hollow, rugged, rocky, and wild. Now we were mounted on a high eminence and could see for miles around, whilst under our feet was a confused mass of hills, huddled and thrown together in wild disorder, the little flock of the sublime mountains which towered up from the horizon on either hand. When on top of one of our hills a mountain of great height suddenly broke on our view on our left hand, distant some forty miles. Our road seems to lie to the southward about midway between this lofty peak and the great chain. At other times we were deep in some rich bottomland, hidden from the view of all the world except the feathered tribe and nothing to be seen by us. We passed by a couple of miserable poor little ranches on the road, and after going up and down for fifteen miles, we arrived here at a place called Las Vegas, an old deserted, dilapidated ranch, just halfway between Montemorelos and Linares. There are no people at all here, and the houses do not appear to have been used for a very long time.

Linares is fifteen miles from here, and we shall probably get in there tomorrow at noon, our company first as we have been detailed for advance guard. General Taylor is along with us and will, I believe, keep with us.

Camp near Linares, December 28 ✦ We are fifteen miles farther on our route, my dearest wife, and are now encamped on the southern bank of Linares River just opposite the town of L. Our march today has been a very pleasant one, especially to our company as we were the advance guard. We started at daylight from our stopping place of last night and soon found that our road of today was even more hilly and rocky than that of yesterday. But the scenery was even more beautiful and varied, that is, the scenery immediately around us, for the distant scenery of the mountains was curtained from view for a great part of the march by heavy clouds of mist which made us fear lest we were threatened with approaching rain. No rain visited us, however, and after a while we had the satisfaction of seeing the sun come out warm to dry our clothes, which we had wet in fording the streams. We waded through beautiful mountain streams, clear, rapid, and cool, the last one waist-deep.

Whilst fording the first one early this morning, just after sunrise, I had the misfortune to burst both of my shoes all along the sides, which of course made the remainder of my march more disagreeable than it would otherwise have been. I have said adieu to the old shoes, and I suppose that by tomorrow some Mexican will be sporting around with them as large as life.

We passed two or three fine sugar plantations, that is, for Mexicans, just before we arrived at Linares, and at one of them I stopped for a moment and took a good drink of syrup and a good big cane under my arm. I believe that since then I must have chewed at least four yards of sugarcane.

When we arrived at Linares I was quite agreeably surprised with the appearance of the town, for I had been induced to believe that it was as small and ugly a place as Montemorelos. But it is larger and very nicely policed, with better and prettier houses. I think it quite a good place, but I have not cared about going over to see it since we marched through.

Camp at Villa grande, December 31   •   So here we are at this little village of Villa Grande, taking a day's rest. We are two days' march beyond Linares, when I last wrote in this, and about five days' march yet from Victoria. In the last two days we have marched but twenty-five miles.

We left our encampment at Linares at daylight day before yesterday and marched three hours over a long, rich bottomland without any water. After going nine miles we forded a mountain stream, where we stopped for half an hour, drank, took a snack, and again went on. And after two hours more at a rapid pace, we encamped near a little miserable old hut in a thick chaparral through which meandered a small stream. . . .

Yesterday morning at daylight we left that camp, and after marching nine miles for three hours over a mighty dusty road we came to a very large plantation or hacienda, "Cerro de Villa." It was a fine sugar plantation and was situated along the bank of a deep, clear, and rapid stream which gave evidence on its banks of a high overflow whenever it rained much. Here is the only place except parts of the Rio Grande where we have seen anything like driftwood, and the piles on the banks looked really like home.

We forded this river, which I think is a branch of the Tigre which empties into the Gulf, and halted on its opposite bank for half an hour to water and eat a snack and rest. I felt pretty tired because since my shoes gave out I have marched in a pair of heavy boots. . . .

Well, on we went at a very rapid pace amounting almost to a dogtrot, and soon we had to turn to the right to bend around the point of a young mountain which was directly in our way. After marching four miles farther in clouds of light dust, just as we turned the hill we saw before us on the opposite side of it a stream with high banks, to the happy surprise of us all, the village of Villa Grande. It is a very small but very old place. The people look tolerably well, but they complain that General Quitman's division of volunteers which passed through here seven days ago ate them out of house and home, and they have hardly an egg or chicken left. What chickens they do have they ask six bits apiece for.

We have encamped just on the suburbs of the village, have had our muster, and now it is almost dinnertime. All hands are taking advantage of the halt to wash clothes and have a clean shirt again. We will, I presume, be off again at daylight in the morning on our way to Victoria. . . .

This, my own dear Sue, is the last day of old '46, the most eventful year of our lives thus far.

Camp near Hidalgo, January 1 ✦ Last night at tattoo, or rather after tattoo, as it was New Year's Eve, the band of the Second Infantry played before the camp for an hour or so. Many of us went out and stood around the fires to listen to the music, and the little town of Villa Grande seemed to have poured out all of its yellow population. Captain Miller and Backus and some others tried their unaccustomed toes once more at the waltz and the polka, but about nine o'clock, knowing that we were early risers, we all retired to our lodgings on the cold ground.[1]

I had pulled off my pants and so forth and was just going to creep into my blankets when a regular gust of a norther came over the mountains and the tent of poor [illegible] just made out to stand and that was all. Little and myself had to hold it up until the fastenings were tightened. I went out to do this and saw that some dozen tents had fallen under the blast and the unlucky inmates were crawling out from under the ruins. Soon I heard a voice calling to me, "Dana, for God's sake come and help a poor fellow in distress." It was old Miller. His tent was facing right towards the wind and had well-nigh turned wrong side out whilst the old captain was holding onto the front pole like a good fellow. Well, I got an axe and helped him out of his scrape and then went to bed and let it blow without minding it until the reveille called us up again at half past four o'clock.

We were off at daylight, and the morning was mighty cold, so our pace was soon quickened almost to what is vulgarly called a dogtrot until we were stopped about eight o'clock at the foot of a large steep hill, where we "doughboys" had to wait for the artillery to get their carriages over. But after we did get over, we went even faster than before. The roads were exceedingly dusty, and we breathed nothing but light dust all the way. We passed two little settlements, one a sugar plantation called San Martin, the other a farm called Animas.

About eleven o'clock we came up with a beautiful piece of woods through which our road lay for a couple of miles. This sight was beautiful to us, as it was the only piece of real woods we had seen since we left the United States. It reminded us of home and looked like the woods on the Fort Wood pass, only the growth was much thicker. But just like that it was here and there spotted with canebrake. At the edge of the woods after we had passed through we forded a river, the same I believe which we crossed at Montemorelos. And about half past twelve o'clock we arrived at the little old town of Hidalgo.

This is about the same size as Villa Grande, probably containing some six or eight hundred souls, but like all the other Mexican places it must have a plaza, or public square, and a church with three or four bells. At the edge of the town we again forded the same river we had tried before, and after having marched another mile, we encamped here in a large open space near an old ranch.

This is the same ground General Quitman occupied eight days ago, and from the abundance of feathers I should suppose that the volunteers did not let the poor peoples' turkeys get off altogether free. I suppose they were determined to have a Christmas Eve supper even if they were on a march.

We have accomplished about eighteen miles today, and I felt almost as fresh at the end of it as when I commenced.

1. Albert S. Miller was commissioned a second lieutenant in 1823, first lieutenant in 1829, captain in 1836. He was brevetted for Monterrey and died in 1852 (Heitman, I, 709).

Hacienda Caballeros, January 3 ✦ It is now tattoo, my own darling wife, so I can write but a few lines tonight, for I am very tired and must get some sleep. I had made an hour's mistake in the time when I finished my writing the other night on guard, and on account of having a fast watch I had reveille beat at half past two o'clock instead of half past three. And at half past four we commenced our march and until the sun rose on us it was very cold indeed. And as bad luck would have it, we were obliged to ford before sunrise the deepest and most rapid river we had yet met with. It is no fun on such a cold morning to wade up to one's waist in the coldest kind of water. Then our road was exceedingly dusty, so that our nostrils got filled with it. And our march, too, was very long and wearisome, especially to me, as I had been up since half past eleven o'clock.

We passed through some finely wooded country and at one o'clock we arrived at Santa Engracias, the largest, most wealthy, and most beautiful hacienda I have seen. And there we encamped. I have never in our country or any other seen any plantation near as large as that of Santa Engracias. The owner of it must be immensely wealthy. His place is of immense size, with a great deal of it planted in sugar: thousands of acres of the richest land, finely walled or hedged, large buildings, a sugar mill and a sugar refinery, an orange grove of about 150 acres, and 100 hands to do his work.

We were aroused again this morning at half past three o'clock, and I felt mighty little like getting up. I had not had half enough sleep, and as I had marched twenty miles the day before, I felt not much inclined to take the road again. But we got off as usual and after having traveled the same dusty road we arrived here, twelve miles from Santa Engracias.

This place is also a very fine and wealthy plantation, though not so good as the last. There are several acres of bananas here, but I am sorry to say that none of them are ripe. The owner of this place gave $30,000 for it and owns here 1,200,000 acres. Wouldn't that make a man rich in our country?

Colonel May has returned to us with the loss of his baggage and eleven men and thirteen horses of his rearguard. He had been on the duty assigned to him to Labradores and was returning through a very narrow pass through which they were even obliged to dismount and lead their horses single file, when a fire was spewed on them from the heights on one side whilst huge masses of rock were thrown down on them from the precipices on the other. No one was hurt, but the officer commanding the rearguard left it very unaccountably, and the supposition is that the men of the guard got bewildered and frightened and, finding themselves without an officer, retraced their steps. They have probably been taken prisoners. May went back and waited an hour and a half for them and then sent back to the alcalde of the next town to inquire after them. And the alcalde sent word that the men had passed through his town shortly after the attack but did not say whether they were prisoners or not. The lieutenant (Sturgis) who commanded the rearguard is arrested and will be tried for his unfortunate conduct.[1]

1. Samuel D. Sturgis graduated from West Point in 1846 and was a second lieutenant at this time. He served as a brigadier general in the Civil War and died in 1889 (Heitman, I, 934). Also see *DAB*, vol. 9, pt. 2, pp. 182-83.

Camp near Victoria, January 5 ✦ We arrived here, dearest Sue, yesterday forenoon after marching twelve miles. We did not stop in the town but passed right through and encamped here on a fine piece of ground two miles beyond the city. We found all well here, the town full of volunteers, and a large camp of them on the other side of it. General Patterson had not arrived from Matamoros, but he got in in the afternoon with about two thousand men.[1] I do not know as yet what troops came along with Patterson except that there is one regiment of Tennessee cavalry. We have here now altogether over six thousand men, and it is understood that we are to move again in a couple of days. . . .

I am on guard again and have been sitting up the greater part of the night and employed the most of my watch in making out a muster roll for Captain Holmes. He is a poor helpless man and cannot even take care of his clothes. Every day he loses something and never thinks of a towel until after he has washed his face, and then he cannot find his half the time and calls for mine. I keep a dirty one purposely for him because I won't have everyone wiping on the same towel which I use.

As soon as breakfast was done this morning I got a horse and rode into Victoria to try and get a Mexican baker to exchange bread for flour which had been issued to the company. It is too hard after a hard march to issue flour to men which they have to mix for the most part in their tin cups and bake it on shovels.

1. Robert Patterson was born in Ireland, was brought up in Pennsylvania, served in the War of 1812, and afterward established himself in Philadelphia as a grocer and commission merchant. He served in the Mexican War as a major general of volunteers. After participating briefly in the Civil War, he returned to his considerable business interests in Philadelphia. He died in 1881 (*DAB*, vol. 7, pt. 2, pp. 306-7).

January 9 ✦ For the last three days, dearest Sue, we have had a tremendously cold snap for this climate. It came up in a real norther right from your direction. The first night when it came up, many of the tents were prostrated and mine just made out to hold itself up. We had ice here that night, a quarter of an inch or thereabouts, and of course many of us poor soldiers slept pretty cold. We all had big fires though and have got through with the cold snap pretty well. . . .

Now, my own dearest Sue, I must go and drill some recruits, and after drill I will come and have another talk with you.

Now I have come from drill, my own sweet Sue, and feel a little cross, of course, for of all things to try one's patience, a stupid recruit is the worst.

Camp of First Division, near Forton, January 17 ✦ Why, just look at it, my darling little Sue, here I am, forty-five miles from where my letter was commenced, hard on my march for Tampico.

On the evening of the thirteenth I had to pack up and arrange for traveling again, for the whole army corps had been ordered in the direction of Tampico, and the First Division of regulars, which was ours, was to march at early daylight on the fourteenth, to be followed on the fifteenth and sixteenth by the two divisions of volunteers under Generals Patterson and Quitman, each of our divisions numbering about seventeen hundred men.

Well, our division left at dawn on the fourteenth, marched through Victoria again (and it was the only time I had been there since I last wrote you), and got onto one of the Tampico roads. We marched over a tolerable road and encamped at Santa Rosa, a ranch ten miles from Victoria. . . .

Well, until we arrived at Santa Rosa, we believed our destination to be the hacienda Alamitas, only halfway to Tampico. But at Santa Rosa we received an express from General Taylor, ordering us directly to Tampico and ordering the light artillery to return to him and at the same time writing to us his farewell, wishing us all success and happiness.

Well, without knowing it we had indeed parted from our brave old chief and had seen him for the last time during this war. I have no doubt the lion-hearted old fellow felt the separation as keenly as any of us, and we would all have liked to have shaken him by the hand before leaving him. . . .

So here we are, three columns of us, in all about five thousand men, on the high road for Tampico. There General Patterson will command until General Scott arrives. When he arrives there, we will have more than ten thousand men there. And I suppose by the last of February we will land near Veracruz. . . .

Our second day's march, the fifteenth, was a short but a hard one, the road very bad, filled with stones and very rugged, no water, and the country entirely barren, owing to the impossibility of irrigation. The road was so bad that we were obliged to keep the sappers and the miners with two companies of infantry several miles ahead of us to repair and improve it with shovels and picks. On the night of the fifteenth we encamped along a little stream at a deserted place called El Pasta.

Our road on the sixteenth was still worse and exceedingly tiresome. We only marched nine miles, and I felt as if I had marched twenty. We had to march slowly because the road had to be worked so much by the pioneers. At night (last night) we encamped in a rough place along a little stream called Arroyo Alajilla, and I was on guard again with my own company.

This morning, the fourth day out, we had reveille at half past four o'clock, and at daylight we were off again on a better road, and it kept improving all the way. And moreover it is said that we have a fine road again all the way to Tampico. Tomorrow morning we are to have reveille at half past three and start at five, an hour before day, as it is the intention to march eighteen miles. Today our march was about thirteen, and as soon as we arrived here, I threw myself on the ground under the shade of a tree and slept mighty tight for a couple of hours.

The country around here is a decided improvement on what we

have passed over for the three days previously, and we are en-camped on one of the largest and finest streams we have met. I believe it is the Rio San Fernando and is pure, fresh, and rapid. Its banks show signs of very heavy overflows during the rainy season. The hacienda Forton on the other side is a tolerably large one but not to be compared in any way with those of Caballeros and Santa Engracias.

As we are going to join General Scott we will expect to have to pay more attention to the regulations of dress, hair, whiskers, and so forth. And as I prefer to do things of my own accord, instead of waiting to be ordered to do it, I shaved off my beard again this afternoon, and my clean, smooth face feels mighty funny.

Camp First Division, near Rancho El Pratill, January 18 ✦ We have marched about sixteen miles today, my own dearest wife. This is our fifth day from Victoria, and we are now about sixty miles from it. Our bugles and drums aroused us from our soldiers' slumbers this morning at half past three o'clock, and at five, an hour before sunlight, we were stretched out along the road on our march again. I can tell you it was mighty hard to get up when the reveille sounded, but I am so smart that I am always the first in our "rancho." The morning was of a good temperature, and thinking we had a much longer march before us than we really had, we stretched our legs to it to a rate of over three miles an hour, our battalion in the lead. We walked mighty fast, and as it was cloudy, before we saw the sun through the fog we had reached La Panocha, a rancho or hacienda about seven miles from where we started. And here again we forded the same big river we forded yesterday and halted for a half an hour on its banks for the train to come up and so forth. And then we set off again at a pretty merry pace.

The country we passed over was very barren, no water, and the growth confined almost altogether to the palmetto and another tree, the queerest thing I ever saw of the kind, like this:[1] It is not a palm, and we, none of us, ever saw anything like it before. Its foliage is on the top of high branches and just like grass, and its bottom bulges out just like a huge globe. We also found another great curiosity in the way of vegetation, a tree bearing thorns exactly like a cow's horns in every respect, the funniest things you ever saw.

Well, we tramped smartly along over hill and stones, and just before we reached here one of the strangest-looking mountains I ever saw came up over the horizon right ahead of us. It appears to be very high and rises up perpendicularly in a high hump. All day we have been [illegible] the southern extremity of the Sierra Alva, having left the Sierra Madre far behind us. We arrived here about twelve o'clock and went into camp pretty well fatigued and pretty warm, too.

1. Here Dana inserted a small drawing to illustrate. The tree is a species of palm, called "sun palm" by the Mexicans.

Rancho Los Estavos, January 21 ✦ For the last two days, my own darling wife, I have not been able to add more to my letter, so I will commence where I left off and keep up the chain of my march for you.

In the first place, dearest one, we left El Pratill on the morning of the nineteenth at six o'clock, and we did not press ourselves hard. Our road was somewhat hilly and the country barren, and after we had marched about ten miles, we arrived at Alamitas. This was the place near which we were to have encamped when we left Victoria. This is a very large hacienda, the largest we have yet seen, though not quite so flourishing as some we have seen. It has a very fine dwelling house, a pretty little church, and a plaza. The place contained about a hundred people. We encamped here as usual only one night, and we left there yesterday morning at an early hour.

The main column started at four o'clock, but Captain Holmes' company was detailed together with Hamilton's of the First to form the rearguard.[1] And as Hamilton himself was sick and no other officer was with his company, I was detailed to take command of it. So we did not start till after the rear of the train had passed, and as the whole line of march extended about three miles, we did not start till about sunrise. But when we did start we heeled it, I can tell you, at the rate of three miles an hour. We kept along at that rate till we had gone sixteen miles, when we arrived at a hacienda called Las Timas, and there of course we expected to halt for the night. But imagine our surprise on arriving at the top of the hill to see our wagon train stretching on over the prairie as far as the eye could reach. So we nursed our wearied legs as much as we could to go another five leagues. I for one was pretty much disgusted, and I imagine everyone on foot was. And I would have cheered to see General Twiggs rolled the whole distance.

From Las Timas our road lay over an immense rolling prairie, limitless as far as we could see and covered by wild horses, here and there a clot of bushes, but no trees. Well, we went on and on, and even when we came over we expected to see the camp. But no, there was no water, and every hill we mounted showed us our train miles ahead. We did not get into camp until sunset, and then how far do you think we had marched? Twenty-eight miles! Some call it thirty-three, but I say twenty-eight. It was a very long march and one which is seldom exceeded. And the best of it was, the men all stood it well and your husband like a hero! But I was mad as all fun all the way because I thought Twiggs was making a fool of himself. . . .

Well, at six we left Chocoyo on this same prairie road. No sun had shown itself for two days, and it was fine weather for marching, especially if we were to make forced marches. We saw high hills far ahead, and I made up my mind that I had to foot it to the other side of those for this day's work. After we had come six miles, we entered a wooded bottom, the road of which is deep under water in wet weather, and now it is uneven and hard and to march on it is like marching on bricks set up endways. Of course it was painful to our feet rendered somewhat tender from yesterday's march, and I thought that road never would come out of those miserable woods. Our stupid general, too, did not halt us once today, so that we arrived here, about thirteen miles from Chocoyo, very tired. I would not at all have been surprised if we had kept on for another five leagues. But we halted and are not to start tomorrow till seven o'clock. Tomorrow we shall march to a town called Altamira, and the next day we shall go through to Tampico where we will get heaps of news from the States and from our Congress. Who knows but that I am a first lieutenant now?

1. Schuyler Hamilton graduated from West Point and became a second lieutenant in 1841. He was promoted to first lieutenant in 1848 after two brevets, resigned in 1855, served as major general in the Civil War, 1861-63, and died in 1901 (Heitman, I, 494).

11

Tampico

January-February 1847

Clearing the Division Ground. Tampico a Beautiful City. A Fine Dinner. Marriage of Mother to General Peaslee. Invitation to Whiting's Mess. Drilling by Brigades. A Norther. Capture of Seventy of the Kentucky Cavalry. Whiting Receives Corpus Christi Engraving. Division Drill. General Scott Arrives.

Camp near Tampico, January 24 • Yesterday I left a letter at the quartermaster's office in Tampico for you. It contained a draft on Colonel Hunt for fifty dollars. It may be that the quartermaster has sent that letter in a sail vessel, and I understand that today the *Massachusetts* is to go with the regular mail. So I just write these few words for fear the *M.* might get first to New Orleans, and you would be disappointed if you did not receive a word. The letter I have sent by the quartermaster is one of two sheets, and you must be patient until you can get that.

I am up to my eyes in work now, clearing ground for the camp. We are three miles from town. We are well. So if you receive this letter, dearest one, before No. 67, try and be content till you get the other. I must now go to work. God bless you all and goodby.

January 26 • We have been so hard at work ever since we have been here, or rather since I sent you my last letter, which was only three days ago, that I have been unable to commence another sheet. We encamped here in a brush so thick that a man could not walk in it till a path had been cut. And we have been, since we arrived, constantly occupied in clearing and cleaning this ground for the division, and still our labor is not half done. We shall probably be at work from reveille until dark for some time, cutting and grubbing. . . .

Last Friday we arrived at Altamira, having marched that day fifteen or sixteen miles. After reaching there, Lieutenant Hanson and myself got permission to ride on to Tampico, so we got horses and set off from our camp at about three o'clock. The distances given to us for the road varied from eighteen to twenty-three miles. We found it the former with a road of deep sand all the way. Well, we galloped for ten miles, and then, finding ourselves by inquiry only about eight miles from the town, we slackened our pace and took it more leisurely. As we advanced, everything looked more civilized, more American, and the country itself more like home, the wild hills of Missouri. I really felt like emerging from a wilderness and as if we were come home from a long voyage.

When we got within a few miles of Tampico we met small parties of soldiers working on the roads, and here and there along the road were quite nice Mexican farmhouses. About dusk we came within sight of the suburbs of the city and our eyes were once more delighted by the sight of a broad sheet of water. The sea is too distant to be seen, but the lagoon was to us a cheering sight. We were tired of prairies and mountains and were delighted to get a sight of a broad sheet of water of any kind.

As we rode through the town, it was candlelight, and the stores, which were lighted up quite brilliantly, still more made us feel that we were really in the land of the living and getting nearer home. We passed many fine stores and houses. Another thing which delighted us much was the American style of the houses. There are but few of the flat-topped houses in town, and the greater part of them are American-built, with roofs of shingle or slate.

We rode first to the quartermaster's office, where we found Colonel Belton, Captain Babbitt, and others who welcomed us as fortunate heroes of the grand army.[1] They were anxious to hear all we could say, and as we were the first of the Monterrey army at Tampico, we were quite lionized. I told them that I felt exactly like a country boy who had come to the city and would cry out at every pretty thing he saw, and indeed it was very much so. H. and I would point out to each other as we passed all the cafes and night places we saw. We were just like two green ones going to see the sights, the glass chandeliers in the exchanges, the marble black floors, the porches before some of the houses, the vessels in the river, the fine billiard tables, and the large barrooms like those of Orleans—all tickled us very much.

After we had talked for some time at the quartermaster's office and satisfied the curiosity of all, we got the quartermaster to take care of our horses. And as we knew that they were not well able to accommodate us with beds, we refused their invitations and asked them to refer us to a good place where we could get a bed and supper and a breakfast. The clerk of the office carried us to an "Italian fonda" which is now kept by a man from New Orleans, and after securing the only two beds in the house, we got a most excellent supper which we did great credit to as we had eaten nothing since nine o'clock in the morning. We had for supper coffee and milk, fine Goshen butter and bread, tender beefsteak, boiled eggs, fried oysters, and so forth.

Whilst we were at supper a couple of my old classmates came to look after us, and after we had eaten until we could eat no more, we went with them to an extensive establishment called the Commercial Exchange, which like the barrooms of the St. Charles is the place for general rendezvous for all. Here we met a great many. When there I almost forgot that I was in the field, and it seemed almost as if I were in the midst of New Orleans once more. During the evening Beauregard came in. I had not expected to meet him in this country, and the surprise was quite agreeable.[2] I met several naval officers and among them the Mr. Nelson who came over with us on the *Alabama* from Pensacola. Don't you recollect him, a very large young man?

I did not go to bed till twelve o'clock, and then I did not sleep very soundly, for in the next room was a ronda table which kept up a great racket until daylight. After breakfast in the morning we went to call on General Shields, the commanding officer, whom we found out.[3] And after looking well through the town, we got our horses again and came out to find the division.

We found it cutting a line to encamp on here, right in the middle of the chaparral, three miles from town. And here we have been ever since, cutting, grubbing, and burning. The officers, many of them, go frequently to town, but I shall visit it but seldom. I prefer to stay at home, since I cannot spend money among those who can afford to let it go as carelessly as they please.

Yesterday morning, my darling Sue, I received another letter from you and one from mother. They both came out by the same mail, which we received on the road, but were detained behind in Quitman's column. I was delighted to hear that you and our little one were so well and that she had commenced walking. Our mother's letter, dearest one, was dated some days after the one she wrote you. Julia has been married, and she herself was going down to Portsmouth next day where she was to be married in eight or ten days at grandmother's to General Peaslee with no one present but the family.

---

1. Francis S. Belton served in the War of 1812 and rose to the rank of lieutenant colonel during the war. A colonel in 1857, he died in 1861 (Heitman, I, 209). Edwin B. Babbitt, who graduated from the Academy in 1826, was a brevet brigadier general in the Civil War. He died in 1881 (Cullum, I, 300-1).   2. Pierre Gustave Toutant Beauregard was born in 1818

near New Orleans and served during the Mexican War as an engineer on the staff of General Scott. In 1861 he was superintendent at West Point when he resigned to join the forces of the Confederacy. Soon thereafter he commanded the batteries that fired on Fort Sumter. Throughout the war he served as a general officer. Afterward he engaged in railroading and was superintendent of the Louisiana lottery. He died in 1893 (T. Harry Williams, *P.G.T. Beauregard: Napoleon in Gray* [Baton Rouge, 1955]; and T.H. Williams, ed., *With Beauregard in Mexico: The Mexican War Reminiscences of P.G.T. Beauregard* [Baton Rouge, 1956]).   3. James Shields was born in Ireland in 1806 and arrived in the United States in the mid-1820s, settling in Illinois, where he became a lawyer and politician. Commissioned brigadier general of Illinois volunteers during the Mexican War, he was wounded at Cerro Gordo, shot through a lung. A Mexican doctor inserted a silk handkerchief and drew it through the wound, and Shields survived the injury. He served on the Union side in the Civil War. He moved from state to state and was elected to the Senate three times, from Illinois, Minnesota, and Missouri. He died in 1879 (*DAB*, vol. 9, pt. 1, pp. 106-7).

January 27   ✦   By the way, my darling one, I must tell you that in a day or two I am going to commence messing with Whiting, and I must tell you all about messing for the last two months. On the first of December, I got Captain Holmes to let me leave his mess. Our mess bill was seldom less than sixteen dollars a month, and I told him that I would not have money enough and did not want to borrow but was anxious to get out of debt as fast as I could. Holmes told me he would always be glad to have me return to his mess whenever I felt inclined, but he would not persuade me to stay at present, as he thought my reasons were very plausible. So I broke off on the first of December and ever since then I have been living on soldier's fare. I would buy regular soldier's rations from the commissary, turn them in to the company, and Robb would bring me my rations. The fare was hard, of course, but I have always been satisfied. The other evening Whiting asked me to join his mess and told me that his mess bill was never over twelve dollars and generally less than that. And as the doctor had told me that I must change my diet entirely in order to get rid of those boils on my face, I agreed to it. . . .

February 1   ✦   We have got our ground tolerably well cleared now, so that this morning we commenced drilling by battalions twice a day. In a short time we are to drill at evolutions of the line, with the whole division on a large plain on the borders of the town. That will be something of a day's work, to march three miles through deep sand, then have a fatiguing drill and march back again. . . .

I marched off guard this morning, dearest Sue, and had the

pleasure of spending the day and night out of doors, for we have not been able as yet to procure any tents for the guard. But I had a big fire built under a large tree and laid there beside it on my cloak, reading by the light of a lantern.

February 3 ✦ We dined at the First Artillery mess, loafed about town all day, and went to the theater at night and did not get home till one o'clock. Don't you think we made a spree of it? The theater is a miserable place, fitted up for the occasion, but some of the actors are very good. It is the same company which has been performing for the army at Corpus Christi and at Matamoros.

February 6 ✦ Yesterday we received twenty-five recruits which came on from Brazos with Lieutenant Carpenter of the First, and we hear that seventy more arrived for us last night. . . .[1]

I have not been into the city, dearest wife, since I last wrote you. For the last two days I have been engaged in drawing up a petition in this division to Congress for an asylum for old and invalid soldiers. I did it for an old friend (Captain Anderson, Third Artillery).[2] It has been a hobby of his for several years, and he is continually urging it before Congress. I promised him to draw up a petition in this division whilst he drew up one in the city. And this morning I have sent him the paper by Van Dorn with seventy-five names on it, with Generals Twiggs and Smith at the head. . . .

We have received no news of late, dearest, from the interior except that a corps belonging to General Kearny's command had fought and badly flogged a superior force of the enemy at Paso del Norte on the Rio Grande on the road from Santa Fe to Chihuahua. It is nearly a thousand miles from here.[3]

1. Stephen D. Carpenter, an 1840 graduate of the Academy, was a major in the Civil War and was killed in 1862 (Cullum, I, 616).   2. Robert Anderson, commander of Fort Sumter in April 1861, was born in Kentucky, graduated from West Point, and during the Mexican War was wounded at Molino del Rey. Partly through his efforts the government established the Soldiers' Home. He served as a brigadier general in 1861-63, retiring because of ill health, but was brevetted major general and sent to raise the flag over Sumter in 1865. He died in 1871 (*DAB*, vol. 1, pt. 1, pp. 274-75). His letters are in Eba Anderson Lawton, ed., *An Artillery Officer in the Mexican War* (New York, 1911).
3. Stephen W. Kearny was one of the principal soldiers of the American West. He was born in New Jersey in 1794 and served in the War of 1812. He received assignments in the West until, in May 1846, he was placed in command of the Army of the West. Shortly thereafter he was made a brigadier general. In August, with sixteen hundred men, he occupied Santa Fe. From there he struck out with a small force for California, where he

took part in the capture of Los Angeles. He proceeded east to Mexico, where a tropical disease contracted at Veracruz destroyed his health. He died in St. Louis in 1848. See Dwight L. Clarke, *Stephen Watts Kearny: Soldier of the West* (Norman, Okla., 1961).

February 7 ✦ I am going to finish this letter now and carry it into town myself tomorrow, for I have got to go in to act as a pallbearer at a funeral. Lieutenant Gibson of the artillery, a classmate of mine, died last night and is to be buried tomorrow at ten o'clock. He died of the same old disease, dysentery. I have seen him but once since we left West Point and knew him but very little there. But all his classmates are invited to attend as pallbearers.[1]

1. David Gibson graduated with Dana in 1842 and had served in garrison duty until the Mexican War (Cullum, II, 52).

February 9 ✦ We have a mighty hot day on hand and have had very hot weather for three days past. I wonder if this heat reaches as far as where you are? The sun here is beginning to show his power, so much so that the horses and mules are reeking even whilst they are standing at their picket ropes. By and by the sun will become terrible, and all our duties must be done early and late. But you recollect that we marched from Reynosa to Camargo in the middle of last July and that we marched from Camargo to Monterrey early in September, so that I expect we will be able to stand anything that is put upon us here on the seacoast.

I am sitting here now, with my tent walls raised in order to get as much circulation of air through the tent as possible, and with my jacket off and my suspenders slipped off. Only to think that at this time last year we were in the midst of snow in St. Louis. . . .

We are drilling now by brigades, and although the ground is rough, we make out to drill very well. The maneuvers in the evolutions of the line are so extended that it takes about two hours to drill. And after drill we are tolerably well tired.

Two or three days ago tickets were circulated in camp that a "respectable ball" would be given at one of the "fondas" last night, and we had heard a great deal of what a grand affair it was to be, that all the decent females in town were to go, three dollars a ticket. Well, last night some of our officers went, and there was no ball at all because no ladies would come. So they just set in and made a regular frolic of it, ate up the supper, and all got high. I heard some of our officers coming home this morning at two o'clock rather noisy.

February 10   ✦   It is blowing a very severe norther again today, my dearest Sue, and out of doors and in camp it is extremely disagreeable. Everything is full of dust and dirt, and when we go out, our hats blow off and our eyes are filled with sand. And in our tents everything is covered with the dirt which is constantly blowing about. When we sit down to meals our plates and dishes get full of grit immediately. And now whilst I am writing, my paper is getting covered with the same uncomfortable, disagreeable stuff.

February 14   ✦   That norther which had commenced when I was finishing my last letter turned out to be worst by far that we have experienced, and we had a gale for three days. And yesterday it finished off with a rain. Today the sun is trying hard to get out but only partially appears and that only for a little while at a time. But the day appears so much like a spring day in Louisiana clearing up after a storm it makes me feel almost homesick. So much do I feel what happiness would be ours if we could only spend this Sabbath together. . . .

I am on guard today, my dearest Sue, and without any tent or other convenience to write on. I am now sitting on a log and am writing on a piece of a box which I have laid hold of for the occasion. I have the wind occasionally blowing around me but am shaded from the little sun that occasionally comes by a tree under which I am sitting. Near me I have forty-eight noisy prisoners. It is only a few days since the men were paid off, so we are somewhat troubled with liquor and have a number of prisoners all the time. . . .

A queer sight has just passed by on the road, dearest one, two bare-legged Mexican women mounted on the same horse, or rather mule. A Mexican woman sits square right on the side of a horse and not halfway to the front as our ladies ride. All of these funny sights are so common and I am so accustomed to them now that I seldom notice them at all. I look upon what I see as I would look at the Negro women on the levee from the barracks where you are to the city. It appears so sappy and foolish and silly for some men like Kendall, Haile, and so forth to be writing about the beautiful faces, lovely features, bewitching forms, and so forth which they have seen in this country.[1] It is all a lie, or else these people have very strange tastes. Indeed I believe I have seen mulatto girls in the United States as good looking in person and face as any I have seen in Mexico. And as for ugliness, I have never seen any old Negro half so hideous and disgusting in appearance as very many of the wretched hags of this ill-famed race. I do think that take the brown order of Mexican women as a race and they are without exception the most revolting, forbidding, disgusting creatures in the world, not even excepting our own Indians. There was an old hag of about sixty without a tooth brought up yesterday as a witness before our court martial against an Irishman who was accused of committing violence on her person! The very idea was enough to make one throw up a breakfast which had been on the stomach for several hours. . . .

We have received information here of the capture of seventy of the Kentucky cavalry near Saltillo by about two thousand Mexican lancers. It was a foraging party under Major Gaines of Kentucky, and they were surprised and obliged to surrender at discretion with all their wagons and baggage. Their Mexican guides were taken out and shot without mercy as traitors to their country, and all the wagons, mules, and so forth were divided among the soldiers for booty. Cassius M. Clay was one of the officers taken. They were all sent by General Miñón, who took them to Santa Anna at San Luis Potosí. The Mexicans proclaim it as a great victory, although not a shot was fired or a blow struck. It is just about the same kind of a scrape as Thornton's was, except T. fought and tried to get clear, and Gaines did not. Those are the only kind of victories they can get, though, and they ought to make the most of it. They were just thirty to one, and that is just about the difference between us. . . .[2]

Beauregard came out to see us a little while ago. He called to see me, and finding I was on guard, he dropped in for a few minutes. He is at work all the week fortifying and can only come to see his friends on Sunday. This town has been very strongly fortified in order that a garrison of one thousand men may hold it against a large force after the forces here now leave it. We have here now all told about seven thousand troops, and General Scott must have from five thousand to seven thousand more with him. General Taylor has at Monterrey probably about four thousand.

1. Like Kendall, Christopher M. Haile was a correspondent for the *Picayune*. He was the first of Kendall's elaborate staff, and among other assignments reported Monterrey. Having attended West Point, he entered General Scott's army as a first lieutenant during the siege of Veracruz, and Kendall thereafter carried the full load of coverage. See Fayette Copeland, *Kendall of the Picayune*, pp. 158, 172, 188-89.   2. For capture of Maj. John P. Gaines and Captain Clay see David Lavender, *Climax at Buena Vista*, pp. 155-57, also—for Clay—David L. Smiley, *Lion of White Hall* (Madison, Wis., 1962), pp. 123-28.

February 16 ✦ General Scott is still at the Brazos, waiting for his transports. He has been cruelly disappointed in his ships not arriving. Circumstances over which he has had no control have delayed him, and the elements have conspired against him to rob him of most valuable and precious time. We cannot be delayed much longer, and I would not be surprised to get orders in a few days to prepare for embarkation. Our quartermasters are all busy making their preparations for the passage by sea to Veracruz. They are all occupied now in making slings for the horses. Those animals which have been shipped from New Orleans were nearly all of them lost through the mismanagement of the quartermaster's department. There was but one company of rifles which did not lose all their horses, and the horses of this company are so knocked to pieces that they are not fit for use.

Our troops want clothing very badly before they move. Through the negligence of the quartermaster's department, no supply of clothing has been sent here from the Brazos for this "corps d'armie," and our troops are all ragged and will soon be barefooted if no clothing arrives.

The Eighth Infantry embarked from the Brazos on the seventh for the Isla Verde or Anton Lizardo. They probably were out in this last norther and must have had a terrible time. Several ships have passed down in the last few days, loaded with troops and ordnance and so forth from the north.

By the last arrival Whiting received four engravings of his drawing of the Corpus Christi encampment. But two hundred copies have as yet been printed. He is very unfortunate, for his brother is unable to raise the requisite funds to bring them out, and I am afraid the publication of his pieces will be delayed. He is not at all pleased with this first engraving, for the artist has not done it justice. . . .

I have got my letters, my darling one, and have read them all. Four from your own dear self and two from sister Matilda, which I will send you. There are still one or two of your dear letters missing, my own darling one, but I suppose they will come to light yet. The one containing sister's letter which you say you gave with another to Mr. Jones I have not received. I also received a New Hampshire paper containing the unanimous nomination of General Peaslee to Congress. I believe he has been there before. He is a very eloquent man in a speech and is a talented lawyer.. . . .[1]

Tomorrow morning our whole division under General Twiggs, in all about fifteen hundred men, are to march to the plains on the border of town to have a grand division drill at evolutions of the line.

1. Charles Hazen Peaslee was born in New Hampshire in 1804, graduated from Dartmouth College in 1824, was admitted to the bar in 1828, and elected as a Democrat to Congress for three terms, 1847-53. He was adjutant general of the state militia in 1839-47 and collector of the port of Boston by appointment of President Franklin Pierce in 1853-57. He died in New Hampshire in 1866. *Biographical Directory of the American Congress: 1774-1961* (Washington, 1961), p. 1438.

February 19 ✦ I must now make use of this evening to write to you because I am not sure that I shall have another chance for some days. Day before yesterday we had that division drill near the city which I wrote to you about the evening before, and a very fatiguing time we had of it and were nearly cooked by the blazing sun. We had breakfast at an early hour, and at eight o'clock the different battalions of the division were formed and marched to town. We entered and marched through the city with drums beating and colors flying, making a great show before the citizens and all the new troops who were out to receive us. Of course we are looked upon as the veterans of the war, for we have served through two campaigns and have now entered upon the third. Well, we drilled about two hours after having marched about four miles to our drill ground, and then we marched back, with a blazing sun overhead and a burning sand underfoot, and when we arrived at camp, we were tired to excess. Many of the men gave out on account of the heat, and for some time after I reached home I had a severe headache. But an afternoon's nap cured me, and then I was ready for another drill. Today we had the same duty to perform again, but it was a cloudy forenoon, and we did not suffer any.

General Twiggs is a good drill officer, and it is well to take advantage of his instructions in the evolutions of the line as often as we can, for it is very seldom that our troops get a chance to drill in large masses. For whenever they are so collected, they always have work to do or are on the march or something of the kind.

Whilst we were drilling in town today, General Scott with a numerous staff arrived on the *Massachusetts* from the Brazos, and a salute was fired and a great fuss was made over him. He was conducted to General Patterson's quarters, where large numbers of officers called on him, and he told them that the embarkation of troops was to commence from here tomorrow with our division. . . .[1]

There are three or four fellows, dear one, here plaguing Little and scuffling about and it is as much as I can do to collect a few scattered ideas to put on paper. But I must write now, at any rate, for it is now after taps a long time, and we move at eight o'clock tomorrow morning. . . . You have no idea how much these varmints trouble me. They are scuffling so here and pulling each other about so much that I can hardly write a sentence and do not know all I have already written. It is always so the night before we march. . . .

Whiting send his love to you, Kate, and Irene. Give mine to I. also. Tell her I have just read her message to Little. He says give his love to her and says if he can possibly get away from Mexico he will come on forthwith, but she must write to General Scott to ask permission for him. He has been looking all over Tampico to get some Mexican curiosity to send her but cannot find any kind. He would send a lock of hair, but he has actually grown bald by giving his hair to the señoritas, but she shall have a lock of the first growth. He wants to know if the loss of a limb would be an objection. He has a pretty little dimple in his cheek where the alcalde's daughter bit him.

1. See Charles W. Elliott, *Winfield Scott* (New York, 1937).

12

Veracruz

February-April 1847

Waiting at Tampico. Aboard the *Othello*. Waiting off Veracruz. Bivouac on the Sands outside the City. The Batteries Open. The City and Castle Capitulate. Damage Is Immense. A Fort Pike Headache. Waiting in Veracruz.

February 20 ✦ It is just a year, dearest, since we embarked on board the *Highlander* at St. Louis. What a different embarkation this is! We left our camp bag and baggage at eight o'clock this morning and marched through town with colors flying as usual, and we reached here after a tramp of seven or eight miles through the sand about one o'clock. And I acknowledge that I for one was pretty well tired. After we had been in camp some time and I had taken a nap, Whiting and myself took a nice bath in the sea, which was truly grateful and refreshing. It was so long since we had had a chance for such a thing. The sea is a great sight after having seen nothing but dry land for a year.

February 22 ✦ Here we are yet instead of, as I thought when I last wrote, Los Lobos. We could not embark well yesterday or today on account of a fresh norther which has been blowing. . . . There are a large ship, two brigs, and six schooners waiting abreast of us to take us on board, and they are all fine-looking vessels.

We have had no news for the last two days. A large steamship arrived last night and is riding at anchor off the bar, but the sea is so rough that we cannot communicate with her, so that we do not even know who she is and where she is from.

February 23 ✦ The steamship *Eudora* has just come over the bar and passed up. She must have a mail for us and I hope we will get hold of it before we leave. There were several ladies aboard who waved their white handkerchiefs at us as they passed the camp, but we could not see who they were. I suppose Mrs. Gates is one of them, and Paul is dreadfully afraid that his wife may be there.

Wouldn't that be nice now, for her to come here just as her husband is embarking? He would only be able to see her for an hour or so, and then she would have to go right back again by the first chance she could get. She has been writing Paul a great deal about her immense doctor's bills in the city. I don't believe it but believe the money has gone in some way that she is ashamed or afraid to speak of.[1]

Our company, dearest one, embarks on board a brig called the *Othello* with a part of the First Regiment, Whiting's company together with Ross' on a schooner called *Regina*. Captain Waite, I believe, goes on board the ship *Ellslie*.[2]

1. Collinson R. Gates, an 1836 graduate of the Academy, died in 1849 (Cullum, I, 515).
2. Carlos A. Waite became a second lieutenant in 1820, first lieutenant in 1828, captain in 1836, and major in February 1847. He was brevetted colonel for Molino del Rey and brigadier general in 1865. He died the next year (Heitman, I, 993).

On board brig *Othello* at anchor off Lobos, February 28 • We have been anchored here for two days, rolling and pitching and tossing about here like chips at sea. We have all been more or less seasick, and if the sea had not have been so bad I would have had a long letter, but I could not write as it is. There are over fifty vessels anchored here, all loaded with troops. All the regulars are here, besides some three thousand volunteers. We are all afloat and will not go on shore, not even General Scott, who holds his headquarters on board the *Massachusetts*.

On board brig *Othello* off Antón Lizardo, March 5 • You see that we are still on board of our miserable transports, my darling wife, and that we have been obliged to play the sailor much longer than we have fancied. . . .

We are now about three miles outside of the anchorage almost in a calm. At the anchorage we see quite a fleet of our vessels, probably some thirty sails, but there are at least forty more which left Lobos with us still to arrive. But my darling wife, let me commence at our shipment from the mouth of the Pánuco and tell you how [we] got along thus far. . . .

We have had as pleasant a time of it as we could have had on board with any set of fellows. Captain Holmes has been sick all the time, very much so, and Carpenter a good deal. The rest of us have been about on a par and are now tolerably good sailors.

Well, on the twenty-fifth we were all towed over the Tampico bar one by one by the steamboat *Undine*, and before sunset the whole division, thirteen vessels, were under sail for the rendezvous at Lobos. We made a tolerably fine start, but in the night we were becalmed, and by daylight we had drifted back again to the anchorage off the bar. About noon a good norther sprang up, and before it we ran right straight down to the island, where we arrived just before sunset on the twenty-sixth and came to anchor in the midst of our fleet of transports numbering about fifty sail. . . .

Well, the way we pitched and tossed and rolled there wasn't at all slow. It appeared sometimes as if we would almost turn bottom upwards. . . .

There must be letters for me in the fleet, for several steamers have arrived, the *Edith, Alabama, Orleans,* and others. Whiting passed me once on the *Eudora* and held up some letters to me, but the wind blew so hard that it was impossible to hear what he said. . . .

Several orders about disembarking and signals and so forth were issued at Lobos, and after General Worth arrived, we all waited for the signal to weigh anchor and proceed to Antón Lizardo. At eleven o'clock on the second a gun was fired on board the flagship and the yellow flag sent up to the mizzenmast head which was the signal for all vessels to proceed to Antón Lizardo. Immediately the *Massachusetts,* the *Edith,* and the *Eudora* (the three generals) went out to sea. But as there was no breeze, the sail vessels of the fleet could not stand out till next morning, day before yesterday. . . .

This anchorage of Antón Lizardo is some distance below Veracruz, and if we land here we will have to march up some ten or twelve miles by land. But no one knows as yet how we are to approach the city except that we are to approach it from the land side.

March 6 ♦ We came to anchor here shortly after I finished writing yesterday, and I went on board the flagship of Commodore Conner with Colonel Wilson to report our arrival. . . .[1] Very nearly all of our vessels are now here, and this morning I counted more than seventy vessels. I suppose it will be a couple of days yet before we attempt a landing. We received a Mexican paper this morning containing Santa Anna's report of a battle with General Taylor. He states his force at seventeen thousand men. General T. could not

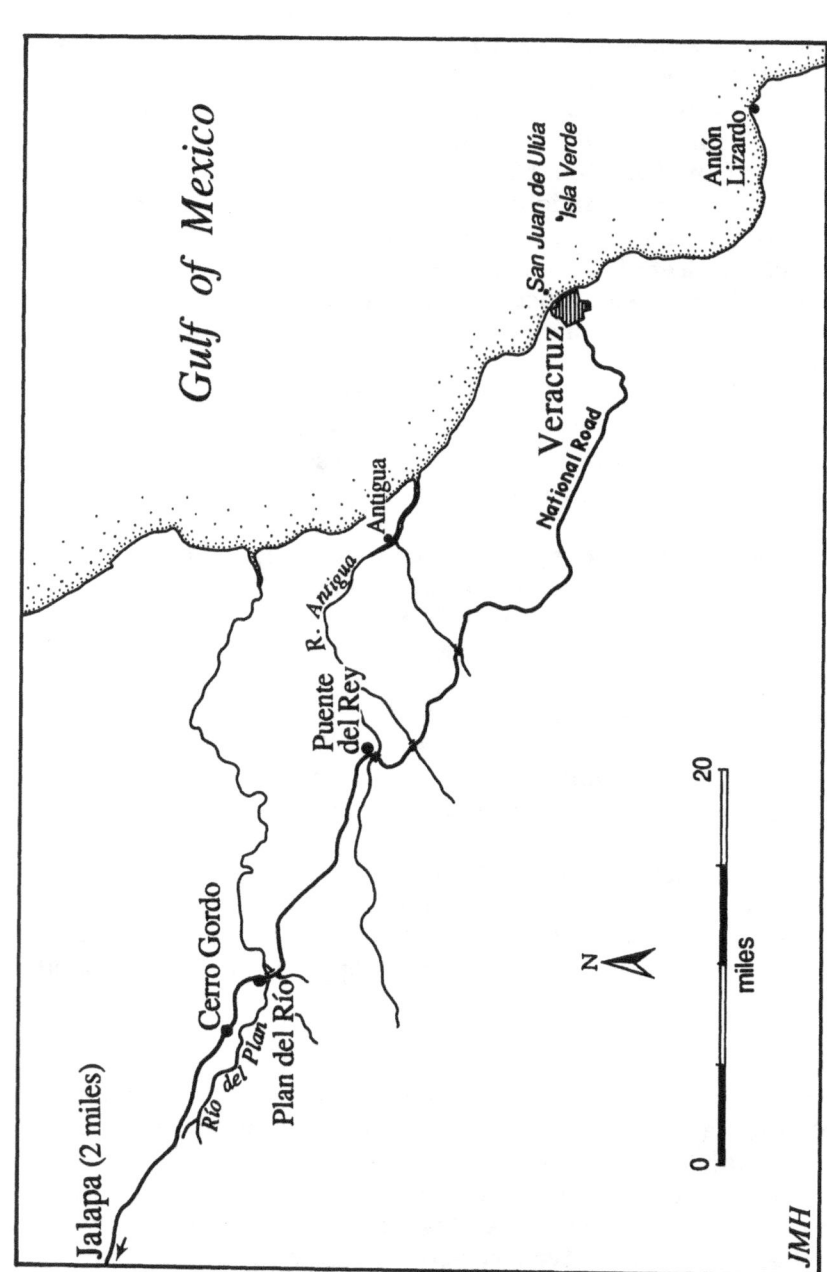

Veracruz and Hinterland

have had over five thousand. They fought two days, and Santa Anna says that he lost one thousand men and was obliged to fall back to get provisions and take care of his wounded. He says that General T. lost two thousand men. This, of course, he knows nothing about, but from the fact of his retreating with such a large force before such a small one we feel sure he has been most terribly bested, and we wait with impatience to hear the report of a signal victory from General Taylor. General Taylor has not more than three hundred regulars with him. I have no doubt that old Zack has added another fresh laurel to all those he has already gained.[2]

1. Henry Wilson fought in the War of 1812 and was a lieutenant colonel during the Mexican War. He was brevetted colonel for Monterrey. He became colonel of the Seventh Infantry in 1851, resigned in 1861, and died in 1872 (Heitman, I, 1,046).   2. The paper was of course reporting Buena Vista (February 22-23).

Anchorage at Antón Lizardo, March 7 ✦ We are still in the same position in which we were, at anchor and making preparations to land. General Scott and all his staff and high officers went yesterday in a steamboat to reconnoiter the castle and city. They were gone pretty nearly all day and went to within a mile and a half of the castle. The enemy threw eleven large Paixhans shells at them which burst pretty near the steamer, but no one was hurt.

March 8 ✦ Here we are still, my darling one, still at anchor for another day. . . . Our brigade under General Twiggs forms the reserve and is to be the last to land. . . . General Quitman arrived last night, and the last of the volunteers are looked for by the first good breeze from the north. . . . We all believe here that General Santa Anna has received a beating from General Taylor, and all the old man's friends are exulting in it.

On board sloop-of-war *St. Mary's*, March 9 ✦ We are all on board the warships now, my dearest one, and I am in the first lieutenant's stateroom. We are now going to land and no prospect of opposition. I leave this on board the *St. Mary's* for you.

Bivouac before Veracruz, March 18 ✦ I cannot enter into a detail of all we have done even if it were interesting. We have had a great deal of hard work and have a great deal more before us. Our brigade is about five miles from the shipping, and we have no tents, no baggage yet, and for nine days I have been rolling in the sand with nothing but my cloak and sometimes in the rain. We have nothing but what we carry on our backs, and in addition to my cloak I have to carry about wth me a haversack with four days' provisions and canteen of water. Quite a load. Our guard duty is very hard, and we have to be constantly on the alert to preventing the enemy from communicating to or from the city. We are all, however, in excellent health and are doing very well, but a little impatient at the delay which the northers have occasioned us.

We landed on the beach about three miles below the city without opposition on the night of the ninth, and next day proceeded to take up our positions to invest the city. On the thirteenth the investment was complete and the city entirely cut off from communication with the world. General Worth's brigade extends from the sea on the south side of the city for about a mile. Our brigade extends from the sea on the north side of the city for about the same distance, and the three brigades of volunteers fill up the interval. When our brigade completed the investment, all the cavalry of the enemy were without grazing, and they are all shut out. We are all beyond the range of the enemy's artillery and in perfect safety. They keep firing with their heavy pieces at Worth's position but without effect.

In taking up our positions we had a little skirmishing in which about ten men were wounded, among them Lieutenant Colonel Dixon of South Carolina. I have heard of but three being killed, a volunteer, a rifleman, and Captain Alburtis of the Second Infantry. He was killed by a chance cannon shot on the eleventh.[1]

There is no danger attending the investment, and I doubt if we experience any more loss. The duty is more tedious and harassing than dangerous. It is evident that the enemy are very weak in the city. They dare not show themselves beyond the walls. They have made several attempts within the last few days to communicate their situation to their friends outside, but we have intercepted all their letters. I have heard of one man being captured who tried to pass for a fool and who was carrying a piece of shingle in his hand, which he carelessly threw down after he was taken. One of our soldiers picked it up and split it to kindle his fire, when out tumbled the same letter to the governor of the department which we had captured copies of twice before. . . .

We have not yet fired a gun at the city. We have but two mortars

The bombardment of Veracruz.

landed yet. A tremendous norther has been blowing for four days past so that nothing could be landed.

1. William Alburtis entered the army as a second lieutenant in 1837, became a first lieutenant in 1839, and was brevetted captain for the campaign against the Florida Indians (Heitman, I, 155).

March 25 ✦ Here we are still in the same place and pretty much the same fix as when I last wrote you. The work is very tedious, but our batteries have been opened for two days, and the city has been severely bombarded. And now whilst I am writing the cannonade is going on very hotly. That poor city is in a bad fix, a constant stream of shot and shells pouring into it all the time, day and night. They still continue to return the fire of our batteries with but little effect, and it is believed by all that they cannot stand this much longer. They are only holding out from day to day in the hope that Santa Anna will advance from the City of Mexico to their relief, but they cannot entertain this hope much longer. Our severe cannonade and bombardment must put them in a very straitened fix, for their city must be completely riddled. And we have ammunition to keep up our cannonade with increased energy for seven or eight days longer.

Scene in Veracruz during the bombardment.

As for us, my dearest wife, we are merely lookers-on. We have as yet had no fighting to do. We are out here in the sand beyond the reach of the city and castle, and we can see all that is going on from the top of our little hillocks without being exposed at all. It is true we are in a very uncomfortable fix still, having no tents and no baggage. I have managed to get my blankets and yesterday borrowed a clean shirt, after having worn one for sixteen days. So if it was not very dirty indeed, your husband must be a remarkably clean man.

We have been very fortunate indeed in not having rain, since we have been here without shelter. We have had hard storms of wind and sand for a great part of the time, but we have had but little rain. This is the most sandy place I have ever seen, nothing but sand hills to be seen as far as the eye can reach, and when the wind blows we are almost buried alive.

Oh, that I could exchange this miserable life for one of harder labor where my labor could be turned to my own advantage and that of my darling wife and my little one. I would willingly exchange my lot, dearest one, for a hard-working one in civil life. What is there longer to induce a young man to remain in the service of the country? Every mail from our government instead of promotion and honor but brings us fresh disappointments and renewed injuries. The army is done for. It is as dead as a doornail, and at the end of the war every young officer who possibly can will leave it in disgust and contempt. I have been in service five years, have served in hard campaigns for upwards of eighteen months, have fought through the whole of the present war, and I am still a second lieutenant and have not risen a single file since the war commenced. Still, new corps have been raised and new military officers created, but the benefits of them are all given to the sovereign people whose friends have votes to give pro or con J.K. Polk. . . .

I am so accustomed now, dearest Sue, to sleeping with my clothes on that I do not know how it feels to go to bed regularly. I have not had off my pants to go to bed for a month, and I pulled off my coat and boots night before last for the first time for a fortnight. And a great part of that time I have also slept with my sword and sash on. . . .

Thus far our siege has been attended with but little loss on our side. I suppose fifteen would cover all our killed, though of course we cannot yet know, our lines are so long. The sailors of the squadron have a heavy battery ashore, and three of them were killed yesterday. Captain Vinton of the artillery was killed two or three days since at one of the batteries. He exposed himself uselessly and was killed by a cannonball striking him on the side. It did not break the skin at all but glanced from him, knocking the breath out of him and killing him immediately.[1] With his exception I have not heard of any officers being hurt since the death of Captain Alburtis. . . .

By the way, dear one, I forgot to tell you of my getting the cake which you sent me. I was out with my company and three other companies the other day on a foraging party and when I returned after a hard day's work Whiting gave me a half of a pound cake with fruit in it which had been left with him for me. He and Van Dorn and myself sat down and made away with it in short order. It was mighty nice, and we thought it a great luxury and vanity in the midst of our hard bread and pork.

1. John R. Vinton graduated in 1817 and was brevetted major at Monterrey (Cullum, I, 164).

March 28 ✦ Well, my darling one, I believe the siege is over and there is but little doubt that both the city and the castle have capitulated. And what has been our loss? A mere nothing! It has all been done by cannonade and bombardment. The poor Mexicans, I expect, have suffered almost incredibly. Since our batteries have been opened, there was a continual stream of shot and shells poured into them night and day without cessation until they sent in a white flag. In the night I have counted five ten-inch shells in the air at one time going into the town and with no cessation. Of course there was no hiding from danger, and they must have suffered immensely. Our batteries of a large number of pieces of very heavy ordnance were opened [with] great violence for the first time on the twenty-second at four o'clock p.m. The fire was kept up constantly till four p.m. on the twenty-fifth, at which hour the enemy hung out a white flag from their walls and sounded a parley. The firing ceased, and negotiations commenced. The enemy agreed to surrender the town, provided the garrison were allowed to march out with the honors of war as they did at Monterrey. This was refused. They then asked for time to bury their dead. This was thought a subterfuge and was also refused. They then demanded that their women and children should be allowed to leave the city. This was also refused on the ground that permission to that effect had been given to them before the batteries opened.

So at half past one o'clock at night, the batteries reopened with increased fury, and they continued to pour in their iron hail all that night and all the day and night of the twenty-sixth. And this was about as long as they could stand it. So at daylight yesterday morning the white flag appeared again, with a letter to General Scott saying that the city proposed to surrender and requesting he would appoint a commissioner to meet their commissioners in the city and arrange the terms.

March 29 ✦ All is done, my darling wife, and the Stars and Stripes are now proudly waving over the city of Veracruz and the castle of San Juan de Ulúa. Captain Holmes came in yesterday and stopped my writing by telling me the news, and since then I have been entirely occupied by duty. . . .

The ceremony of surrender today was very imposing. I did not see it as our brigade did not go into town. At eight o'clock this morning the Mexicans fired a salute from the castle and the town and hauled down their colors. At ten General Worth's and General Pillow's brigades, six thousand men, marched into the city to receive the surrendered places, and the naval vessels took up a position between the castle and town.[1] When our colors were hoisted separately at each position, all the naval vessels, the foreign

The salute from the castle and the American fleet.

navies, the castle, all the batteries, and the town saluted, and such a slam bang of cannon has not been heard since the King of Rome was home. Then the two brigades formed in two lines facing towards each other. The forces of the enemy marched in between them, stacked their arms, hung all their equipment on the stacks, and left them. Poor fellows, they must have felt badly to have left their arms in that way. Then the surrender was complete, and the great place of Mexican strength is in our hands.

1. A law partner of Polk, Gideon J. Pillow was clearly cut out for command during the Mexican War. Born in Tennessee in 1806, he delighted in political manipulation and believed that he secured Polk's nomination for the presidency in 1844. He did have a part in the nomination of Pierce in 1852. In the Mexican War, Polk appointed him brigadier general and subsequently advanced him to major general. After serving briefly with General Taylor, he transferred to Scott and took part in all the campaigns to Mexico City. At Cerro Gordo he shouted at his troops and thereby disclosed their position. The troops hated him, as is evident from the diary remark of a Pennsylvania volunteer: "By this time, Brig.-Gen. Gideon Johnston Pillow, (I am giving you his title and name in full), was seen going down the hill in our rear, and was no more seen or heard from until the engagement was all over" (J. Jacob Oswandel, *Notes on the Mexican War* [Philadelphia, 1885], 126, entry of April 18, 1847). In the Civil War he supported the Confederacy, but his ignominious behavior in 1862 at Fort Donelson, when he escaped just prior to the surrender and left his troops to give themselves up to the Federal forces, further tarnished his reputation. He died in 1878 (*DAB*, vol. 7, pt. 2, pp. 603-4).

March 30 ◆ Just one year this day since we parted, my own Sue.
When will we be able to meet again?

April 2 ◆ I finished your last letter on the thirtieth, and then I
went to town to get it on board some boat which was going with a
mail. But everything in town was confusion, and I could find
neither post office, postmaster, nor anything else. Nothing had
then been established, and nobody knew where anybody was. At
last I met Captain Sanders of the engineers, who told me that he was
to start with dispatches for Washington next day on the *Alabama*. So
I gave him my letter and asked him to be particular not to carry it on
to W. with him but either to mail it at Orleans or to put it in the letter
box of the *Alabama*. Now, I hope he will not carry the letter north
with him, but it is as likely as not that he will, for every other person
he met had some command for him. The letter was a large one, such
as the officers of the army receive on official business and contained
my pay accounts for March ($65.50). I trust you will not be delayed
in getting them. Let me know so soon as you can draw the pay what
paymaster paid them, as that will be necessary on my next account. . . .
    Whilst I was in the city I made up my mind that one visit would
do for me, so I went all over it everywhere, to the castle, too, in a
boat. Well, this walking, together with four miles there and back
from camp, of course, pretty nearly tired me out. I did not get home
till after dark, and then I was comforted by receiving your four
letters to read.
    The damage done to the city by our shot and shells is immense.
The lower half of the city is almost ruined. Whole blocks of buildings are so shattered, so that it will cost as much to repair them as it
would to rebuild them. Our immense shells would fall through the
tops of houses, go through both stories, and then bursting would
shatter the whole house, throw down walls, and blow two or three
rooms into one. Doors and windows are blown to pieces all over the
city. Some houses had as many as a dozen ten-inch shells burst in
them. One of their splendid churches is completely ruined inside.
Several ten-inch shells fell in among the altars, and a number of
forty-two-pounder shot went through it. These splendid altars,
costly and old oil paintings, images of alabaster, wood and marble,
alabaster ornaments, cut-glass chandeliers and large vases and
shades, gilt and silver work, ornamental flowers and drapery,
priests' robes and church linen, books, bricks, mortar shot, and

Gate of Mercy at Veracruz.

pieces of shells formed one confused mass of fragments, the most costly work of a costly Catholic tabernacle totally destroyed.

I went in there and looked all around, and would you believe it, your sacrilegious husband stole from the very altar. I would have liked to have found a little wax image, but there was nothing of the kind there. But in the pile of destruction of one of the altars, I found several little consecrated bags which the priests bless and sell to the people, who wear them around their necks under their shirts and shifts as the Indians wear a charm. Some have a piece of money consecrated and put into it. Dr. Randall will tell you the meaning of the Latin motto. I enclose it here for you.

On the steps of the altar of this church sat two mothers with their babes at their breasts during the bombardment, and the Mexicans say that they were both killed by the first shell which entered the tabernacle. I was told also that a shell killed seven members of one family whilst they were collected in one room. War is a terrible thing at best, but when it comes to killing women and children, it is shocking. It cannot, however, be helped in investing and bombard-

ing a city. If they do not choose to run the risk, they can always clear
out before the investment is complete.

As for the castle of San Juan de Ulúa, it is the most perfect
fortification I ever saw. It is said to be much stronger than Quebec by
those who have seen both places. Probably Gibraltar, the Morro,
and this work are the three strongest forts in the world, and the
Spaniards built all three of them. I believe that if properly defended
it is perfectly impregnable except by starvation. There are some of
the largest cannon there I have ever seen, and ten or fifteen beautiful old Spanish brass twenty-four-pounders.[1] In all, I believe, the
castle has mounted 170 cannon. I have not seen the inventory of our
captures, but I suppose 300 cannon is not an overestimate, and the
military stores of all kinds is immense.

1. Guns in the castle dated to Philip V, and American troops investing Veracruz used
guns taken from Burgoyne in the Revolution. George Furber, *The Twelve Months Volunteer*,
549-50, 569. The war of 1846-48 came just at a time when shells were replacing round shot
and rifled guns the old smoothbores. During the investment the shells proved far more
destructive than the balls, as Dana related.

April 5   ✦   I can only write you a very few lines this time. I have
just heard that the *Edith* is going today, and I am very much afraid
my own little Sue will be so much disappointed if she does not get a
letter by her. I believe, dearest one, that we will start tomorrow on
the road to Jalapa. . . . Colonel Wilson's regiment is to remain as a
garrison for Veracruz. If they are careful to keep the city clean, I
doubt if they will have any yellow fever at all. Nothing but the filth
of the people can breed yellow fever here, for it is just such a place as
Fort Pickens. Out here in these sand hills yellow fever never comes.
It is confined solely, I believe, to the filthy city. Jalapa is said to be
one of the garden spots of Mexico.

Yesterday and the day before, dearest one, I had an attack of one
of my Fort Pike headaches and so forth. I thought I was bilious and
sent for the doctor and asked him to take all the bile out of me. He
took me at my word, having first made me promise that I would
take anything he would prescribe. He gave me an emetic night
before last, a heavy dose of calomel on an entirely empty stomach
yesterday morning, and a Seidlitz powder in the afternoon. So you
may be very certain there is no bile in me now. I was pretty sick
yesterday from the effects of the medicine, but today I am ready for
a fresh start. That physicking will probably be the means of keeping
me well all summer.[1]

My own dear wife, I will pack your box of shells now as well as my limited means will allow, but I fear that some of them will get broken. I wish I had something else to fill up the box. The goblet is the one that Montezuma used when he drank Cortéz' health. . . .

My own darling wife, the doctor has just been in and tells me that he has not a single ounce of transportation for carrying the sick and that if I went I would have to march. But three small tents can be taken for each company, so he advised me to stay here until I got perfectly robust and start again when I could come on. So I shall put myself under the care of our good old friend Laub for a week or so.

1. The nature of Dana's ailment is difficult to discern, but his physician friend evidently took him at his word—about the bile. The result was calomel, as a purgative, and the Seidlitz powder as a mild cathartic. Shortly thereafter, as the reader will see, Dana sensibly took quinine, which may have been what he needed. It was, he related, Sue's favorite remedy. A Missouri resident, Dr. John Sappington, was the nationally known advocate of quinine as a remedy for malaria, and Sue as a Missouri native doubtless knew of Sappington's Pills. See *DAB*, vol. 8, pt. 2, p. 353. Dana was seldom ill, which was his great good fortune, as illness carried off far more of Taylor's and Scott's soldiers than did the battlefield. Like all earlier wars, and even the then approaching Civil War, the Mexican War occurred in the medical dark ages when physicians knew little about the medicines they dispensed. Mortality from illness was very high. Of all men in the U.S. Army in the Mexican War, 1,549 were killed in battle or died of wounds, and 10,970 died of disease, a ratio of seven deaths from camp diseases, chiefly dysentery, to one caused by battle injury. Mortality from disease was 110 per 1,000 per year, compared with 65 and 16 for the Civil War and World War I, respectively. Losses due to disease among the volunteers were nearly twice as high as in the regular army (Stanhope Bayne-Jones, *The Evolution of Preventive Medicine in the United States, 1607-1939* [Washington, D.C., 1968], 86).

April 7 ✦ Our brigade marches tomorrow, so today I am going into town. I am quite well again now but I do not like to take the road again after taking so much medicine until I get thoroughly strengthened. Since I last wrote you I have taken quinine, your old favorite. I shall be ready to start in a few days, probably when General Worth's division leaves.

April 9 ✦ Here I am in Veracruz and right well again. The regiment left yesterday morning on the march, and I came into town and installed myself in a comfortable house where seven other officers board. . . . You may judge the prices of things here. Tomatoes are three for a bit, eggs a picayune a piece, and so forth. However, when I came in here I had not eaten a mouthful of food except one potato for five days and the doctor told me that it was necessary not to mind my purse till I had looked out for my health,

so I am living on lemonade, and the way I can put into the vegetables, cabbage, tomatoes, potatoes, and especially lettuce isn't
slow. . . .

Here am I in a nice, cool room with big doors in a high second
story, and green blinds and shade, and I believe I could live secure
here. . . .

I met our old friend De Leon this morning, and we went and
demolished some such nice oysters. How many raw oysters do you
suppose I ate? Only three dozen. . . .

We have the enemy here trembling before a very fine army for
his capital, and that noble old man, that hero of the north, our brave
old General Taylor, has stricken the enemy so in his quarter that
they shrink from him as he advances. He is a noble specimen of a
soldier and a gallant general. That honest old man, we believe him
the greatest general our country has produced, and there is nothing
the army will not do for that old chief. I believe he can call around
him now if he were so inclined a host of brave spirits from all
sections of our country who would follow him to anything and
guard him to the last. It is useless for such insignificant pygmies as
J.K. Polk to beat their brains out against such men as he!

13
Cerro Gordo
April-May 1847

A Fast March. On the National Road to the City of Mexico. Our Army Reported
Encamped before the Enemy at Paso del Gordo. I Am Now a First Lieutenant. My
Twenty-fifth Birthday. The Puente del Rey, or King's Bridge. Wounded and at Plan del
Río. Jalapa. Sue Must Practice a Good Deal of Patience.

Second halting place from Veracruz, April 14 ✦ Here we are
again on the march, and mighty hard marching it has been. The sun
has been and must always be excessively hot in this climate, and we
ought to do all our marching in the night. If we do march in the
daytime, we must expect our men to break down, as they have been
doing for the last two days. We have just strewed the road with
men, and when we arrive at our halting place for the night, not two-
thirds of the men are up.

I would have written some to you last night, dearest wife, but
our road was so heavy and sandy that my baggage did not get up till
midnight, and I went and took supper and slept with our friend De
Leon, whose baggage had come up.

Day before yesterday, dearest Sue, I had my baggage moved out
from my boardinghouse to the camp of the Fourth Infantry so as to
be ready to start with them yesterday morning. About tattoo after
arriving in camp, I heard that a mail had come, so I walked a mile to
the post office and bothered the postmaster till he allowed me to
look over such letters as he had assorted, and I received three from
your own dear self, one from mother, and one from sister. The
letters I have not even been able to read yet. Two of yours are old
ones, one of them written before last Christmas which I suppose
had been 'way up to Monterrey and back. It was the letter in which
you have so much to excuse yourself for in buying an old guitar. I am
only sorry you did not buy a better one whilst you were about it. But
you have never said anything about it since. Have you learned to
play on it yet? . . .

We started for the encampment near Veracruz yesterday morning at five o'clock, and our march was a very hard one indeed, for
the most part over a road of deep sand and under a blazing sun, not

one ray of which seemed to be reflected from us. We had to halt very frequently, and still the men broke down and laid down by the roadside in great numbers. And even when we started this morning some of the men were not up.

I loafed about after we halted till about tattoo, when I went and "rung in" on De Leon. We did not start this morning till late, and although the road was excellent, being the grand National Road to the City of Mexico, the excessive heat made the march very distressing. Yesterday we marched fourteen miles and today not more than ten, but we were obliged to halt to recruit the men.

We found and buried this morning the bodies of two dragoons who were murdered. They were evidently express men returning to Veracruz from General Twiggs. Twiggs evidently drove a body of the enemy before him for some distance along the road.

A wagon train passed us today returning from General Twiggs to Veracruz for supplies. They report our army encamped twenty-five miles from here before the enemy. Santa Anna has chosen a position in a strong mountain pass called I think "Paso del Gordo" and has fortified himself there upon the hills. General Twiggs intended to attack him today, but I rather think that General Scott got up in time to stop him until he gets all ready. He will probably wait for us to come up, and then he will put Santa Anna in a mighty bad fix. I trust we may be able to give him such a whipping that the war will be finished at a blow. If we can annihilate this army of his and catch him, the City of Mexico will probably be taken without another struggle.

Santa Anna is said to have several heights crowned with field-works and cannon, and our army is encamped within three miles of him as near as they can obtain water. Our engineers have been busy reconnoitering, and the different parties have been fired on. Captain Johnston of the topographical engineers received two musket balls whilst making a reconnaissance.[1] He has just been appointed a lieutenant colonel in one of the new regiments. We must have eight thousand men ahead, and when we get there we will be about twelve thousand.

The order for my promotion came among many others, my darling Sue, the evening before I left Veracruz. I am now a first lieutenant and belong to Captain Gatlin's company, and so long as he remains away I shall command the company. I trust he will remain absent for a long time, for it will be worth ten dollars a month to me as long as he does.

The National Bridge from the bluffs on the east.

1. Joseph E. Johnston, a graduate in 1829, was brevetted colonel for his reconnaissance. Achieving the rank of brigadier general in 1860, he resigned the next year and became one of the principal commanders of the Confederacy (*DAB*, vol. 5, pt. 2, pp. 144-46).

Puente del Rey, April 15 ✦ This is my twenty-fifth birthday, my own darling wife and I wonder if you have forgotten it again this year. Now before this reaches you yours will probably be past, but I shall not forget it. What an old girl you are, twenty-five, only think of it. Five more and you will be thirty. . . .

We made an early start this morning from our last halting place, and our march was a very easy and comfortable one. We only marched nine miles, and here we are at the great national bridge called Puente del Rey, or King's Bridge. It is a grand and beautiful piece of masonry, a solid mass of heavy masonry arches. It must have cost a very large sum of money and have been built by a very skillful engineer. It is a credit to any nation and any road and is one of the finest works of the kind I ever saw.

Indeed this whole road is as fine and expensive a one as I ever traveled on. It is regularly built and sometimes for miles it is paved with stone. Sometimes it is built up like a stone bridge and then again it is cut through limestone rock. It is a great work of Old Spain, on a par with the castle of San Juan de Ulúa. Mexico never would have done such a work of herself.

This bridge runs through a defile which is strongly fortified by a

fort situated on the heights on each side of it. One of the forts has
high walls of stone and is about eight hundred feet above the
bridge. The Mexicans had eight pieces of cannon here and intended
to dispute the pass, but when we sent the expedition to Antigua,
they thought that it was our whole army coming round in their rear
to cut them off, so they cleared out of this. And afterwards Santa
Anna came and concluded to post himself in the Paso del Gordo,
which is a much more difficult defile than this. We shall see how
much good his strong position will do him.

He attacked General Taylor with an immensely superior force,
and our general repulsed him with fearful harm. Now we will show
him what we can do when we attack with equal force. We have
heard several cannon today and suppose it is the Mexicans firing at
our reconnoitering parties. It may be that the fight will be over
before we can reach there. But I should think General Scott would
wait till we come up in order to cut off the enemy's retreat. We are
now sixteen miles from our army, and I expect we will reach them
tomorrow night.

On the road today I found some bananas and plantains, the first
thing like fruit that I have seen in this deserted country. We have
passed a great many ranches, but they are all deserted. I suppose
the families have all gone to Jalapa, and the men I suppose have all
been pressed into the service. I have no doubt there are a good
many in Santa Anna's army who surrendered and were paroled at
Veracruz. If so and we can get hold of any of them and detect them,
they will be shot to a certainty.

April 16 ✦ We are still here, my own dearest Sue, at the National
Bridge and will probably not move now till tomorrow morning.
After we had all gone to bed last night we were woken up to be told
that reveille would be sounded at twelve o'clock and that we would
march at one in order to join in the conflict when the positions of
Santa Anna were assaulted today. Well, sure enough, we had reveille at midnight, and at one we were on the road expecting to come
up with General Scott about ten o'clock this morning. When we had
gotten about three miles on our route, we were stopped by an aide
from General Scott, so we laid down by the road and slept till
daylight, when we returned again to our old position. We do not
know exactly what General Scott's orders to General Worth were,
but we think that the attack was postponed and that we were

The hills of Cerro Gordo and Telegrafo.

ordered to remain here until the train of wagons comes along from Veracruz and then escort it. This train will probably be along this afternoon, and we will probably join General Scott tomorrow. I suppose the general has concluded to wait for some more mortars and heavy cannon and shell them out of their position as he did at Veracruz.

The Battle of Cerro Gordo on April 18, 1847, proved a triumph for General Scott's army, and especially for the West Pointers in its midst. In part through advice of Captain Robert E. Lee and the captain's assistants, Scott found a way to outflank Santa Anna's positions and virtually cut the Mexican troops to pieces. Considering their stolid leadership the Mexicans fought surprisingly well, and unit actions often were fierce. One of the most notable was the defense of Telegraph Hill. Lieutenant Dana was moving up the hill with his men when a ball struck him down. Left on the field for dead, he lay there for thirty-six hours until a burial party brought him in. On April 19, Captains Hanson and Whiting wrote Sue what had happened. "When shot," Hanson related, "he was gallantly engaged on the left of the company, under my command, in charging the most formidable of the works which defend the pass of the 'Sierra Gorda.' This wound was soon dressed by the surgeon of the regiment, Dr. McLaren, and as soon as the fort was in our posses-

sion and my duties would permit, I had him conveyed in a litter to the work.[1] Whilst engaged in contributing to his comfort as far as the means in my power would allow, I received an order to take my company and join my regiment upon the Jalapa Road. I left him in the care of attentive medical officers who will, I doubt not, do all in their power to relieve him. I left with him also a man of my company to attend to him solely.

"In a few days I hope to see him established in comfortable quarters at that place, when I and his numerous other friends will do everything we can for him.

"It is in compliance with the request of my friend, Mr. Dana, that I have written to you. When the request was made I felt that the task would be a painful one as I then feared that his wound was a dangerous one. The task is no longer painful as I am now gratified to be able to assure you that he is considered out of danger."

Whiting added the following: *"I have only time before Captain Hanson closes his letter and the mail is about off to add a line. Don't be alarmed about our friend your husband. He will do well. He is not now considered in danger. His wound threatened at first to be very serious, being struck on the right side, but the ball passed through without injuring vitally any of the internal parts. Everybody, especially his surgeon, [illegible], is [sure] he will soon be well and so far recovered as to be able to go home and be placed under your loving care.*

"I have to keep with my company and regiment. I cannot see him. I wrote him a cheery note this evening. This affair has been one of the most brilliant of the war. Our regiment deserves a great share of the applause. Dana himself will be one of the heroes. He will also get a brevet, that's certain.

"So console yourself and be not distressed and all will be well and you will soon be happy in his return. I will soon write you and when your husband joins us, which he soon will, he will have every comfort and attendance. I will give you report by every chance.

"God bless you."

To which he added a postscript: *"Do not think of going. Take the advice of your friends and husband."*

1. Adam N. McLaren, appointed assistant surgeon in 1833 and major surgeon in 1839, was brevetted lieutenant colonel during the Civil War and died in 1874 (Heitman, I, 674).

Depot at Plan del Río, April 22   ✦   Isn't it funny that such a sweet little wife as you should have an old cripple of a husband lying on

The Battle of Cerro Gordo. Amon Carter Museum, Fort Worth.

his back and writing on his breast at this distance from her? And what would you say if I were by and by to make my appearance among you for *you* to take care of *me*, and *me* to sit in *your* lap? Won't it all be nice business? But let me tell you something about things here, for I can write you but a very short note. You know how exhausting it is to write in such a constrained position.

Well, I had hardly finished my little pencil note to you on the eighteenth [sixteenth?] from the field of battle when our regiment was ordered immediately with the rest of our division in pursuit of the routed army. Well, I remained on the hill under a bower two days and a night and then was brought on a litter on the shoulders of four men to this place from which we started to make the attack.

And here I am in a Mexican house occupied by Dr. Cuyler, who is attending me, and I am doing mighty well.[1] I suffer as little as a man could with the same wound. I show it to all my friends who come to see me as a genteel mark. I don't think I shall wear clothes any longer between the waist and knee in order to exhibit my battle scars. But I will give them to you. They shall be your scars.

All the army is in Jalapa and General Worth's still following up beyond. The Mexican army is entirely scattered. Santa Anna fled

Flight of Santa Anna from the Battle of Cerro Gordo.

through Jalapa with only a guard of cavalry. They are used up now.

I received notes from Whiting and Hanson yesterday. My friends sent me down all kinds of luxuries and among other things oranges. They sent a little of everything. W. promised to write you.

And now you want me so much to say something about coming home, don't you? When do you expect me? Tomorrow, I'll bet! You must be patient a little. A wounded man cannot be carried fifty miles in a wagon until his wound is on the mend. And the doctor tells me that this will probably be in ten or twelve days. I shall start at the earliest possible chance.

My friends in Jalapa are trying to get me an order from General Scott to go on recruiting service, as that would pay my traveling expenses, but if he objects I will go out on sick leave and pay my own expenses. I know you would not have me start from here too soon. I do not wish you to calculate on any day for my arrival, for you may meet with a half dozen disappointments. I cannot leave here in less than a week and the probability is that I will not stay longer than twelve days.

In the meantime keep up a light heart and cheerful spirits. I myself am in first-rate spirits at the prospect of being once more in the bosom of my sweet family and of living once again like a gentleman except wearing fine clothes.

Now, my darling one, I must say goodby for I am tired. Love to Kate and kisses for Mary.

1. John M. Cuyler, assistant surgeon in 1837 and major surgeon in 1847, became a colonel in 1876, retired in 1882, and died two years later (Heitman, I, 350).

Jalapa, April 30 • Here you see I am at Jalapa. Doubtless you have heard of it before now from Whiting, and to him I will leave to tell about me generally because I do not like to write too much. I was brought up here on a litter on men's shoulders, together with all the rest of the wounded at Plan del Río. I did not suffer at all from the journey, and it has been of immense benefit for me to be here. In the first place your old friends chills and fever, which had fastened me down there, have left me, and I am doing remarkably well. My wound is fast recovering, as fast as possible, and soon I hope the doctor will allow me to take the road to Veracruz. Once there I can easily get to you, but my own darling wife, you must wait patiently for me and not worry yourself at all about my coming.

Whiting has told you before now that I am ordered to New York to report for recruiting service. Haven't you got a delightful journey before you? And I expect we shall have a chance to spend some time with all my friends and perhaps go to Washington and West Point and so forth. But I am sure I do not know what I shall do for money, and unless I can get hold of my trunk, I cannot make a decent appearance in dress. Who shall I borrow from? I do not know how to dispose of those things you left at the barracks. I want them all sold, but I am sure I do not know how I shall manage it. It is a puzzler. . . .

My own sweet Sue, I write in such a constrained position that it is very tiresome, so I must write short letters, just enough to tell you how well I am getting on.

Colonel Scott was in here the other day and says he would give five years' pay and take my wound now for the honor of it. He says he knows I'm glad I got hit.[1] Well, dear Sue, to tell the truth I do not regret it in the least, and you won't either by and by. I lie here on a comfortable cot, dearest one, all day, reading, eating oranges and so forth, and thinking of my darling ones at home and laying plans for our happy future.

In the morning the doctor comes about eight o'clock to dress my wound and congratulate me on its fair appearance, and this, with talking with Whiting, passes my time away. So be patient and do not

Dana recuperated from his wound at Jalapa, seen here in a drawing by American soldier James T. Shannon.

make yourself at all uneasy, for I am mighty comfortable and am doing mighty well.

Kiss our little one for me and give love to all the family.

1. Martin Scott served in the War of 1812 and was promoted over the years to lieutenant colonel. He was twice brevetted, for Palo Alto and Resaca de la Palma and again for Monterrey (Heitman, I, 869). Years later Dana wrote the following recollection: "Colonel Martin Scott was the man of whom the story is related that the coon told him he need not shoot as he would come down for he knew that he would hit him. He always had a pack of hounds with him. He was a great hunter. Some of his dogs got to chasing Mexican artillery projectiles across the field at Palo Alto and were killed. He always said the Mexican bullet was not molded which could hit him. Being a lieutenant colonel of a regiment of infantry at the storming of Molino del Rey and leading it to the assault, a bullet struck him. He immediately said, pointing to the rear, 'That bullet came from that direction,' showing that the ruling passion was strong in death. He dismounted from his horse. 'Forward, my men, my word is always Forward,' [he said]. He laid himself on the ground in the position of a soldier and died" (undated typescript in Dana MSS).

May 6 ✦ I have just heard that several regiments of discharged volunteers leave today, and as it may be the last chance we may have of sending a mail for a long time, I make haste to take advantage of the opportunity, but I am almost afraid I am too late. Oh, that I were stout enough to go along with this column, but I haven't quite strength enough yet.

My wound is doing wonderfully well, but gunshot wounds are slow in healing. For two days I have been taken out of bed and sat up in a rocking chair for three hours at a time. In addition to this, I am frequently propped up with a chair in bed. My wound gives me so little trouble and pain that I hardly know I had one except the doctor comes to dress it every morning. The doctor says he will get me on crutches before long, and then I suppose he will allow me to go by the first strong escort for Veracruz. You must have patience, loved one, as well as myself.

Three companies of our regiment left here yesterday for the National Bridge to wait there to reinforce the escort of a very large train coming from Veracruz. The train has a valuable load. Whiting's company was among them. Tomorrow the remainder of the regiment together with the Third Infantry march also to reinforce them.

My darling Sue, if you are well enough and can find time, won't you write mother a line for me? We are all doing mighty well here and will soon recover.

We have had a great deal of rain for a few days, but today it is bright and sunny.

Now I must say goodby, my beloved wife. By the way, last night my heart was made glad by two of your dear letters, as late as April 19. I am glad you have got quarters at last. Are you making preparations for the north? I also received a letter from Sister Matilda last night. She is now in Concord.

Now goodby. Kiss our sweet little Mary for her papa. Love to Kate, your sister Orph, and all. Tell your sister that Whiting was in fine health and spirits when he left. He says he wishes he was wounded too and had an order in his pocket to go out of the country. A thousand kisses, my dear Sue, and a whole heartfull of love right from your own deeply devoted husband.

May 11 ✦ Here I am, you see, still in this distant place, but I am better now than I have been yet. My wound always does well, but these miserable chills and fever have reduced me down so that I am very weak. You see that my hand trembles so that [I can] hardly write at all. I rather think I have got rid of those chills altogether. The doctor said this morning that my skin was in a better state than it had been yet and that I was much better in every way. All I want is a little strength and then I shall do well enough.

I am now sitting up in a rocking chair writing on a little table by my side, so you may judge that I am getting right smart. In fact, my dearest Sue, I feel perfectly well, only I want a little strength. My appetite is getting good, and today I am going to dine on stewed tomatoes and stewed chicken and potatoes.

You must practice a good deal of patience, dearest Sue, about my coming home. These wounds are very tedious things. Even that little trifling wound of Gatlin's kept him at Monterrey a month, and Potter's kept him on his back two months, and then he went away on crutches.[1] Well, my wound is much more tedious than either of those. So you must have patience, dearest one, and I shall be home by and by.

I feel like a hero today in all except my weakness, and I shall soon find means to get rid of that.

Van Dorn was in here this morning and told me that he could get a letter off for me if I could get it written by eleven o'clock. Well, it is near that now, and I suppose he will be sending for the letter soon. I believe he is going to send it by a sutler who is going in the Mexican diligence on stages. I am rather doubtful about the safety of the conveyance. Chances to send letters will in future be very rare, but I hope now and then to find one.

Captain Penrose has just been in and requested me to give you his remembrances.[2] My darling wife, you must try and be cheerful and keep in good spirits. I shall get home after a while, and then we shall have such a nice time traveling.

Now I must say goodby. Kiss our own dear little Mary for her papa. Give love to Kate, your sister Orph, and all.

Your own devoted husband.

1. Joseph H. Potter, an 1843 graduate of the Academy, wounded at Monterrey, was brevetted brigadier general during the Civil War and retired at that rank in 1886 (Cullum, II, 87-88).   2. James W. Penrose graduated in 1828 and was brevetted for Cerro Gordo. He died in 1849 (Cullum, I, 336-37).

Acknowledgments

Many people helped with this book, especially the former manuscript librarian at the U.S. Military Academy, Marie Capps, who offered a welcome to the Academy's archives and pointed to a stack of manuscripts—the Dana letters. Her enthusiasm was downright contagious, for as she pointed she smiled and said that *there* was something really new. Marie is largely responsible for *Monterrey Is Ours!*

Thanks also to Alan C. Aimone, for late afternoons when he kept the archives room open, and to Marie's successor, Judith A. Sibley, who answered mail queries. At an early point Lt. Col. Jim Blake made a list of the letters. Colleagues in the Academy's history department in 1987-88, under headship of Col. Robert A. Doughty, were likewise supportive.

Lynne McCaffry transcribed most of the letters, and her unerring eye made work much easier. She caught Spanish misspellings, and enlivened her comments by droll description of life in Kansas.

Ben W. Huseman and Nancy Stevens of the Amon Carter Museum furnished proof of their catalog of published eyewitness illustrations of the war, for which Ben did the collection and annotation and Nancy the editing. Ben spent two days with me at the museum, and among other kindnesses brought out all the Mexican War holdings in the storage rooms.

At the University of Texas at Arlington, Katherine R. Goodwin produced contemporary books, newspapers, broadsides, prints, and a sketchbook. And thanks to the head of special collections, Gerald D. Saxon, and to Jenkins Garrett whose generosity enabled the university to acquire its collection.

Richard J. Sommers and Michael Winey of the U.S. Army Military History Institute at Carlisle Barracks sent a copy of the daguerreotype of Dana and wife and daughter in the Civil War Library and Museum in Philadelphia. Thomas B. Grier photographed the daguerreotype and other Dana items in the Museum, and Constance E. Williams, librarian, arranged the eventual photographic copy.

Robert Ryal Miller sent proof of his book on the San Patricio Battalion, in answer to an inquiry (inspired by the classic narrative of Justin Smith) as to whether the Seventh Infantry, Dana's regiment, produced more deserters than any other unit of the army.

Calvin D. Davis of Duke University searched the manuscript

holdings of the Duke library. Richard D. McKinzie of the University of Missouri at Kansas City investigated photographs in the Library of Congress and National Archives.

John S.D. Eisenhower, fellow historian, made the way much easier with publication of his excellent book on the war, *So Far From God*.

For detailed readings, many thanks to Oakah L. Jones, Jr., Grady McWhiney, Allan R. Millett, and David M. Pletcher. And to Ken and Nancy Stevens, Paul F. Boller, Jr., and Joyce Goldberg and Steve Maizlish, for hospitality in Fort Worth.

Thanks are also due to the staff of the University Press of Kentucky, and to Marcia Brubeck, for most helpful editing.

Again a thank-you to Lila and Carolyn.

Illustration Credits

Maps in this book were created by John M. Hollingsworth, Staff Cartographer of Indiana University.

Except as otherwise noted, other illustrations in the text are courtesy of the Special Collections Division, The University of Texas at Arlington Libraries, Arlington, Texas, including those from the following published sources: pages 3, 147, and 150 from Daniel P. Whiting, *Army Portfolio* (New York: G. and W. Endicott, 1847); pages 40, 43, 51, 73 from Thomas Bangs Thorpe, *"Our Army" on the Rio Grande* (Philadelphia: Carey and Hart, 1846); page 77 from J.H. William Smith, *Rough and Ready as He Is* (n.p., n.d.); pages 82, 100 and 195 from the *New York Herald* (8 Mar. 1847, 8 Dec. 1846, and 11 Apr. 1847); pages 121, 127, 130, 137 from Samuel Chester Reid, *The Scouting Expeditions of McCulloch's Texas Rangers* (Philadelphia: G.B. Ziegler, 1847); page 125 from T.B. Thorpe, *Our Army at Monterey* (Philadelphia: Carey and Hart [1847]); pages 191, 192, 197, 203, 205 from George C. Furber, *Twelve Months Volunteer* (Cincinnati: J.A. and U.P. James, 1850).

Courtesy of the Amon Carter Museum, Fort Worth, are page 63, from *The War between the United States and Mexico* (New York and Philadelphia, 1851) and pages 68, 84, 136, 207.

The caricatures on pages 70 and 80 are courtesy of the Historical Society of Pennsylvania.

Sources of the illustrations in the photographic insert following page 178 are given in the insert.

Index

Boldface numbers refer to illustrations.